Islamic Business and Finance Series
Series Editor: Ishaq Bhatti

There is an increasing need for Western politicians, financiers, bankers, and indeed the Western business community in general to have access to high-quality and authoritative texts on Islamic financial and business practices. Drawing on expertise from across the Islamic world, this new series will provide carefully chosen and focused monographs and collections, each authored/edited by an expert in their respective field all over the world.

The series will be pitched at a level to appeal to middle and senior management in both the Western and the Islamic business communities. For the manager with a Western background, the series will provide detailed and up-to-date briefings on important topics; for the academics, postgraduates, business communities, and managers with Western and Islamic backgrounds, the series will provide a guide to best practices in business in Islamic communities around the world, including Muslim minorities in the West and majorities in the rest of the world.

The Informal Economy and Islamic Finance
The Case of Organization of Islamic Cooperation Countries
Shabeer Khan

Digital Transformation in Islamic Finance
A Critical and Analytical View
Edited by Yasushi Suzuki and Mohammad Dulal Miah

The Islamic Finance Industry
Issues and Challenges
Edited by Burak Çikiryel and Tawfik Azrak

Shariah Governance in Islamic Banking Institutions
Edited by Shafiullah Jan and Muhammad Ismail

For more information about this series, please visit: www.routledge.com/Islamic-Business-and-Finance-Series/book-series/ISLAMICFINANCE

Shariah Governance in Islamic Banking Institutions

Shariah governance assumes the primary instrument through which Islamic Banking Institutions (IBIs) ensure the Islamicity of their products, services, operations, and internal environments. It is considered to be one of the fundamental elements that differentiates IBIs from their traditional counterparts.

Shariah Governance in Islamic Banking Institutions provides a critical overview of the key aspects pertaining to Shariah governance within Islamic financial institutions and presents a detailed analysis of its conceptual background. The authors have identified the unique issues that have emerged due to the integration of Shariah, namely the involvement of the Shariah supervisory board (SSB), in the corporate governance arrangements of Islamic banks. These issues relate to disclosure, transparency, independency, consistency, confidentiality, competency, and reputation. The book details the doctrines of Shariah pronouncements in Islamic banks, the importance of having a central advisory board at a regulatory level in the standardization of Islamic banking practices, as well as the competence required for Shariah supervisory board members. It provides a critical analysis of the Shariah governance framework in Pakistan and introduces the authors' vision of an ideal Shariah governance framework. Furthermore, the chapters offer guidance in promoting effective policies for improving Shariah governance.

This is one of the core challenges facing Islamic banks, namely, to ensure compliance with faith and provide legitimacy to the business of IBIs and, as such, the book will appeal to both the research and professional communities.

Shafiullah Jan is associate professor and Head of the Centre for Excellence in Islamic Finance, Institute of Management Sciences, Peshawar, Pakistan.

Muhammad Ismail is assistant professor at Iqra National University, Peshawar, Pakistan.

Shariah Governance in Islamic Banking Institutions

Edited by Shafiullah Jan and
Muhammad Ismail

LONDON AND NEW YORK

First published 2023
by Routledge
4 Park Square, Milton Park, Abingdon, Oxon OX14 4RN

and by Routledge
605 Third Avenue, New York, NY 10158

Routledge is an imprint of the Taylor & Francis Group, an informa business

© 2023 selection and editorial matter, Shafiullah Jan and Muhammad Ismail; individual chapters, the contributors

The right of Shafiullah Jan and Muhammad Ismail to be identified as the authors of the editorial material, and of the authors for their individual chapters, has been asserted in accordance with sections 77 and 78 of the Copyright, Designs and Patents Act 1988.

All rights reserved. No part of this book may be reprinted or reproduced or utilised in any form or by any electronic, mechanical, or other means, now known or hereafter invented, including photocopying and recording, or in any information storage or retrieval system, without permission in writing from the publishers.

Trademark notice: Product or corporate names may be trademarks or registered trademarks and are used only for identification and explanation without intent to infringe.

British Library Cataloguing-in-Publication Data
A catalogue record for this book is available from the British Library

Library of Congress Cataloging-in-Publication Data
Names: Jan, Shafiullah, editor.
Title: Shariah governance in Islamic banking institutions /
edited by Shafiullah Jan and Muhammad Ismail.
Description: 1 Edition. | New York : Routledge, 2023. |
Series: Islamic business and finance |
Includes bibliographical references and index.
Identifiers: LCCN 2022061189 (print) | LCCN 2022061190 (ebook) |
ISBN 9781032350011 (hardback) | ISBN 9781032350028 (paperback) |
ISBN 9781003324836 (ebook)
Subjects: LCSH: Banks and banking–Religious aspects–Islam. |
Finance–Religious aspects–Islam. | Islamic law.
Classification: LCC HG3368 .S43 2023 (print) | LCC HG3368 (ebook) |
DDC 332.10917/67–dc23/eng/20230216
LC record available at https://lccn.loc.gov/2022061189
LC ebook record available at https://lccn.loc.gov/2022061190

ISBN: 978-1-032-35001-1 (hbk)
ISBN: 978-1-032-35002-8 (pbk)
ISBN: 978-1-003-32483-6 (ebk)

DOI: 10.4324/9781003324836

Typeset in Times New Roman
by Newgen Publishing UK

Contents

List of Figures		*vii*
List of Tables		*viii*
List of Contributors		*ix*
1	A Critical Analysis of Conceptual Background of Shariah Governance Framework for Islamic Banking and Finance SHAFI'I ABDUL AZEEZ BELLO	1
2	Assessing Shariah Disclosure in Pakistan: The Case of Islamic Banks MUHAMMAD ISMAIL, SHAFIULLAH JAN, AND KARIM ULLAH	21
3	Fatwa in Islamic Legal Tradition and Its Implications for Shariah Pronouncements of Islamic Banks MUHAMMAD TAHIR MANSOORI	36
4	Central Advisory Board and the New Shariah Governance Framework for Islamic Banks in Turkey: A Qualitative Approach MURAT YAŞ AND AHMET FARUK AYSAN	65
5	From Confidentiality to Concealment: An Issue of Shariah Governance in Islamic Banking Institutions MANSOOR KHAN	80
6	Paradox of Shariah Governance and Price Competitiveness in Islamic Banking SALMAN AHMED SHAIKH	94

7 Issues in Shariah Governance Framework of Islamic Banking Institutions 110
ABDUL BASIT

8 Shariah Audit Practices in Islamic Financial Institutions 131
YASIR AZIZ, MUHAMMAD ASIF KHAN, AND FADILLAH MANSOR

9 Shariah Governance for Islamic Financial Institutions 152
IMRAN HUSSAIN MINHAS

Index *176*

Figures

1.1	Principles of Shariah Governance Framework.	4
7.1	Dimensions of the Intentions of the Islamic Law in Traditional Classification. Author's Diagram.	113
7.2	Al Ghazali's Maqasid al-Shariah Theory. Author's Diagram.	114
7.3	Components of Shariah Governance in IBIs.	117
7.4	The Allocation of Shariah Supervision at the Macro and Micro Levels.	118
7.5	Role of Shariah Supervisory Board in IFIs.	121
7.6	Responsibilities of SSB.	121
7.7	Characteristics of the Shariah Supervisory Board.	123
7.8	Capacities Required for SSB.	124
8.1	Pictorial Representation of the Audit Process.	138

Tables

2.1	List of Annual Reports Collected from Pakistan's Full-Fledged Islamic Bank Websites	25
2.2	Themes Extracted from IBD-SBP's Shariah Governance Framework – 2018	27
2.3	Themes Extracted from AAOIFI's Governance Standards	29
2.4	Voluntary Shariah Disclosure Themes Extracted from Prior Research Studies	30
2.5	Summarized Table Showing Shariah Disclosure in Pakistan's Full-Fledged Islamic Bank	31
4.1	Background of Interviewees	69
6.1	Performance Indicators of Islamic Banking in Muslim-Majority Countries	104

Contributors

Ahmet Faruk Aysan
Hamad Bin Khalifa University, College of Islamic Studies, Qatar

Yasir Aziz
PhD Scholar in Islamic Finance, University of Malaya, Malaysia

Abdul Basit
PhD Scholar in Islamic Business & Finance, Institute of Management Sciences, Peshawar, Pakistan

Shafi'i Abdul Azeez Bello
Lecturer, Islamic University of Minnesota Benin Republic Branch

Muhammad Ismail
Assistant Professor, Iqra National University, Peshawar, Pakistan

Shafiullah Jan
Associate Professor, Institute of Management Sciences, Peshawar, Pakistan

Mansoor Khan
Lecturer and Editorial Assistant, Ripha University, Islamabad, Pakistan

Muhammad Asif Khan
Assistant Professor, University of Swabi, Pakistan

Muhammad Tahir Mansoori
Resident Shariah Board Member, Askari Islamic Bank Limited, Pakistan

Fadillah Mansor
Professor, University of Malaya, Malaysia

Imran Hussain Minhas
Head of Learning and Development, Askari Bank Limited, Pakistan

Salman Ahmed Shaikh
Project Coordinator & Editor, Islamic Economics Project, Pakistan

Karim Ullah
Associate Professor, Institute of Management Sciences, Peshawar, Pakistan

Murat Yaş
Marmara University, The Institute of Islamic Economics and Finance, Turkey

1 A Critical Analysis of Conceptual Background of Shariah Governance Framework for Islamic Banking and Finance

Shafi'i Abdul Azeez Bello

1.1 Introduction

Over the last decade, a significant increase of interest in Shariah-compliant investment can be seen worldwide. This interest has not been confined to the Islamic world or to Muslims. Economists and politicians have shown interest in Islamic banking. However, there are challenges. One major problem in the development of Islamic banking services and products is lack of uniformity; the diversity of views that exists among the schools of jurisprudence on certain key issues. This creates not only tension within the industry, but also a degree of legal uncertainty which undermines confidence and therefore the long-term viability of Islamic financial services.[1]

Aligned with moving forward the Islamic banking and financial industry worldwide with the responsibilities of the Shariah board and the intricacy of their duties towards different shareholders, it is submitted that a standard and proper Shariah governance system must be established. The Shariah governance system is the best instrument that can strengthen and elevate the functions of the Shariah board and its connected institutions for the aim of Shariah compliance. The concept of Shariah governance in Islam refers to a set of organizational arrangements on how to govern, manage, control and direct the corporate affairs of the structure. This provides the governance structure through which all stakeholders' interests are protected, the company's objective is achieved and the principles of Shariah are complied with. This is, to a certain extent, consistent with the definition of the Organisation for Economic Co-operation and Development (OECD) Principles of Corporate Governance, which explains it as:

> A set of relationship between a company's management, its board, its shareholders and other stakeholders. Shari'ah governance also provides the structure through which the company goals are set and the means of attaining those objectives and monitoring performance are determined.[2]

DOI: 10.4324/9781003324836-1

1.2 Definition of Shariah Governance in Islamic Banking

Shariah literally means, 'the road to the watering place', 'the straight path to be followed'. This shows that Shariah is the road to salvation. By way of illustration, a traveller lost in the desert will be glad to find a path to the oasis. The Qur'an used the word Shariah with this meaning in the following verse:

> Then we have put you (O Muhammad, *(p.b.u.h)* on a plain way of Our commandment. So, follow you that (Islamic monotheism and its laws), and follow not the desires of those who know not.[3]

As a technical term, however, the word Shariah was defined by *Al-Qurtubi* as the canon of Islam, as all the different commandments of Allah (SWT) to mankind.[4] Some scholars limited the meaning to law-related matters, while others confined Shariah to its linguistic meaning by saying that this word means 'following strictly the injunctions of Allah or the way of Islam (din)'.[5] A comprehensive definition of the word Shariah can be deduced from the different definitions given above as follows.

It is the sum of the Islamic teachings and system, which was revealed to Prophet Muhammad (p.b.u.h) recorded in the Qur'an as was deducible from the Prophet's Sunnah. Some scholars opine that all commandments of Allah (SWT) to mankind are part of Shariah. Each one of these commandments is called a *hukm* (Rule). Shariah regulates all human actions. This is why it is not 'law' in the modern sense as it contains a comprehensive set of dogmas and legal ethical doctrines.

It is basically a doctrine of duties and a code of obligations. In the context of Islamic banking and finance, the word Shariah is regularly used to denote the compliant aspect of Islamic banking and financial products and services. Currently, two key words are commonly used by the Islamic finance industry, namely Shariah 'compliant' and Shariah 'based' products and services. Shariah–compliant products refer to products which have their origin from the conventional market and are 'Islamized' by modifying them to suit Shariah requirements. This is usually done by inserting certain contracts and peripherals in the structure in order to make it Shariah compliant. A classic example of that structure is in the *ijarah* contract coupled with the option of buying the asset at the end of the contract which is also known as *al-ijarah thumma al-bay' bittamlik*. This contract is similar to the hire purchase contract in conventional products. On the other hand, Shariah-based products refer to products which do not originate from conventional practice. Examples of those products are those used in the contract of *salam* or *isitsna*.[6] The IFSB-3 explains Shariah governance in the context of Islamic financial Industries to encompass:

> A set of Organisational arrangements whereby the actions of the management of institutions offering Islamic financial services are lined up, as

A Critical Analysis of Conceptual Shariah Governance Framework 3

far as possible, with the interests of its stakeholders; provision of proper inducements for the organs of governance such as the board of directors (BOD), Shari'ah Supervisory Board and management to pursue objective that are in the interests of stakeholders and facilitate effective monitoring, thereby encouraging IIFS to use resources more efficiently; and comply with Islamic Law rules and principles.[7]

This definition can be grouped into three essential components:

1. 'A set of Institutional and Organizational arrangements – this refers to the Shariah board and its related institutions such as internal audit department and Shariah division.'
2. 'An effective independent oversight of Shariah compliance – this indicates the aims and objective of the Shariah governance system to provide an efficient mechanism for the purpose of Shariah compliance.'
3. 'Shariah pronouncements, dissemination of information and an internal Shariah compliance review – this involves the overall Shariah governance process that covers both ex-ante ex-post aspects of the Shariah compliance framework.'

This definition implies that the institution of the Shariah board is crucial to the Shariah governance system as an authoritative body ensuring Shariah compliance.[8] The Accounting and Auditing Organisation of Islamic Financial Institutions (AAOIFI) governance Standards No.1 defines Shariah governance as an independent body entrusted with the duty of directing, reviewing and supervising the activities of Islamic financial institutions (IFIs) for the purpose of Shariah compliance, and issuing legal rulings pertaining to Islamic banking and finance.[9] A similar definition is given by the IFSB-10 where it refers to it as 'a body comprised of a panel of Shari'ah scholars who provide Shari'ah expertise and act as special advisors to the institutions in carrying out this duty'. The Shariah board needs a clear framework and structure to ensure its effectiveness, particularly in the matters of its independence, the binding force of its rulings, its objectivity and full mandate. On this basis, any formal or informal arrangement as to how the Shariah board is directed, managed, governed and controlled for the purpose of Shariah compliance is also part of the Shariah governance system.[10] See Figure 1.1 for the Principles of Shariah Governance Framework.

(i) Shariah Governance Structure: Islamic Financial Institutions must establish a sound & robust Shariah governance structure.
(ii) Accountability & Responsibility: Board of Directors, Management & Shariah Committee to play significant role in ensuring Shariah compliance.
(iii) Independence: Independence of Shariah Council to make decisions, access to non-compliance.

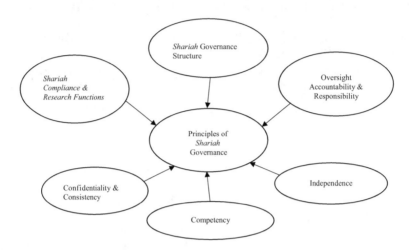

Figure 1.1 Principles of Shariah Governance Framework.

(iv) Competency: Shariah Council to have sufficient knowledge on Shariah and must be 'fit and proper'.
(v) Confidentiality: Internal and privileged information obtained by the SC shall be kept confidential at all times.
(vi) Professionalism: Professional ethics, judgment and consistency of Shariah decisions.

Robust Shariah Compliance Functions: Shariah review and audit; Shariah risk management; Shariah research; Shariah secretariat.

1.3 Significance and Purpose of Shariah Governance in the IBF System

The requirement for the establishment of the Shariah governance in Islamic banking is generally based on the elementary arguments in Islamic tenets. Though the arguments are in the form of general principles applicable to the Shariah, however, since Islamic banking falls under the area of *mu'āmalah*, these general principles also apply to Islamic banking. At least two prominent principles can be raised in the subject matter, particularly the principle of *al-amr bi al-ma'rūf wa al-nahy 'an al-munkar* and the obligation of *ḥisbah*.[11] *Al-Amr bi al-ma'rūf wa al-nahy 'an al-munkar* means 'commanding for doing the good deed and preventing from doing the bad deed'. The term is derived from the Qur'an:

> Let there arise out of you a band of people inviting to all that is good, enjoining what is right and forbidding what is wrong: they are the ones to attain felicity.[12]

A Critical Analysis of Conceptual Shariah Governance Framework 5

With regard to the Qur'an above, the *hadīth* from *Abū Sa'īd* deserves mentioning. The Prophet (p.b.u.h) was reported to have said:

Whoever amongst you sees something abominable should rectify it with his hand; and if he has not strength enough to do it, then he should do it with his tongue; and if he has not strength to do it, (even) then he should (abhor it) from his heart, and that is the least of Faith.[13]

This verse and *hadīth* of Prophet command for performing the *al-amr bi al-ma'rūf wa al-nahy 'an al-munkar* principle. Aside from the exhortation for doing it, the Qur'an emphasizes the danger of not doing so.[14] In a nutshell, *al-amr bi al-ma'rūf wa al-nahy 'an al-munkar* are the two principles that prevent Muslims from committing wrong. In relation to Islamic banking, this principle is highly suitable for maintaining Shariah compliance. In this regard, to maintain that the banks are always well bound by ideological orientation and not merely profitable orientation, *al-amr bi al-ma'rūf wa al-nahy 'an al-munkar* is a highly recommended remedy.[15] Another important principle pertinent to Shariah governance in Islamic banking is the principle of *ḥisbah*. *Ḥisbah*, according to *Ibn Taimiyah*, which is commanding for *al-ma'rūf* when it is left, and prevents *al-munkar* when it is done.[16]

Therefore, the Shariah governance system[17] is meant to address a specific type of risk exclusive to IFIs – the Shariah non-compliance risk.[18] Moreover, the significance of Shariah non-compliance risk to the Islamic finance industry can be illustrated in the case of declining *sukuk* issuances due to the statement made by the Chairman of the AAOIFI Shariah board, the Organization of the Islamic Conference (OIC) *Fiqh* Academy's declaration on the impermissibility of *tawarruq*, and the Malaysian High Court's judgment on the issue of *bay' bithaman ajil* (BBA). All of these major cases indicate the very significance of Shariah governance system as a risk management tool to mitigate Shariah non-compliance risk.[19] The Islamic Financial Services Board (IFSB) Guiding Principles on Risk Management specifically classifies the Shariah risk as part of the operational risks which can be managed through a sound and proper Shariah governance system.[20]

1.4 The Qualification Requirements

Islamic banking and financial business in the present modern practice was unknown in the classical period of Muslim history. Nevertheless, the basic principle of such business was recognized. The modern banking system was recognized by the Muslim society not earlier than after the middle of the twentieth century. In this context, the availability of Shariah governance is important.

Pursuant to the above, the Shariah governance comprises Shariah scholars who are experts in *fiqh mu'amlat* and *uṣul al-fiqh*. In terms of the composition of the Shariah governance, it varies from one IFI to another. Shariah governance at the international and national levels usually comprise leading international and regional scholars, whereas Shariah boards of the domestic IFIs consist of regional and local scholars.[21]

It is contended that the ideal qualification of the board members is those who are experts in the Shariah and law, specifically in the area of *fiqh mu'amalat* and *uṣul al-fiqh*. The reason behind this is that the Shariah board mostly deals with issues relating to commercial law. This is in parallel with appendix 2 of the BNM/RH/GL/_012_3, which requires the Shariah board members to have at least either qualification or possess necessary knowledge, expertise or experience, in Islamic jurisprudence or Islamic commercial law.[22]

Paragraph 2 of the Guidelines on Islamic Private Debt Securities (1 July 2000) issued by the Securities Commission of Malaysia requires that the appointment of the Shariah advisors in relation to the approval of the structure of Islamic bonds must be of good reputation, be well-versed in *fiqh mu'amalat and uṣu al-fiqh*, and have at least three years' experience in Islamic financial transactions. In addition, section 28 of the Regulations of Faisal Islamic Bank of Sudan requires the Shariah board members to be scholars of the Shariah or comparative law. Similar provisions can be found in section 3 of the Guideline of the Supreme Shariah Supervisory Board, Bank of Sudan.[23]

Nevertheless, the AAOIFI Governance Standards and IFSB-10 allow the appointment of a person who has no expertise in *fiqh mu'amalat* to be a Shariah board member to strengthen the ability of the SB to scrutinize and understand banking business and its operation. This position is followed by several countries such as Pakistan and Malaysia. The Shariah board members of BNM comprise experts from various fields, and they include Shariah scholars, chartered accountants, lawyers, judges and central bankers.

The Shariah Board of Pakistan has gone even further by putting very strict conditions on SB members' qualifications. In terms of educational qualification, any board member must have a degree from a recognized institution with a minimum of second-class Bachelor's degree in Economics or degree in *Fiqh* and sufficient understanding of banking and finance or a post graduate degree in Islamic Jurisprudence or *uṣuluddin* or LLM (Shariah) from any recognized university and with exposure to banking and finance.

From the aspect of experience and exposure, all members must have at least three years' experience of giving Shariah rulings or at least five years' experience in research and development in Islamic banking and finance. The SBP also insists on the capability of mastering or having reasonable knowledge of Arabic and English languages.[24] All these requirements indicate the essence of the SB's competency in setting higher standards of practice of Shariah governance in IFIs.[25]

1.5 Duties, Responsibilities and Rights of Shariah Governance

Islamic banks shall set out the duties and responsibilities of every key functionary involved in the implementation of Shariah governance framework

A Critical Analysis of Conceptual Shariah Governance Framework

since the rational for the establishment of Shariah governance is to ensure that the bank complies with the Shariah principles. For this reason, the main aspect of their duties and responsibilities in Islamic banking can be divided into three groups as follows:

(a) Board of Directors
   (i) The Board is ultimately accountable and responsible for the overall SG framework and Shariah compliance of the IFIs, by putting in place the appropriate mechanism to discharge the aforementioned responsibilities. The Board is also expected to perform diligent oversight over the effective functioning of the IFI's SG framework and ensure that the framework is commensurate with the scope, complexity and nature of its business.
   (ii) The Board, upon consultation with the SC, shall approve all policies relating to Shariah matters and is expected to ensure that such policies are implemented effectively.
   (iii) The SC members shall be appointed by the board upon the recommendation of its Nomination Committee. The number of SC members to be appointed must not be less than five (5), the majority of whom must possess strong knowledge in the Shariah and backed by the appropriate qualifications in that area. The Board must ensure that the SC members are aware of their fiduciary responsibilities in discharging their duties.
   (iv) The Board may consider appointing at least one (1) member of the SC as a member of the board that could serve as a 'bridge' between the Board and the SC. The presence of a director with sound Shariah knowledge would foster greater understanding and appreciation amongst the board members on the decisions made by the SC.
   (v) The board must ensure that an effective communication policy among the key functions of the IFIs is in place to facilitate smooth escalation of material matters relating to Shariah to the Board. The communication policy should also ensure that staff in the IFIs is fully aware on the need to observe the Shariah requirements at all times.
   (vi) The board shall remunerate the SC members appropriately as advised by its Remuneration Committee. Such remuneration shall reflect and be commensurate with the accountability, duties and responsibilities of the SC.

(b) Shariah Committee
   (i) The Shariah Committee shall be responsible and accountable for all its decisions, views and opinions related to Shariah matters. While the Board bears the ultimate responsibility and accountability on the overall governance of the IFIs. The Board is expected to rely on the SC on all Shariah decisions, views and opinions relating to the business of the IFIs. As the Shariah decisions, views and opinions

bind the operations of the IFIs and the SC are expected to rigorously deliberate the issues at hand before arriving at any decisions.

(ii) The SC is expected to perform an oversight role on Shariah matters related to the institution's business operations and activities. This shall be achieved through the Shariah review and the Shariah audit functions. Regular Shariah review reports and the Shariah audit observations should enable the SC to identify issues that require its attention and where appropriate to propose corrective measures.

(iii) In discharging its duties, the SC is expected to disclose sufficient information in the IFI's annual financial report on the state of compliance of the IFIs, as per the requirements under the Guidelines on Financial Reporting for Licensed Islamic Banks (GP8-i) and Guidelines on Financial Statements for Takaful Operators (GPT6).

(iv). The SC is expected to understand that in the course of discharging the duties and responsibilities as a SC member, they are responsible and accountable for all Shariah decisions, opinions and views provided by them.

(c) Management

(i) The management shall be responsible for observing and implementing Shariah rulings and decisions made by the SAC and the SC respectively. The management is also responsible to identify and refer any Shariah issues to the SC for decisions, views and opinions.

(ii) Given that the accountability of Shariah decisions rests with the SC, the management is expected to provide information and disclosure which are complete and accurate to the SC in a timely manner, and shall be transparent on any areas that need clarification by the SC to enable them to discharge its duties effectively.

(iii) It is the responsibility of management to allocate adequate resources and manpower to support the SG framework that are commensurate with the size, complexity and nature of the IFI's business. The infrastructure and resources to be provided shall include, among others, budget allocation, reference and research materials, trainings and development, etc.

(iv) The management is responsible to provide continuous learning and training programs to the key internal stakeholders including the board, the SC, and the relevant staff in Shariah and finance matters. This is to ensure that every function in the SG framework is sufficiently exposed to current developments in Shariah-related matters.

(v) It is the responsibility of the management to develop and adopt a holistic culture of Shariah compliance within the organization. A holistic culture of Shariah compliance refers to the way in which the IFI complies with Shariah principles in its overall Islamic financial business operations. For example, the management should regularly remind the frontline staff on the importance of Shariah and the impact to the IFI if Shariah principles and practices are not observed,

A Critical Analysis of Conceptual Shariah Governance Framework 9

and to always place the Shariah as the overarching requirement in the formulation of any procedures and activities relating to Islamic financial business carried out by the IFI. In addition, all relevant staff are expected to be conversant with Islamic products offered by the IFI, as well as the underlying Shariah concepts and the similarities and differences with conventional products and concepts.

(vi) The management must ensure that Shariah policies and procedures are accessible at all times to those involved in the implementation of SG and the Shariah policies and procedures shall provide clarification on matters related to the end-to-end process of SG in the IFI. The management shall also be responsible in ensuring that the operations are executed according to the policies and procedures, and to constantly review and update the policies and procedures to reflect current market practices and developments.

(vii) In the event the management becomes aware that certain operations are found to be carrying out businesses which is (are) not in compliance with Shariah, or against the advice of its Shariah Committee or the rulings of the SAC, the management shall: (i) immediately notify the board and SC as well as the Bank of the fact; (ii) immediately cease to take on any new business related to the Shariah non-compliant business; and within thirty (30) days of becoming aware of such non-compliance or such further period as may be permitted by the Bank, furnish a plan to rectify the state of non-compliance with the Shariah, to be duly approved by the board and endorsed by the SC.

(viii) In cases where the Bank has reason to believe that an IFI is carrying on operations that are non-compliant with Shariah, the Bank may direct and require rectification measures to be instituted by the IFI.[26]

1.6 Competency of Boards of Shariah Governance

Any person bearing responsibilities outlined in the Shariah governance framework for an IFI shall possess the necessary competency and continuously enhance their knowledge and understanding on the Shariah as well as keep abreast of the latest developments in Islamic finance. The board and management are expected to have reasonable understanding on the principles of the Shariah and its broad application in Islamic finance. The SBs are expected to have sufficient knowledge on finance in general, and Islamic finance in particular, to enable the SC to comprehend Shariah issues brought before them. The SB members are expected to constantly equip themselves with relevant knowledge on the Shariah and finance as well as attend relevant training programs.

The IFI shall develop a set of proper criteria for the appointment of any Shariah Committee member, using the minimum criteria set by the bank as a base to ensure that only competent persons are appointed as SC members. The competency and credibility of the SC members provide the assurance that the IFI's operations are being monitored by a credible and competent committee. The Bank may prescribe other criteria or requirements in addition to those set by the IFIs, as and when the bank considers it necessary. The IFI shall engage other professionals such as lawyers, accountants and economists to provide appropriate assistance and advice. The IFI is required to adopt a formal process of assessing the performance of the SC members.

The assessment should be designed to evaluate individual performance based on the competence, knowledge, contribution and overall effectiveness of the SC members on Shariah deliberations. The process should also identify relevant gaps to enable proper training and exposure for the SC members. The IFI should develop a succession planning programme for the SC members by identifying, hiring and nurturing new members with the view to entrusting them with greater responsibilities as and when appropriate.[27]

1.7 Independence of Shariah Board

The Shariah board should play a strong and independent oversight role with adequate capability to exercise objective judgment on Shariah–related matters. No individual or group of individuals will be allowed to dominate the Shariah board's decision-making. In order to uphold the integrity and credibility of the Shariah board, its members must not only be able to exercise independent judgment without undue influence or duress, especially from the management of the IFIs, but also be seen to be truly independent. In this respect, it would be required for an IFI to formalize the independence of the Shariah board and its members by recognizing the Shariah board's roles and mandate. IFIs must have in place an appropriate and transparent process for resolving any differences of opinion between the BOD and the SB.[28] This process may include having direct access (after duly informing the supervisory authority) to the shareholders as a 'whistle-blower'.

The supervisory authorities may be involved in this process of resolving differences, without compromising the binding nature of the pronouncements/resolutions of the SB. A SB can only be deemed 'independent' when none of its members has a blood or intimate relationship with the IFIs, its related companies or its officers that could interfere, or be reasonably perceived to interfere, with the exercise of independent judgement in the best interests of the IFIs by the SB. In the case of Shariah advisory firms, it can only be deemed independent from the IFIs if they are not related parties, such as in terms of having common shareholders or common directors.[29] Adapted from international best practices usually applicable to independent, nonexecutive members of the BOD, the following are examples of relationships that would deem a member of a SB as lacking independence from the IFIs he or she is serving, and thus must be avoided:

(i) a member of the SB being under full-time employment by the IFIs or any of its related companies for the current or during the last financial year;

A Critical Analysis of Conceptual Shariah Governance Framework 11

(ii) a member of the SB who has an immediate family member such as spouse, children or siblings who are, or who were during the last financial year, employed by the IFIs or any of its related companies as a senior executive officer;
(iii) a member of the SB, or his or her immediate family member, accepting any compensation or financing from the IFIs or any of its subsidiaries other than compensation for service on the SB; or
(iv) a member of the SB, or his or her immediate family member, being a substantial shareholder of or a partner in (with a stake of 5% or more), or an executive officer of, or a director of any for-profit business organization to which the IFIs or any of its subsidiaries made, or from which the IIFS or any of its subsidiaries received significant payments in the current or immediate past financial year.

The relationships set out above are not intended to be comprehensive, and are examples of situations that would deem a member of the SB or a Shariah advisory firm to be perceived as not independent. If the IFIs still wish to consider a member of the SB or Shariah advisory firm as independent, in spite of the existence of one or more of these relationships, it should disclose in full the nature of that relationship and bear the responsibility for explaining why the member or the firm should be considered independent. The disclosure can be made, where appropriate, to the supervisory authority or to the public through the annual report of the IFIs. In addition, wherever a conflict of interest is unavoidable, the member of the SB or Shariah advisory firm should declare it in writing to the IFIs. They must similarly report any such conflict in regard to members of their family, business associates or companies in which they have an interest.

Where there is such a conflict of interest, or a duty to another party, then they should abstain from participating in the relevant decision or action on behalf of the IFIs. Where a notification is made of a conflict, it should be recorded and retained by a designated officer. When a member of the SB has multiple SB responsibilities/appointments, he or she must ensure that sufficient time and attention is given to the affairs of each IFI. The IFIs should decide if a member of the SB is able to and has been adequately carrying out his or her duties in serving his or her SB. Internal guidelines should be adopted that address the competing time commitments that are faced when members of the Shariah board serve on multiple SBs.[30]

1.8 Models of Shariah Board

The existing framework of Islamic finance in various jurisdictions demonstrates diverse practices and models of Shariah governance system. Some jurisdictions prefer greater involvement of regulatory authorities while some countries do not. Until now, it is still debatable whether the former or the latter is more prevalent and appropriate for possible adoption. To illustrate these diverse approaches, this study identifies five Shariah governance models in the context of regulatory perspective.

1.8.1 Reactive Approach

This model is more prevalent in non-Islamic legal environment countries such as the United Kingdom and Turkey. Although several Islamic banking licences have been issued to IFIs, the regulatory authority is silent upon the Shariah governance framework. Like any other conventional bank, IFIs are required to comply with existing legislations and regulations. IFIs have a duty to make sure that all their business operations and products are Shariah compliant. There is no specific legislation governing IFIs as well as any directive specifying Shariah governance framework. At this point, the regulators will only react and intervene in the Shariah governance matters if there is any significant issue involved which may affect the industry. For instance, the UK Financial Services Authority is only concerned about the role played by the Shariah board of IFIs to be advisory and supervisory and not executive in nature.

1.8.2 Passive Approach

This model is exclusive to Shariah governance model in Saudi Arabia. Saudi Authority Monetary Agency (SAMA) treats IFIs equal to their conventional counterparts. SAMA is yet to issue legislation pertaining to Islamic finance and guidelines on Shariah governance system. There is no national Shariah advisory board or any institutions to be the sole authoritative body in Islamic finance. The existing Shariah governance system as practised by IFIs in the Kingdom is a product of self-initiative rather than regulatory requirement or regulator's direction.

1.8.3 Minimalist Approach

This model is mainly practised by the GCC countries with the exception of Oman and Saudi Arabia. Unlike the reactive approach, the minimalist model allows slight intervention on the part of regulatory authorities. The regulatory authorities expect IFIs to have proper Shariah governance system without specifying the requirements in detail. There is no restriction on multiple appointments of the Shariah board to seat in various institutions at one particular time. Some jurisdictions in the GCC countries such as Bahrain, Dubai and Qatar favour the adoption of the AAOIFI Governance Standards. The minimalist approach prefers the market to develop its own Shariah governance system rather than greater intervention on the part of regulators.

1.8.4 Proactive Approach

This model is favoured by the Malaysian regulatory authority. The proponent of this model has strong faith in a regulatory-based approach in strengthening Shariah governance framework. With this motivation, the Malaysian regulator initiates comprehensive Shariah governance framework from regulatory and non-regulatory aspects. There are several laws passed and amended by the parliament such as the Islamic Banking Act 1983, which has been replaced by Islamic Financial Service Act (2013) (IFSA), the TA 1984, the Banking and Financial Institutions Act 1984 which was replaced by Financial Service Act 2013 and the Securities Commission Act 1993. The Central Bank of Malaysia Act 2009 confirms the status of National Shariah Advisory Council (SAC) to be the sole authoritative body in Islamic finance. Furthermore, the Bank Negara Malaysia (BNM) has issued the Guidelines on the Governance of Shariah Committee for the Islamic financial institutions known as the BNM/RH/GL/_012_3. To complement this, the Securities Commission of Malaysia issued the Registration of Shariah Advisers Guidelines 2009 which set up the criteria for the registration of a Shariah advisor in the capital market sector.

1.8.5 Interventionist Approach

While a passive approach is exclusive to Saudi Arabia, an interventionist model is unique to Shariah governance model in Pakistan. The interventionist model allows third party institutions to make decisions on Shariah matters pertaining to Islamic finance. In the case of Pakistan, the Shariah Federal Court is the highest authority in matters involving Islamic finance despite the establishment of Shariah board at the State Bank of Pakistan level.[31]

1.9 Appointment Procedures

The most important element of Shariah governance is its process of appointment. The Shariah governance process represents the instrument functions of the Shariah board as part of the institution of corporate Islamic finance institutions. This section provides an explanation on the Shariah governance process, which is an attribute of the SBs with respect to its appointment.[32] The establishment of the SAC in some jurisdictions is statutory/legal requirement by the country. In countries where there is no specific Islamic banking law, the provision is made through IFIs Articles of Association without any force of law.[33]

According to AAOIFI standard, the authority to appoint members of the SSB (Shariah Supervisory Board) must be vested in the Annual General Meeting (AGM) of all shareholders of the institution. The reason for this is to ensure that the members of the SSB are free from any undue influence of the management board because the latter does not have the authority to appoint or to dismiss them. It is acceptable for the management board to propose the names of prospective members of the SSB to the AGM for deliberation and endorsement. The rationale of AAOIFI'S standard is to prevent any undue influence of the management board on the Shariah advisors which might exist if the former were given the authority to appoint.[34]

In contemporary practice, the members of Shariah board are appointed by the shareholders or the Board of Directors (BOD) with the approval of the shareholders at the AGM. In actual practice, numerous IFIs appoint members of Shariah board through their BODs, as in the case of Malaysia and Pakistan. Section 8 of the BNM/RH/GL/_012_3 places the power of appointment in the hands of the BOD upon recommendation of its nomination committee and by obtaining prior written approval of BNM. In Pakistan, the appointment of the Shariah board is approved by the BOD in the case of domestic IFIs. In case foreign banks have Islamic banking subsidiaries, the appointment shall be made by the management.[35]

There are different practices in the case of the appointment of Shariah board members at the central bank level, where the power is vested in the government, as in the case of the SB of the central banks of Sudan, Malaysia and the UAE. In Malaysia, the SB of the BNM is appointed by the Yang di-Pertuan Agong (King),[36] on the recommendation of the finance minister pursuant to the Central Bank of Malaysia Act 2009. In the case of the UAE, the SB of the Central Bank of UAE has the authority to approve and endorse the appointment of the SBs at the respective banks by virtue of Section 5, Federal Law No. (6), 1985. On this basis, it can be said that there is no standard practice on the method of appointment of SBs.[37]

1.10 The Role of Shariah Board

The role of Shariah board in Islamic banks shares some similarities with the general concept of corporate governance in other types of corporations. The best explanation of the objective of SB can be simplified as: promoting corporate fairness, transparency and accountability. Good SB is crucial in order to protect the rights and interest of all stakeholders. This is the main reason why there has been growing interest in the topic of SB, particularly in financial institutions.[38] In the context of SB in Islamic banks, its framework goes beyond the relationship between the shareholders, BOD, management and stakeholders as it includes maintaining the relationship with Allah (SWT). In this regard, Islamic banks require an additional framework of Shariah in its character to safeguard and maintain not only the relationship with Allah (SWT) but also its correlation with humankind as well as the environment. As one of the most essential components of Shariah governance in IFIs, the institution of SB plays an essential role in the aspect of the Shariah supervision, monitoring, auditing and issuing legal rulings.[39]

There are broad sets of Shariah board roles which are exclusive to Islamic banks which are as follows:

1. There is a need to reassure stakeholders that their activities fully comply with Shariah principles.
2. The stakeholders also need to be assured that Islamic banks maintain and improve growth and are able to prove efficiency, stability and trustworthiness. The role of Shariah board hence includes harmonizing these two

functions so as to meet the requirements of the Shariah and satisfy the aim of a profit-generating corporation.[40]
3. Shariah board in Islamic banks is also crucial as a means to address numerous types of risk, especially governance risk. Failure to institute appropriate corporate governance measures to mitigate risk may lead to corporate collapse, such as in the case of Ihlas Finance in Turkey, Islamic Bank of South Africa and Islamic Investment Companies of Egypt, and huge commercial losses as in the case of Dubai Islamic Bank and Bank Islam Malaysia Berhad.[41] As an Islamic corporation, Islamic banks have to avoid involvement with all kinds of Shariah prohibitions such as *ribā* (interest), *ghara* (uncertainty), speculation and *maysir* (gambling).
4. It also has to observe the principle of Islamic morality. In this respect, Shariah governance in Islam is a dire necessity to Islamic banks not only to foster and gain confidence of the stakeholders, but also of the general public that all its products, operations and activities adhere to Shariah rules and principles.[42]
5. It has a role as control mechanism to monitor the IFIs' business transactions for the purpose of Shariah compliance including assuring *zakat* payment.[43] This is affirmed by a scholar that Shariah board is to guide IFIs in the setting of policies and regulations according to the Shariah in approving their financial transactions from a legal side and in preparing their contracts for future transactions according to Islamic law.[44]
6. In addition, Abomouamer describes the role of the Shariah board as being proactive rather than reactive. He mentions that the Shariah board has fiduciary duties to force the management of Islamic banks to disclose and dispense revenue from any unlawful transaction to charity as well as to conduct an audit on zakat funds.[45]
7. On the other hand, Banaga outline the Shariah board responsibilities from an auditor's perspective to include answering enquiries, issuing legal opinions, reviewing and revising all business transaction also operations to be in compliance with Shariah principles.[46] Abdallah seems to agree with the contention that the Shariah board must be proactive rather than reactive. He holds the view that the Shariah board should set up the accounting policies to ensure that the formula used in allocating profit between shareholders and account holders is fair, and should ensure that all revenues are generated from lawful transaction and *zakat* funds are properly calculated, and should influence the Islamic banks to perform their social responsibilities towards the community and other stakeholders.[47]

1.11 Functions of Shariah Governance System

Appendix 4 of the guideline on the Shariah governance framework for the Islamic financial Institutions (BNM/RH/GL_012_3) establishes the main functions of the Shariah advisers: to advise the management of the IFI on Shariah matters in order to ensure that is business operations comply with Shariah principles at all times. To endorse and validate relevant documentations such as the proposal forms, contract, legal documentations, product manuals, advertisements as well as brochures. To advise and provide assistance to the various parties of the IFI such as its legal counsel, auditor or consultant on Shariah matters upon request. To advise the IFI to refer to the SAC matters which have not been resolved or endorsed. To assist the SAC by giving explanations on any Shariah matters that have been referred to besides ensuring that all of the SAC's decisions are implemented by the IFI.[48]

1.12 Conclusion

Compliance with Shariah is vital to enhance the confidence of the stakeholders of Islamic banks and finance. This is one of the reasons that all Islamic banking and finance around the globe needs to establish the Shariah governance to be implemented by the Islamic banks and conventional banks that operate Islamic business windows. Moreover, it is the objective of this work to examine the impact of the Shariah Governance functions on the roles of Islamic banks. So far, there is a growing concern regarding the Islamic principles of the Shariah governance because one major ethical component of any economic activity in Islam is to provide justice, honesty, fairness and to ensure that all parties do their rights and duties.

Furthermore, the vital roles played by sound Shariah governance ensures the ultimate success of the economy. Good Shariah governance has long been considered a crucial role for stakeholders in the business environment. Though the goal of Shariah governance differs from one firm to another or from one country to another, the main important concern is to motivate a good code of mechanisms to uplift and govern the organization. But with the current business pressure, sound Shariah governance practices have become critical to worldwide efforts to stabilize and strengthen good capital markets and protect investors.

In addition, there is empirical evidence to suggest that countries that have implemented good Shariah governance measures have generally experienced strong growth of corporate sectors and higher ability to attract capital than those that have not. The good Shariah governance helps to bridge the gap between the interests of those who increase investor confidence and lower the cost of capital for the company. Furthermore, it also helps in ensuring company dignities, its legal commitments and forms value-creating relations with stakeholders. Finally, it is found that companies with better Shariah governance enjoy higher appraisal around the globe.

Notes

1 Nethercott C.R., & Eiseenberg, D.M. (Eds) *Islamic Finance Law and Practice* (Oxford: Oxford University Press, United Kingdom, 2012), at 133–34.

A Critical Analysis of Conceptual Shariah Governance Framework   17

2 OECD, OECD Principles of Corporate Governance (Revised). (Paris: OECD. Available at: www.oecd.org/dataoecd/32/18/31557724.pdf. Accessed on 25 October, 2013), at 17.
3 Abdullah Yusuf 'Ali. *Qur'an Translation* (Q, 45: 18).
4 Al-Qurtubi, Muhammad Ahmad. *Al-Jāmi' al-Ahkām al-Qur'an, vol 16.* (Beirut: Dār al-Fikri, 2011), at 11.
5 Lee, M.P., & Detta. I.J. *Islamic Banking & Finance Law.* (Selangor Darul Ehsan: Longman Pearson Malaysia, 2007), at 41.
6 Ibid., at 148.
7 IFSB-3. *Guiding Principles on Governance for Collective Investment Schemes* (Kuala Lumpur, 2006), at 33.
8 IFSB, *Guiding Principles on Governance for Collective Investment Schemes* (2009) at 2.
9 AAOIFI, Governance Standard No. 1 at 4.
10 Dusuki A.W, et al. (Eds) *Islamic Financial System Principle & Operations* (2012), at 702.
11 Abu Dāwūd, As-Sijsitaanī. *Sunan Abu Dāwūd.* (Al-Urdun: Baitu al-Afkār al-Daoliyah, 2009) at 17–18.
12 Abdullah Yusuf 'Ali. English Qur'an translation (Q, 3:104).
13 *Ibn Rojab al-Anbalī. Jāmiu' al-'Ūlum wa al-Hkam.* (Beirut: Mua'sasah ar-Risālah, 2001). Vol. 2 No. 34, at 243.
14 Id., 24, (Q, 5:78).
15 Regarding the above mentioned, part of conducting *al-amr bi al-ma'rūf wa al-nahy 'an al-munkar,* is to educate people to understand Islamic principles on trade and finance before they get involved in the business or market. The classical Muslim scholars such as *'Umar ibn Khattāb and Shafi'ī,* stress on the importance of the understanding *Shariah* when people are entering the market. *Nazīh Ḥammād, 'Al-Mas'ūliyah al-Shar'iyyah wa al-Qānuniyyah lī A'ḍā' al-Hai'ah al-Shar'iyyah,'* paper presented in *al-Mu'tamaral-Thanī li al-Hai'āt alShar'iyyah li alMu'ssasāt alMāliyah al-Islāmiyyah,* 29-30/10/2002 in Bahrain, at 2.
16 Ibn Taimiyyah. *Public Duties in Islam; The Institution of the Hisbah,* translated by Muhtar Holland (Leicester: The Islamic Foundation, 1983), at 26.
17 AAOIFI Governance Standards for IFIs, No. 1–5, Bahrain, AAOIFI. Annual Report (2011).
18 Bangladesh Bank, Guideline for conducting Islamic banking (2009), at 30–31.
19 Dusuki, A.W. *Ethical and Social Responsibility Models for Islamic Finance* (Kuala Lumpur: ISRA, Malaysia, 2011), at 3–30.
20 IFSB, *Guiding Principles of Risk Management for Institutions (Other Than Insurance Institutions) Offering Only Islamic Financial Services.* (Kuala Lumpur, IFSB, Malaysia, 2002).
21 Dasuki, A.W, et al. (Ed.) Islamic Financial System Principle & Operations, 2012), at 715.
22 Appendix 2 of the BNM/RH/GL/_12_3.
23 Al-Darir, 2001.
24 State Bank of Pakistan, 2008a).
25 Ibid., 36, at 715–16.
26 BNM/RH/GL_012_3 *Shari'ah* Governance Framework for Islamic Financial Institutions (Kuala Lumpur: *Islamic Banking and Takaful Department,* Malaysia, 2010), at 10–14.

27 Ibid., at 17–18.
28 Rammal, H.G. The Importance of *Shari'ah* Supervision in IFIs. *Corporate Ownership and Control* (Spring, 2006) vol. 3, Issue 3, at 204–208.
29 Lahsasna, A. *Fatwa, Shari'ah Supervision & Governance in Islamic Finance.* (Kuala Lumpur: CERT, Malaysia, 2010) at 245–46.
30 IFSB, Guiding Principles on *Shari'ah* Governance Systems for Institutions Offering Islamic Financial Services (Kuala Lumpur, *IFSB,* Malaysia, December 2009), at 14–15.
31 Hasan Z. Regulatory Framework of *Shari'ah* Governance System in Malaysia, GCC Countries and the UK, (Kyoto Bulletin of Islamic Area Studies, 3–2 (March 2010), at 82–84.
32 Dusuki, A.W, et al. (Eds), Islamic Financial System Principle & Operations (2012), at 714.
33 Mahyuddin K. D. *Shari'ah* Advisory Council (SAC) ACIS, UiTM on 14 December 2012 Retrieved from < www.slideshare.net/emkay84/shariah-advisory-council-sac>, accessed on 6/11/2013.
34 Ibid.
35 State Bank of Pakistan, 2008.
36 The King appointed for every 5 years rotation to be regarded as the constitutional monarch.
37 Ibid., 61, at 714–15.
38 Macey, J.R., & O'Hara, M. The Corporate Governance of Banks, *Academic journal article from Federal Reserve Bank of New York Economic Policy Review, Vol. 9, No. 1 April* (2003) at 91.
39 Ibid., 66, at 684.
40 Grais, W., & Pellegrini, M. Corporate Governance and *Shari'ah* Compliance in Institutions Offering Islamic Financial Services, *World Bank Policy Research Working Paper No 4054.* November, 2006).
41 Ibid., 68, at 684.
42 Ibid., at 685.
43 Briston, R., & El-Ashker, A. Religion Audit: Could It Happen Here? *Accountancy, October* (1986) at 113–127.
44 Dāwūd, H.Y. *Shari'ah* Control in Islamic Banks. Herndon (Virginia: *International Institute of Islamic Thoughts* 1996).
45 Abomouamer, F.M. An Analysis of the Role and Function of *Shari'ah* Control in Islamic Banks. (PhD dissertation. University of Wales, 1989).
46 Banaga, A., Ray, G. & Tomkins, C. *External Audit and Corporate Governance in Islamic Banks: A Joint Practitioner-Academic Research Study* (Aldershot: Avebury, 1994)
47 Abdallah, A.A. The Role of *Shari'ah* Supervisory Board in Setting Accountability and Governance: An Islamic Perspective. *The American Journal of Islamic Social Sciences, Vol. 15. No. 1, 1994),* at 55–70.
48 Mahyuddin K. D., *Shari'ah* Advisory Council (SAC) ACIS, UiTM on Dec 14, 2012 Retrieved from <www.slideshare.net/emkay84/shariah-advisory-council-sac>, accessed on 6/11/2013.

References

AAOIFI, Governance Standard No. 1 at 4.
AAOIFI (2011). Governance Standards for IFIs, No. 1–5, Bahrain, AAOIFI. Annual Report.

Abdallah, A.A. (1994). The Role of Shari'ah Supervisory Board in Setting Policies in Islamic Banks. Development of an accounting system for Islamic banks. Selected readings (Chapter 10, pp. 129–142). London: Institute of Islamic Bank and Insurance.

Abomouamer, F.M. (1989). *An Analysis of the Role and Function of Shari'ah Control in Islamic Banks*. PhD dissertation. University of Wales.

Abu Dāwūd, As-Sijsitaanī (2009). *Sunan Abu Dāwūd*. Al-Urdun: Baitu al-Afkār al-Daoliyah.

Al-Qurtubi, Muhammad Ahmad (2011). *Al-Jāmi' al-Ahkām al-Qur'an, vol 16*. Beirut: Dār al-Fikri.

Appendix 2 of the BNM/RH/GL/_12_3.

Banaga, A., Ray, G., & Tomkins, C. (1994). External Audit and Corporate Governance in Islamic Banks: A Joint Practitioner-Academic Research Study. Aldershot: Avebury.

Bangladesh Bank (2009). Guideline for conducting Islamic banking.

BNM/RH/GL_012_3 (2010). Shari'ah Governance Framework for Islamic Financial Institutions. Kuala Lumpur: Islamic Banking and Takaful Department.

Briston, R., & El-Ashker, A. (1986). Religion Audit: Could It Happen Here? Accountancy, *October*.

Dāwūd, H.Y. (1996). *Shari'ah Control in Islamic Banks*. Virginia: International Institute of Islamic Thoughts.

Dusuki, A.W. (2011). *Ethical and Social Responsibility Models for Islamic Finance*. Kuala Lumpur: ISRA, Malaysia.

Dusuki, A.W, et. al. (Ed.) (2012). *Islamic Financial System Principle & Operations* Kuala Lumpur: ISRA, Malaysia.

FSB (2009). *Guiding Principles on Governance for Collective Investment Schemes*. Kuala Lumpur.

Grais, W., & Pellegrini, M. (2006). Corporate Governance and Shari'ah Compliance in Institutions Offering Islamic Financial Services, *World Bank Policy Research Working Paper No 4054*. November.

Hasan, Z. (2010). Regulatory Framework of Shari'ah Governance System in Malaysia, GCC Countries and the UK *(Kyoto Bulletin of Islamic Area Studies, 3–2 March*.

Ibn Rojab al-Anbalī (2001). *Jāmiu' al-'Ūlum wa al-HkamI*, translated by Maher Fahel. Beirut: Mua'sasah ar-Risālah,

Ibn Taimiyyah (1983). *Public Duties in Islam; The Institution of the Hisbah*, translated by Muhtar Holland. Leicester: The Islamic Foundation.

IFSB (2002). *Guiding Principles of Risk Management for Institutions (Other Than Insurance Institutions) Offering Only Islamic Financial Services*. Kuala Lumpur: IFSB.

IFSB (2009). *Guiding Principles on Shari'ah Governance Systems for Institutions Offering Islamic Financial Services*. Kuala Lumpur: IFSB.

IFSB-3 (2006). *Guiding Principles on Governance for Collective Investment Schemes*. Kuala Lumpur: IFSB.

Lahsasna, A. (2010). *Fatwa,* Shari'ah *Supervision & Governance in Islamic Finance*. Kuala Lumpur: CERT.

Lee, M.P., & Detta, I.J. (2007). *Islamic Banking & Finance Law*. Selangor Darul Ehsan: Longman Pearson Malaysia.

Macey, J.R., & O'Hara, M. (2003). The Corporate Governance of Banks, *Academic Journal Article from Federal Reserve Bank of New York Economic Policy Review*, Vol. 9, No. 1, April.

Mahyuddin, K. D., Shari'ah Advisory Council (SAC), ACIS, UiTM (2012). Retrieved from <www.slideshare.net/emkay84/shariah-advisory-council-sac>, accessed on 6/11/2013.

Mahyuddin, K. D., Shari'ah Advisory Council (SAC) ACIS, UiTM on Dec 14, 2012 Retrieved from <www.slideshare.net/emkay84/shariah-advisory-council-sac>, accessed on 6/11/2013.

Nazīh Ḥammād, 'Al-Mas'ūliyah al-Shar'iyyah wa al-Qānuniyyah lī A'ḍā' al-Hai'ah al-Shar'iyyah,' paper presented in al-Mu'tamaral-Thanī li al-Hai'āt alShar'iyyah li alMu'ssasāt alMāliyah al-Islāmiyyah, 29-30/10/2002 in Bahrain.

Nethercott C.R., & Eiseenberg, D.M. (Eds) (2012). *Islamic Finance Law and Practice*. Oxford: Oxford University Press.

OECD, OECD Principles of Corporate Governance (Revised). Paris: OECD. Available at: www.oecd.org/dataoecd/32/18/31557724.pdf. Accessed on 25 October 2013.

Rammal, H. G. (2006). The Importance of Shari'ah Supervision in IFIs. *Corporate Ownership and Control*. Spring, 3(3).

2 Assessing Shariah Disclosure in Pakistan

The Case of Islamic Banks

Muhammad Ismail, Shafiullah Jan, and Karim Ullah

2.1 Introduction

Islamic banking and finance is a unique kind of banking phenomenon, which is purely based on the Islamic law of business transactions/muamlat (Jan & Asutay, 2019). Islamic banking is also known as ethical banking as it also stands on the Islamic business ethical values. Furthermore, the involvement of Shariah in the banking operations, activities, governance, investment, and products and services design give rise to a special kind of disclosure issue called Shariah disclosure. Thus, it is not the additional, but fundamental responsibility of the Islamic banks to ensure full disclosure and transparency of their internal governance environment and compliance with Shariah. Many scholars argue that to protect their ideological stance and religious commitments, Muslims customers are very keen to know the Islamicity of the Islamic banks' operations, activities, governance, investment, and products and services design (Gilani, 2015; Grais & Pellegrini, 2006; Al-Mehmadi, 2004). Normally, the existing customers select their investment and business decisions provided by Islamic banking institutions based on Shariah disclosure. Therefore, Shariah disclosure is essential not only for the existing Muslims customers but also for other potential customers across the world including non-Muslims.

This chapter attempts to assess the level of Shariah reporting and disclosure in Pakistan's five full-fledged Islamic banks. To meet the objective we first developed a Shariah Disclosure Index (ShDI) by considering the Shariah reporting requirements of State Bank of Pakistan (SBP) Shariah governance framework 2018, AAOIFI, and others Islamic reporting literature. The sample size of the study is Pakistan's five full-fledged Islamic banks. Their annual reports were analysed over the period 2015–2017. Survey design is used to achieve the objectives of the study. The research provides a benchmark for the Islamic bank's stakeholders in making their investment and business decisions based on Shariah reporting and disclosure.

DOI: 10.4324/9781003324836-2

2.2 Significance of the Research

The current research is the first of its kind, which is primarily focusing on the Shariah reporting and disclosure in Pakistan's Islamic banking institutions. The study also is an attempt to provide a benchmark for Islamic reporting to Pakistan's Islamic banking institutions. By constructing ShDI, the study primarily focuses on the existing regulatory disclosure requirements, AAOIFI disclosure requirements, and other disclosure items as discussed in the pertinent literature. The study will contribute to the existing literature of Shariah reporting in Islamic banking and finance especially in Pakistan's perspective. This study also helps in designing optimal policies on Shariah reporting and disclosure for Pakistan's Islamic banking and finance industry. Furthermore, the research will provide a benchmark and indicator for all concerned and potential stakeholders who are making their investment and business decisions based on the Islamic banks' Shariah reporting and disclosure. Besides, this study also provides important concern on the inclusion of the financial investors, who are excluded because of their difference ideological stance and commitment to Shariah.

2.2.1 Research Gap

The literature available related to the Islamic corporate governance principles and disclosure covered a lot about financial, governance, and corporate statements disclosure. Meanwhile, there is not much literature available related to the Shariah disclosure framework in IBIs. Furthermore, so far in Pakistan, there is no study for assessing the Shariah reporting and disclosure in IBIs. Therefore, the present study is an attempt to fill this gap through developing ShDI by considering the existing regulatory disclosure requirements, AAOIFI disclosure requirements, and volunteer disclosure items explored in the prior pertinent literature.

2.3 Literature Review

According to Grassa (2013), Shariah governs all aspects of the IBIs which adds additional values to the existing corporate governance (CG) structure of Islamic banks. Therefore, Shariah generates special kinds of corporate governance challenges in the Islamic banks. The involvement of Shariah experts in the CG activities of an Islamic bank gives rise to some unique issues, such as independence, confidentiality, competency, consistency, and disclosure (Grais & Pellegrini, 2006; Zainuddin & Nordin, 2016; Hasan, 2011). Meanwhile, Hamid et al. (2016) and Grassa (2013) added transparency and reputation, respectively, in the list of issues that arise due to the engagement of Shariah advisors in the Islamic banks' corporate governance system. Shariah reporting and disclosure refers to the communication of Shariah information to all the concerned stakeholders. Gilani (2015) argues that Islamic business ethical values are the salient features of the Islamic financing modes that attract the financial stakeholders. Stakeholders, whether existing or potential, usually rely on the Islamic bans' annual reports while making their decisions on investment or any other sort of financial decisions (Othman et al., 2009). This prove that they are protecting their ideological stance and religious commitments, Muslims customers are very keen to know the Islamicity of the Islamic banks' operations, activities, governance, investment, and products and services designing (Jan et al., 2018; Jan et al., 2015; Jan et al., 2016).

Raharja (2011) also argues that IFIs must comply with the Shariah in all conditions. Therefore, there is high demand on the Shariah compliance to ensure full disclosure for all banking activities, operations, products, and services. The involvement of Shariah in the corporate governance arrangement of Islamic banks gives rise to a special kind of disclosure issue called Shariah disclosure and reporting (Grassa, 2013; Grais & Pellegrini, 2006; Hasan, 2012; Srairi, 2015; Askari et al., 2010). Disclosing information, concern about Islamic products and services, attract the potential investors who are conscious about the Islamicity of a bank's activity (Grassa et al., 2018). It means that Islamicity and Islamic ethical identity are the fundamental determinants which make Islamic banking become the first choice of Muslims investors. Therefore, higher Shariah reporting and disclosure strengthen the confidence of both the existing and potential investors in IBIs.

Ismail et al. (2018) establish a detailed study on the Shariah attributes that should be disclosed in the annual reports of Islamic banks. Their inquiry is very comprehensive in the sense that it covers three important dimensions of the Shariah disclosure framework, i.e. Shariah disclosure information, mechanisms of Shariah disclosure, and adaptability in Shariah disclosure. Regarding disclosure of Shariah information in the annual report of IFIs, the authors recommended that institutions shall disclose their investment avenues along with proof of Islamicity, Shariah appraisal of the developed products and services, and showing Shariah compliance through actions. Said et al. (2018) constructed the Maqasid index, based on disclosure analysis, for evaluating the performance of Islamic banks. They assess Islamic banks based on the disclosure of Islamic banks' contributions toward the objectives of Shariah. Maali et al. (2006) emphasize the disclosure of IFIs justly dealing with their employees, customers, and all other stakeholders. Sugianto and0 Harapan (2017) suggest that IFIs shall disclose details of their charities given to the poor and needy. Zubairum et al. (2012) explore an important attribute that an IFI shall disclose in their annual report and that is the disclosure of an institution's commitment towards its debtor.

In the established Shariah governance disclosure literature, there are different indexes developed for evaluating the Islamic business ethical and Shariah reporting of IBIs. Abdullah et al. (2015) develop a Voluntary Corporate Governance Disclosures Index (VCGDI) for evaluating reporting level in southeast Asian and GCC Islamic banks; Albassam and Ntim (2017) develop a Islamic Values Disclosure Index (IVDI) for measuring the level of

Islamic reporting in Saudi Arabia's Shariah-compliant companies; Inten and Devi (2017) construct a Islamic Social Reporting Index (ISRI) for evaluating Islamic social reporting in Indonesian and Malaysian Islamic banks; Masruki et al. (2018) develop a Shariah Supervisory Board Index (SSBI) for measuring the level of Shariah supervisory board related information in Malaysian Islamic banks; Noordin et al. (2015) develop a Shariah governance Disclosure Index (SDI) for measuring the level of Shariah governance reporting in Malaysian Islamic banks; Ousama and Fatima (2010) construct an Islamic Disclosure Index (IDI) for assessing the level of Islamic reporting in Shariah-approved companies listed on Bursa Malaysia; Abdullah et al. (2013) develop a Shariah Supervisory Board Index (SSB Index) for measuring Shariah reporting in Malaysian and Indonesian Islamic banks; El-halaby et al. (2015) develop a SSB Disclosure Index for measuring Shariah compliance in 23 Islamic banks globally; Haniffa and Hudaib (2007) construct an Ethical Identity Index (EII) for measuring ethical reporting in Malaysian and Indonesian Islamic banks; Asutay and Harningtyas (2015) develop a Maqasid al-Shariah Index for evaluating Maqasid al-Shariah through Islamic banks' activities.

2.4 Methodology of the Research

2.4.1 Type of Research and Research Design

The research is applied in nature in which the purpose is to assess the level of Shariah disclosure and reporting in Pakistan's full-fledged Islamic banks. Research design is based on the nature of the data collection technique. Primarily, survey design used in this study in which items of the self-constructed index were investigated in the sample Islamic banks' annual reports. Therefore, based on the established evidences, survey design is an ideal and the most appropriate method for indexation and comparing studies (Belal et al., 2015; Blancone et al., 2016; Hassan & Syafri Harahap, 2010). In this study all five full-fledged Islamic banks, listed on SBP website, are used for data collection. Total 27 reports, including both annual reports and Shariah reports, were analysed over the period of 2015–2017. ShDI will be constructed based on the SBP's Shariah governance framework-2018, AAOIFI disclosure requirements, and some prior Islamic reporting literature.

2.4.2 Data Collection and Information

The secondary data will be collected from the annual reports of Pakistan's full-fledged Islamic banks. Currently, there are five full-fledged Islamic banks in Pakistan namely Meezan Bank Limited (MEBL), Bank Islami Pakistan Limited (BIPL), Dubai Islamic Bank Limited (DIBL), Al-Barakah Bank Pakistan Limited (ABPL), and MCB Islamic Bank Limited (MIBL). Three years of data, both financial report and Shariah report, were collected over the period 2015–2017 (as shown in Table 2.1). The reason is that MIB is comparatively a

Table 2.1 List of Annual Reports Collected from Pakistan's Full-Fledged Islamic Bank Websites

Name of the Islamic Bank	2015	2016	2017	Total
Meezan Bank Limited	FR*+SR**	FR+SR	FR+SR	6
Bank Islami	FR+SR	FR+SR	FR+SR	6
Dubai Islamic Bank Pakistan	FR	FR	FR+SR	4
Albaraka Bank Pakistan	FR+SR	FR+SR	FR+SR	6
MCB Islamic Bank	SR	FR+SR	FR+SR	5
Total Reports				27

* FR–Financial Report, ** SR–Shariah Report

new bank established in 2015 and their annual reports are available from 2015. Both the financial reports and Shariah reports of these Islamic banks are available on their respective websites. Therefore, these websites are approached for data collection.

2.4.3 Data Analysis

The data collected from the annual reports is analysed by using disclosure analysis approach in which ShDI items were investigated. Disclosure analysis approach is an ideal approach when the study aims to investigate for items in documents (Platonova, 2014; Zafar & Sulaiman, 2018; Ahmed & El-belihy, 2017) already on the ethical banking horizon, the Islamic banking model. For scoring the index themes, binary or dichotomous value approach were adopted which is frequently followed in the prior similar studies (Albassam & Ntim, 2017; Triyuwono & Kamayanti, 2014; Harun, 2016). Annual reports of GCC Islamic banks for the period 2010–2014 are analysed using manual content analysis, which involves 195 observations of 39 Islamic banks. The CSR disclosure index is constructed based on 11 dimensions using AAOIFI standard no. 7, 2010. An ordinary least square (OLS; Rahman et al., 2014; Ibrahim et al., 2004; Haniffa & Hudaib, 2007; Darmadi, 2013; Abdullah et al., 2015). According to the approach, if an Islamic bank is disclosing a particular theme in their annual report, so it will score 1 otherwise 0, if not disclosing. Furthermore, the following formula for calculating ShDI is inspired from the work of Haniffa and Hudaib (2007); Ibrahim et al. (2004); and Kamla and Rammal (2013). ShDI for a bank calculated as:

$$ShDI = \Sigma ADT \times 100 \text{ Nth EDT}$$

Where ΣADT = Sum of actual disclosed themes
Nth EDT = Total number of expected disclosure themes

Higher the ShDI value represents best Shariah disclosure and reporting practices and vice-versa.

2.5 Developing Shariah Disclosure Index (ShDI)

ShDI is a specific kind of index developed to compare the expected disclosure items with the actual Islamic banks' Shariah disclosure practices. Indexation is a process in which the developer compared designed models with real system parameters (Ullah, 2014). In addition, it is also the Shariah responsibility of the Islamic banks to ensure full disclosure especially Islamicity disclosure (Abdullah & Syariati, 2016; Herwiyanti et al., 2005; Obid & Hajj, 2011). Therefore, to ensure full Shariah disclosure, the present study is an attempt to develop a comprehensive and adequate index for evaluating the Shariah disclosure level of Islamic banks. ShDI were constructed by following the below fundamental steps.

Step-I: Reviewing of prior literature on Shariah and Islamic corporate governance indexation. These literatures include SPB's Shariah governance framework-2018, original and high-quality journal papers regarding Shariah disclosure, and AAOIFI's governance standards.

Step-II: Key Shariah disclosure themes were identified from the prior literature and then categorized it in three different sets. According to Raharja (2011) in accounting and financial system, there are three broad categories of disclosure: mandatory, recommended, and voluntary. In the present study, mandatory disclosure refers to the native regulator(s), recommended disclosure refers to the standards or guidelines by the international standard-setting agencies, and the voluntary disclosure refers to the recommendations of the prior original studies. The themes are categorized based on SBP's mandatory themes, AAOIFI's recommended themes, and prior studies' voluntary disclosure themes. There are total 53 themes in which 27 were extracted from SBP-Shariah governance framework-2018, 6 from AAOIFI's governance standards, and 20 from prior studies.

Step-III: Coding of themes is the third step of ShDI development. In this step themes were coded based on their respective class and number. SBP's mandatory themes represented by SSDR which means SBP's SGF Disclosure Requirements, AAOIFI's recommended themes represented as ASDR which refers to AAOIFI's Shariah Disclosure Requirements, and themes extracted from prior studies were symbolized as VSDI which means Voluntary Shariah Disclosure Items. All the extracted themes and their respective codes are mentioned in the Tables 2.2, 2.3, and 2.4.

Step-IV: In fourth step, themes of each set were scored based on dichotomous or binary value system approach. According to this approach, each theme scored by 0–1 or 0–0.75 or 0–0.5. If the SSDR's theme disclosed in the bank annual report so it will score 1 otherwise 0. In the same way, if a particular ASDR theme disclosed in the bank annual report so it will score 0.75 otherwise 0. Similarly, if the bank disclosed a particular VSDI theme in their annual report so it will score 0.5 otherwise 0. The score of the entire 53 themes is 41.5.

Assessing Shariah Disclosure in Pakistan 27

Table 2.2 Themes Extracted from IBD-SBP's Shariah Governance Framework – 2018

No	Theme's Code	Description of Theme	Theme's Score
1	SSDR*-1	The bank's annual Shariah report published in English in its annual report.	0–1
2	SSDR-2	The bank's annual Shariah report published in Urdu in its annual report.	0–1
3	SSDR-3	Opening of annual Shariah report with the name of Allah	0–1
4	SSDR-4	Statement that the 'Board of Directors and Executive Management are solely responsible to ensure that the operations of the bank are conducted in a manner that comply with Shariah principles at all times, we are required to submit a report on the overall Shariah compliance environment of the bank'	0–1
5	SSDR-5	There is an effective mechanism for BODs to frequently oversight the Shariah compliance mechanism of the bank	0–1
6	SSDR-6	The bank has established an independent and effective SSB and the SBP's Fit and Proper Criteria (FAPC) properly adopted in the appointment of SSB's members	0–1
7	SSDR-7	The bank has at least three Shariah advisors in their SSB.	0–1
8	SSDR-8	The bank has Resident Shariah Board Member (RSBM) to frequently oversee the Shariah compliant status of bank's products, services, and operations.	0–1
9	SSDR-9	To assist SSB, the bank has an effective Shariah Compliance Department (SCD) which also serve as a conduit between SSB and bank's management	0–1
10	SSDR-10	Reporting concerning SCD's verification and approval of the distribution of profit and loss sharing mechanism with depositors, prior to its disbursement in the concern depositors.	0–1
11	SSDR-11	Disclosure of the avenues and their Shariah conformity wherein the bank deploy of funds of investors especially IAHs.	0–1
12	SSDR-12	The BOD meted the SSB at least twice a year regarding strengthen the bank Shariah compliance environment and enforcement of SSB's pronouncements.	0–1
13	SSDR-13	The bank frequently arranges trainings and learning seminar concerning Islamic finance for their management.	0–1
14	SSDR-14	The SSB meted at least on a quarterly basis.	0–1
15	SSDR-15	The bank's SCD conducted Shariah reviews, on test check basis, of each class of transactions, the relevant documentation and process flows.	0–1

(*Continued*)

Table 2.2 (Continued)

No	Theme's Code	Description of Theme	Theme's Score
16	SSDR-16	The bank conducted internal Shariah audit.	0–1
17	SSDR-17	The bank conducted external Shariah audit.	0–1
18	SSDR-18	SSB's opinions concerning bank's Shariah the compliance environment of the bank in the light of SSB's issued fatwah	0–1
19	SSDR-19	SSB's opinions that whether or not the bank's products, services, and operations are in accordance with the SBP-IBD's directives, rulings of SBP's Shariah Board's, and SBP's Shariah governance framework.	0–1
20	SSDR-20	Reporting concerning 'SSB's opinions that whether or not the bank has a comprehensive mechanism in place to ensure Shariah compliance in their overall operations'	0–1
21	SSDR-21	The bank's earnings realized from sources or by means prohibited by Shariah have been credited to charity account	0–1
22	SSDR-22	Charity fund are being properly utilized.	0–1
23	SSDR-23	Disclosure of the SSB's opinions that whether or not the bank efficiently followed the SBP instructions concerning profit and loss distribution, before disbursement, and pool management.	0–1
24	SSDR-24	Disclosure concerning the level bank's management awareness toward Islamic finance and acknowledging their sincerity and efforts in the promotion of Islamic banking	0–1
25	SSDR-25	SSB opinions concerning that whether or not SSB facilitated and well-informed while discharging their duty effectively	0–1
26	SSDR-26	Report of the outstanding Shariah-related issues.	0–1
27	SSDR-27	Signatures of the entire SSB's members on the annual Shariah report.	0–1

* SSDR–SBP's SGF Disclosure Requirements

Step-V: Calculation of ShDI or indexation for each Islamic bank is the fifth step of ShDI. In this step the achieved score of each Islamic bank is multiplied with 100 and then divided by the ideal desired score of ShDI which is 41.5. The final value is the ShDI score in term of percentage. Higher the ShDI value indicates higher Shariah disclosure in the particular Islamic bank while lower the ShDI value indicates lower Shariah disclosure.

2.6 Findings and Discussion

Besides other disclosure arrangements, Islamic banks need to ensure adequate Shariah reporting and disclosure. The established literature suggested different

Assessing Shariah Disclosure in Pakistan 29

Table 2.3 Themes Extracted from AAOIFI's Governance Standards

No	Theme's Code	Description of Theme	Theme's Score
28	ASDR**-1	Disclosure of fatawa/ Shariah pronouncements guidelines of the SSB	0–0.75
29	ASDR-2	A proper title of bank's SSB report	0–0.75
30	ASDR-3	The calculation of Zakat is in compliance with the Shariah rules and principles	0–0.75
31	ASDR-4	The bank has clear policy for waqf management	0–0.75
32	ASDR-5	Greetings the addressee by Assalamu Alaykum Wa Rahmatu Allah Wa Barakatuh	0–0.75
33	ASDR-6	Closing the Shariah report by Wassalamu Alaykum Wa Rahmatu Allah Wa Barakatuh	0–0.75

** ASDR–AAOIFI's Shariah Disclosure Requirements

Shariah reporting and disclosure attributes in which the Islamic banks' stakeholders are interested. These attributes include SSB-related disclosure, disclosure about investment avenues and their proof of Islamicity, Islamicity of the products and services, disclosure of the Shariah pronouncements, disclosure of the bank annual Shariah report, disclosure of the bank annual Shariah audit report, and disclosure of bank charity account details, etc. Therefore, based on all these attributions, we developed a disclosure index called Shariah Disclosure Index (ShDI) and then evaluated the Shariah disclosure practices of the Pakistani full-fledged Islamic banks by using their annual report for the years 2015–2017. The result shows that the overall Shariah disclosure levels for the five full-fledged Islamic banks in Pakistan are 53.74%. However, the level of Shariah disclosure in Pakistani Islamic banks and foreign Islamic banks are 69% and 30.35% respectively, which shows that Pakistani Islamic banks are the more satisfactory in terms of Shariah disclosure and reporting. In addition, bank wise Shariah disclosure, Bank Islami is on top by securing score of 75% followed by MEBL, MIBL, ABPL, and DIBL by securing score of 71%, 62%, 39%, and 23% respectively. In addition, Islamic banks disclosed about 80%–90% of the SSDR and ASDR themes, whereas, on the other hand, these banks disclose very low percentage of VSDI themes. Furthermore, it is also noticed that Shariah disclosure level is improving with time in all Islamic banks except in BIPL which remain the same throughout 2015–2017. The findings are summarized in Table 2.5.

2.7 Conclusion

The results show that Islamic banks in Pakistan have a low level of Shariah disclosure. It is observable that Islamic banks do not disclose adequate Shariah information related to the activities that may attract criticism, such as the Shariah appraisal of ambiguous transactions. On the other hand, they did

Table 2.4 Voluntary Shariah Disclosure Themes Extracted from Prior Research Studies

No	Theme's Code	Description of Theme	Theme's Score	Reference
34	VSDI***-1	Amount subject to Zakat	0–0.50	Abdullah et al. (2013)
35	VSDI-2	A proper title of bank's SSB report	0–0.50	Abdullah et al. (2013)
36	VSDI-3	Zakat beneficiaries	0–0.50	Abdullah (2014)
37	VSDI-4	Statement concerning 'bank's financing strategies includes formal exclusions of any engagement that deals with haram or unlawful goods and services'	0–0.50	Abdullah (2014)
38	VSDI-5	The bank discloses Qard Al-Hassan statement	0–0.50	Abuhmaira (2006)
39	VSDI-6	The bank debt written off policy for insolvent debtors.	0–0.50	Ahmed & El-belihy (2017)
40	VSDI-7	Definition of the Islamic products offered	0–0.50	Al-baluchi (2006)
41	VSDI-8	Shariah screening during investment	0–0.50	Amran et al. (2017)
42	VSDI-9	The bank Shariah examination procedures	0–0.50	Darmadi (2013)
43	VSDI-10	The bank disclosed experience of SSB's members	0–0.50	Elamer, Ntim, & Abdou (2017)
44	VSDI-11	Are the report shows that the bank complies with the AAOIFI's Shariah standards	0–0.50	El-halaby et al. (2015)
45	VSDI-12	The bank future directions in serving the needs of Muslim community	0–0.50	Haniffa & Hudaib (2007)
46	VSDI-13	The bank involvement in non-permissible activities-% of profit	0–0.50	Haniffa & Hudaib (2007)
47	VSDI-14	SSB's approval for new products and services	0–0.50	Obid & Hajj (2011)
48	VSDI-15	The bank policy on Late Repayments	0–0.50	Othman & Thani (2010)
49	VSDI-16	BOD and top management knowledge and competence in banking and Shariah	0–0.50	Rashid & Hassan (2014)
50	VSDI-17	The bank just dealings with its employees.	0–0.50	Maali, Casson, & Napier (2006)
51	VSDI-18	The bank has a formal policy on duties and responsibilities of SSB.	0–0.50	Srairi (2015)
52	VSDI-19	Remuneration of SSB	0–0.50	Setyawan & Permatasari (2017)
53	VSDI-20	The bank disclosure toward Maqasid al-Shariah	0–0.50	Said et al. (2018)

*** VSDI–Voluntary Shariah Disclosure Items

Table 2.5 Summarized Table Showing Shariah Disclosure in Pakistan's Full-Fledged Islamic Bank

Rank	Name of the Islamic Bank	$ShDI_{2015}$	$ShDI_{2016}$	$ShDI_{2017}$	ShDIA*	Pakistani vs Foreign	ShDIC**
1	Bank Islami	75%	75%	75%	75%	69%	53.75%
2	Meezan Bank	68%	70.5%	74.7%	71%		
3	MCD Islamic Bank	48.8%	66.8%	70.5%	62%		
4	Al Baraka Bank	38%	38%	40.4%	39%	30.35%	
5	Dubai Islamic Bank	0	0	65.7%	23%		

*ShDIA–Average ShDI, **ShDIC–Cumulative ShDI

provide more disclosures regarding their charitable activities and their involvement in social upbringing of the society. The scope of the study is limited to disclosure of Shariah information and the Islamicity evidence of products, services, operations, and activities. Therefore, other type of disclosure such as social disclosure, corporate disclosure, ethical disclosure, moral disclosure, cultural and environmental disclosure may not be discussed in this study. This limitation become the opportunity for the Future study and other improvement can be made by including the Shariah disclosure requirements of Islamic Fiqh Academy Jeddah, Islamic Financial Services Board (IFSB), Securities and Exchange Commission of Pakistan (SECP), and fatwa giving department/Darul Ifta of Pakistan's prominent religious institutions like Darul Uloom Karachi, Jamia tur Rasheed Karachi, Shariah Academy–IIU Islamabad, etc. Furthermore, this study has ranked Islamic banks on the basis of their Shariah disclosure only without taking into consideration other elements such as the bank assets, branches, time, business, market shares, bank management, technological advancement, etc.

The research provided a benchmark and indicator for all concerned and potential stakeholders who are making their investment and business decisions based on the Islamic banks' Shariah disclosure. In addition, the study is equally important for IBIs to comply with ShDI and ensure full Shariah disclosure for attracting new investors and protect their ideological and religious commitments as well. Furthermore, to keep the confidence of stakeholders in Islamic banks, it is recommended to IBIs to ensure adequate disclosure of the attributes explored in this study. In addition, in order to evaluate the Shariah disclosure practices of Islamic banks, the regulator is also recommended to adopt ShDI. Islamic banks' stakeholders are also recommended to ShDI before making their business decisions towards any Islamic bank. In order to achieve a robust finding, it is recommended to add more mandatory, voluntary, and standard attributes concerning Shariah disclosure and reporting.

References

Abdullah, B. H. (2014). *An exploratory examination into the relationship between corporate governance and risk management in Islamic banks: Disclosure and survey analysis* (Doctoral thesis, Durham University, Durham, United Kingdom). Retrieved from http://etheses.dur.ac.uk/10817/

Abdullah, W. A. W., Percy, M., & Stewart, J. (2013). Shari'ah disclosures in Malaysian and Indonesian Islamic banks: The Shari'ah governance system. *Journal of Islamic Accounting and Business Research*, *4*(2), 100–131. https://doi.org/10.1108/JIABR-10-2012-0063

Abdullah, W. A. W., Percy, M., & Stewart, J. (2015). Determinants of voluntary corporate governance disclosure: Evidence from Islamic banks in the Southeast Asian and the Gulf Cooperation Council regions. *Journal of Contemporary Accounting and Economics*, *11*(3), 262–279. https://doi.org/10.1016/j.jcae.2015.10.001

Abdullah, W., & Syariati, A. (2016). Islamic bank as bank of ethics. *Journal of Research in Business and Management*, *4*(4), 1–4. Retrieved from www.researchgate.net/publication/325140019_Islamic_Bank_As_Bank_of_Ethics

Abuhmaira, M. A. (2006). The impact of 'AAOIFI' standards on the financial reporting of Islamic banks: Evidence from Bahrain (Doctoral thesis). Available from British Library e-theses database. (Order No. 429476)

Ahmed, A., & El-belihy, A. (2017). An investigation of the disclosure of corporate social responsibility in UK Islamic banks. *Academy of Accounting and Financial Studies Journal*, *21*(3), 1–31.

Al-baluchi, A. E. A. (2006). *The impact of AAOIFI standards and other bank characteristics on the level of voluntary disclosure in the annual reports of Islamic banks* (Doctoral thesis, University of Surrey, Guildford, United Kingdom). Retrieved from http://epubs.surrey.ac.uk/801/

Al-Mehmadi, F. B. S. B. S. (2004). The external reporting needs of investors in Islamic banks in Saudi Arabia: An exploratory study of full disclosure (Doctoral thesis). Available from British Library e-theses database. (Order No. 496402)

Albassam, W. M., & Ntim, C. G. (2017). The effect of Islamic values on voluntary corporate governance disclosure: The case of Saudi-listed firms. *Journal of Islamic Accounting and Business Research*, *8*(2), 182–202. https://doi.org/10.1108/JIABR-09-2015-0046

Amran, A., Fauzi, H., Purwanto, Y., Darus, F., Yusoff, H., Zain, M. M.,... Nejati, M. (2017). Social responsibility disclosure in Islamic banks: A comparative study of Indonesia and Malaysia. *Journal of Financial Reporting and Accounting*, *15*(1), 99–115. https://doi.org/10.1108/JFRA-01-2015-0016

Askari, H., Iqbal, Z., Krichenne, N., & Mirakhor, A. (2010). *The Stability of Islamic Finance: Creating a Resilient Financial Environment for a Secure Future*. John Wiley & Sons.

Asutay, M., & Harningtyas, A. F. (2015). Developing Maqasid al-Shari'ah index to evaluate social performance of Islamic banks: A conceptual and empirical attempt. *International Journal of Islamic Economics and Finance Studies*, *1*(1), 5–64. Retrieved from https://dergipark.org.tr/en/pub/ijisef/ issue/29332/313846

Belal, A. R., Abdelsalam, O., & Nizamee, S. S. (2015). Ethical reporting in Islamic Bank Bangladesh Limited (1983–2010). *Journal of Business Ethics*, *129*(4), 769–784. https://doi.org/10.1007/s10551- 014-2133-8

Blancone, P. P., Shakhatreh, M. Z., & Radwan, M. (2016). Operational risk management disclosure in Islamic banks. In V. Cantino, P. De Vincentiis, & G. Racca (Eds), *Risk Management: Perspectives and Open Issues* (pp. 62–78). McGraw-Hill Education.

Darmadi, S. (2013). Corporate governance disclosure in the annual report: An exploratory study on Indonesian Islamic banks. *Humanomics, 29*(1), 4–23. https://doi.org/10.1108/08288661311299295

El-halaby, S., Hussainey, K., & El-Sood, H. A. (2015). The determinants of the disclosure level of Sharia compliance in Islamic Bank. In *10th International Conference on Islamic Economics and Finance*. Islamic Research and Training Institute.

Elamer, A. A., Ntim, C. G., & Abdou, H. A. (2017). Islamic governance, national governance, and bank risk management and disclosure in MENA countries. *Business & Society, 59*(5), 914–955. https://doi.org/10.1177/0007650317746108

Gilani, H. (2015). Exploring the ethical aspects of Islamic banking. *International Journal of Islamic and Middle Eastern Finance and Management, 8*(1), 85–98. https://doi.org/10.1108/IMEFM-09-2012-0087

Grais, W., & Pellegrini, M. (2006). Corporate governance in institutions offering Islamic financial services issues and options (World Bank Policy Research Working Paper No. 4052). Available at SSRN: https://ssrn.com/abstract=940709

Grassa, R. (2013). Shari'ah governance system in Islamic financial institutions: New issues and challenges. *Arab Law Quarterly, 27*(2), 171–187. https://doi.org/10.1163/15730255-12341254

Grassa, R., Chakroun, R., & Hussainey, K. (2018). Corporate governance and Islamic banks' products and services disclosure. *Accounting Research Journal, 31*(1), 75–89. https://doi.org/10.1108/ARJ-09-2016-0109

Hamid, W., Ubud, S., Djumahir, & Siti, A. (2016). Trade principles and Sharia-Adhehence banking performance analysis by employing maqasid Islamic Shari'ah index approach: Study on Indonesian Sharia bank. *Russian Journal of Agricultural and Socio-Economic Sciences, 11*(59), 66–74. https://doi.org/10.18551/rjoas.2016-11.09

Haniffa, R., & Hudaib, M. (2007). Exploring the ethical identity of Islamic banks via communication in annual reports. *Journal of Business Ethics, 76*(1), 97–116. https://doi.org/10.1007/s10551-006-9272-5

Harun, M. S. Bin. (2016). The impact of corporate governance and its consequences on CSR disclosure: Empirical evidence from Islamic banks in GCC countries (Doctoral thesis, University of Plymouth, Plymouth, United Kingdom). Retrieved from http://hdl.handle.net/10026.1/6608

Hasan, Z. (2011). A survey on Shari'ah governance practices in Malaysia, GCC countries and the UK: Critical appraisal. *International Journal of Islamic and Middle Eastern Finance and Management, 4*(1), 30–51. https://doi.org/10.1108/17538391111122195

Hasan, Z. (2012). *Shari'ah Governance in Islamic Banks*. Edinburgh University Press.

Hassan, A., & Syafri Harahap, S. (2010). Exploring corporate social responsibility disclosure: The case of Islamic banks. *International Journal of Islamic and Middle Eastern Finance and Management, 3*(3), 203–227. https://doi.org/10.1108/17538391011072417

Herwiyanti, E., MA, A. S. W., & Rosada, A. (2005). Analysis of factors influencing the Islamic corporate governance disclosure index of Islamic banks in Asia. *International Journal of Humanities and Management Sciences, 3*(4), 192–197.

Islamic Banking Department, State Bank of Pakistan (2018). Shari'ah governance framework for Islamic banking institutions (updated till June 2018). Retrieved from http://www.sbp.org.pk/ibd/2018/C1.htm

Ibrahim, S. H. B. M., Wirman, A., Alrazi, B., & Pramono, S. (2004). Alternative disclosure & performance measures for Islamic banks. In Second Conference on Administrative Science: Meeting the Challenges of the Globalization Age, King Fahd University of Petroleum and Minerals, Dahran, Saud Arabia (pp. 19–21).

Inten, M., & Devi, F. (2017). Islamic social reporting in Islamic banking: Stakeholders theory perspective. SHS Web of Conferences. https://doi.org/10.1051/shsconf/2017 3412001

Ismail, M., Jan, S., & Ullah, K. (2018). Determinants of Shari'ah disclosure in Islamic banking institutions. *Abasyn University Journal of Social Sciences*, 11.

Jan, S., & Asutay, M. (2019). *A Model of Islamic Development: An Approach in Islamic Moral Economy*. Edward Elgar.

Jan, S., Khan, Z., & Ullah, K. (2018). Institutionalizing justice in Islamic finance. *Journal of Islamic Banking and Finance*, *14*(1), 205–216.

Jan, S., Ullah, K, & Asutay, M. (2015). Knowledge, work, and social welfare as Islamic socio-economic development goals. *Journal of Islamic Banking and Finance*, *32*(3), 11–21.

Jan, S., Ullah, K., & Asutay, M. (2016). Islamic perspective of development: Maqasid Al Shari'ah, Islamic moral economy, and socio-economic development goals. In I. A. Ghafar, A. S. Syed, & H. L. B. B. Mameed (Eds), *Policy Discussion on Maqasid Al Shari'ah for Socio Economic Development* (pp. 45–58).

Penerbit kuis. Kamla, R., & Rammal, H. G. (2013). Social reporting by Islamic banks: Does social justice matter? *Accounting, Auditing & Accountability Journal*, *26*(6), 911–945. https://doi.org/10.1108/AAAJ-03-2013-1268

Maali, B., Casson, P., & Napier, C. (2006). Social reporting by Islamic banks. *ABACUS A Journal of Accounting, Finance, and Business Studies*, *42*(2), 266–289. https://doi.org/10.1111/j.1467-6281.2006.00200.x

Masruki, R., Hanefah, M. M., & Wahab, N. A. (2018). Shari'ah Supervisory Board (SSB) and performance of Islamic banks in Malaysia. *International Journal of Engineering & Technology*, *7*(3.25), 710–714. Retrieved from www.sciencepubco.com/index.php/ijet/article/view/17831

Noordin, N. H., Kassim, S., Prabangasta, D., & Hayeeyahya, N. (2015). Does composition of Shari'ah committee influence Shari'ah governance disclosure? Evidence from Islamic banks in Malaysia. IIUM Institute of Islamic Banking and Finance, Malaysia, (July), 31.

Obid, S. N. S., & Hajj, A. F. (2011). Bank ethical disclosure level: Malaysian Islamic bank. *Asia Pacific Journal of Accounting and Finance*, *1*(2), 199–210.

Othman, R., & Thani, A. M. (2010). Islamic social reporting of listed companies in Malaysia. *International Business & Economics Research Journal*, *9*(4), 135–144. https://doi.org/10.19030/iber.v9i4.561

Othman, R., Thani, A. M., & Ghani, E. K. (2009). Determinants of Islamic social reporting among top Shari'ah approved companies in Bursa Malaysia. *Research Journal of International Studies*, *12*(12), 4–20.

Ousama, A. A., & Fatima, A. H. (2010). Voluntary disclosure by Shari'ah approved companies: An exploratory study. *Journal of Financial Reporting and Accounting*, *8*(1), 35–45. https://doi.org/10.1108/19852511011055943

Platonova, E. (2014). *Comparative analysis of CSR disclosure and its impact on financial performance in the GCC Islamic banks* (Doctoral thesis, Durham University, Durham, United Kingdom). Retrieved from http://etheses.dur.ac.uk/10726/

Raharja, S. (2011). *An examination of social disclosure by Islamic banks in Indonesia. Paper presented at the IIUM International Accounting Conference V (INTAC V)*, Pan Pacific Klia, Malaysia. Retrieved from http://eprints.undip.ac.id/36114/

Rahman, R. A., Danbatta, B. L., & Saimi, N. S. B. (2014). Corporate ethical identity disclosures: The perceived, the publicized and the applied in Islamic banks. *International Journal of Trade, Economics and Finance*, 5(2), 199–203. https://doi.org/10.7763/IJTEF.2014.V5.371

Rashid, M., & Hassan, M. K. (2014). Market value of Islamic banks and ethical identity. *American Journal of Islamic Social Sciences*, 31(2), 43–79.

Said, R., Abd Samad, K., Mohd Sidek, N. Z., Ilias, N. F., & Omar, N. (2018). Corporate social responsibility disclosure index of Malaysian Shari'ah–compliant companies. *International Journal of Ethics and Systems*, 34(1), 55–69. https://doi.org/10.1108/IJOES-09-2016-0068

Setyawan, H., & Permatasari, D. (2017). Corporate governance disclosure practices: Evidence from Indonesian Islamic banks. Paper presented at Seminar Nasional Hasil Penelitian dan Pengabdian Masyarakat UNIMUS 2017,

Semarang, I., & Srairi, S. (2015). Corporate governance disclosure practices and performance of Islamic banks in GCC countries. *Journal of Islamic Finance*, 4(2), 1–17.

Sugianto, & Harapan, N. (2017). The Integration of Disclosure of Islamic Social Reporting (ISR) in Islamic Bank Financial Statements. In M. Y. Jaaffar, A. A. Sani, & A. Muhammad (Eds.), The 2016 4th International Conference on Governance and Accountability (pp. 133–146). EDP Sciences. https://doi.org/10.1051/shsconf/20173600011

Triyuwono, I., & Kamayanti, A. (2014). Islamic values Islamic bank underlying performance assessment. *Research Journal of Finance and Accounting*, 5(24), 106–113.

Ullah, K. (2014). *Adaptable service-system design: An analysis of Shari'ah finance in Pakistan* (Doctoral thesis, Brunel University, London, United Kingdom). Retrieved from https://bura.brunel.ac.uk/handle/2438/8281

Zafar, M. B., & Sulaiman, A. A. (2018). Corporate social responsibility and Islamic banks: A systematic literature review. *Management Review Quarterly*, 69, 159–206. https://doi.org/10.1007/s11301-018-0150x

Zainuddin, Z., & Nordin, N. (2016). Addressing governance issue in Islamic Real Estate Investment (I-REITs): A case study for OIC country–Malaysia. *International Journal of Islamic Business*, 1(1), 60–75.

Zubairu, U. M., Sakariyau, O. B., & Dauda, C. K. (2012). Evaluation of social reporting practices of Islamic banks in Saudi Arabia. *Electronic Journal of Business Ethics and Organizational Studies*, 17(1), 41–50

3 Fatwa in Islamic Legal Tradition and Its Implications for Shariah Pronouncements of Islamic Banks

Muhammad Tahir Mansoori

3.1 Introduction

Fatwa in Islamic finance has played a very significant role in the development and expansion of Islamic banking industry in the last two decades. The credibility of Islamic banking and customer's confidence in it is largely attributed to the religious verdicts issued by a Shariah advisor regarding Shariah legitimacy of Islamic banking products, transactions and operations. A mufti assures a client that this is the mufti, not the client, who is responsible for the prohibition or permissibility of transaction. Thus, relying on the words and integrity of mufti, a client decides to deal with Islamic bank. He deposits money in it and avails its services believing that every transaction he enters into with Islamic bank is *Halal*. Once the fatwa has been issued by the mufti, the onus, burden and responsibility with regard to Halal and Haram is shifted from the client to the Mufti. A mufti speaks in the name of Allah. He is 'Signatory for God Almighty' and 'the heir of Prophets' as prominent Muslim jurists Imam Ibn al-Qayyimand Imam Shatibi call him. A mufti, writes Shatibi, 'Stands before the Muslim community in the same place as the Prophet (S.A.W.S) stood' (Shatibi).

The modern Muftiship or Shariah advisory, whether at the level of Shariah Advisory Committee of State Bank of Pakistan or at the level of Shariah boards of Islamic banks in Pakistan, has been a subject of severe criticism by the scholars. Many scholars have contested the eligibility and competency of Shariah advisors to undertake such a sensitive task that directly pertains to Halal and Haram. They have criticized 'Fit and Proper Criterion' prescribed by the State Bank for Shariah Advisor and have raised many objections on it. In their view, Islamic finance is a multi-disciplinary field. It combines a number of disciplines such as Shariah, business law, conventional finance, economics, etc. A mufti in the field of Islamic finance is supposed to possess sound grounding in Shariah and rich exposure to these disciplines. Beside eligibility and competence of Shariah advisors, the structure of modern fatwa, its substance and content has also been subject matter of debate and discussion among Shariah scholars. The scholars claim that the pronouncements of Shariah boards

DOI: 10.4324/9781003324836-3

regarding products and transactions, do not qualify to be a fatwa in its technical sense. Such pronouncements are merely approvals and certifications not Fatwa per se. It is pertinent to note that majority of the fatawa issued by the Shariah boards or Shariah advisors do not follow the format or structure prescribed for fatwa in classical Islamic juristic literature and fatwa manuals. The current format of so-called fatwa is that a product sheet or process flow of transaction is presented to the Shariah advisor who puts his approval on it with the words: 'I reviewed this product and did not find anything contrary to Shariah.' Sometimes he writes: 'I approve this product.' No Shariah argument or the basis of fatwa is provided by the Shariah advisor in his approval. This assertion may be verified by looking at the Shariah pronouncements or fatawa of the previous 3 years, where it may be observed that no fatwa is accompanied by Shariah basis which, according to fatwa manuals, is a necessary requirement of any fatwa.

In this chapter, we will investigate the concept of fatwa, qualification and qualities of mufti, the ethical standards for mufti, and the methodology of fatwa in classical Islamic jurisprudence. We will also examine the modern fatawa of Islamic banks in Pakistan on the touchstone of the above classical standards and requirements. The chapter has been organized in the following sections:

Concept of Fatwa and Its Significance in Islamic Legal Tradition
Adab al-Mufti: Required Qualification and Qualities of Mufi
Methods and Principles of Fatwa
Fatwa on Trial: Issues in Shariah Pronouncements in Islamic Finance Industry in Pakistan

3.2 Concept of Fatwa in Classical Islamic Tradition

As a juristic concept, fatwa is a non-binding advisory opinion in the matters of Shariah to an individual questioner (mustafti). It is an opinion, verdict or response given by the mufti, the specialist of Shariah on certain questions of Islamic law. Mustafti is the person who asks for fatwa, the questioner or petitioner. Istifta is the act of petitioning or the question submitted for fatwa (Khalid Masud, 1984). The function of Ifta or muftiship is *fard kifayah*, a societal obligation which suggests that Muslim society has collective obligation to provide answers to queries on issues of Shariah. However, if this duty is performed by an individual who is competent to undertake this task, the remaining community of muftis is absolved of its obligation towards the Muslim community. Sometimes, rendering fatwa becomes a personal and individual obligation. This happens where only one mufti is available for fatwa in the community. In that case giving fatwa by that single mufti becomes obligatory on him like performing obligatory prayers and fasting. The Quran instructs the Muslim individuals and society to consult the 'ahl al-zikr', people of knowledge or remembrance on matters of Shariah.

The institution of fatwa occupies a very significant position in Muslim society. A mufti, as interpreter of Shariah and expounder of hukm Sha'ri, owes a very sensitive and heavy role and duty towards Allah and the community. Many texts prohibit a mufti from issuing hasty fatwa without exercising due care and diligence. The early petitioners of fatwa were very cautious about issuing fatwa. The Holy Prophet (S.A.W.S) has warned against issuing hasty Shariah verdicts without proper deliberation.

A mufti is 'heir of the Prophets' as the Muslim jurists describe him. As heir of Prophet (S.A.W.S), his duty is to transmit knowledge of Shariah to the people and to exert his utmost to derive Shariah rules from their sources (Ibn Salah). Imam Qarafi says that a mufti in relation to Allah is like a spokesman of a ruler. A spokesman or representative of ruler is required to communicate the instructions of the ruler without any addition or deletion. In the same way a mufti has an obligation to convey to the people the rulings that he has discovered through his Ijtihad and legal reasoning. This is if he is mujtahid, but if he is only a muqallid mufti, then he is a representative of his mujtahid Imam, and in that capacity he has to reproduce the opinion of his Imam or school with all required honesty and integrity (al-Mallah. p. 586).

3.3 Adab al-Mufti: Qualities and Qualifications of Mufti

Adab al-Mufti or fatwa manuals deal generally with the topics such as definitions of fatwa, istifta, mufti, mustafti, the qualifications and qualities of mufti, requirements for mustafti, the petitioner or questioner, format and pattern of fatwa and broad guidelines and principles for fatwa, etc.

3.3.1 Qualification and Eligibility Criterion

In classical Islamic jurisprudence, the terms 'mufti' and 'mujtahid' have been used as interchangeable words and terms. The early jurist did not make a distinction between mujtahid mufti and non-mujtahid mufti, in terms of qualification and eligibility criterion. Imam Shafi (d. 820) claims that a mufti must be a mujtahid who has the ability to exercise legal reasoning and derive Shariah ahkaam from different sources. He mentions a number of branches of Islamic disciplines in which a mufti should be proficient. In his opinion, he should possess in-depth knowledge of legal verses of the Quran and Sunnah, Arabic language especially its grammar, knowledge of issues on which consensus (Ijma) has taken place and art of derivation of ahkam especially the analogical deduction (Shafi, 1325: 7:274).

Imam al-Haramayh al-Juwaini (d. 1085) has also used the terms 'mufti' and 'mujtahid' interchangeably. A mufti, in his view, must have necessary skill to derive rules for new and novel situations. From this one may safely conclude that in the analysis of Juwaini, a mujtahid alone can be a mufti. Imam Ghazali (d. 1111), another prominent jusrist, upholds the same above position. In his celebrated work on usul fiqh 'al-Mankhul', he affirms that the 'mufti is he who has complete mastery of Shariah rules embedded in the revealed texts as well as those discovered by the means of legal reasoning' (Al-Mankhul, 1980: 463,665).

Imam al-Baghawi, emphasizing Imam Shafi'is view on qualification of mufti, says:

> It is not permissible for an individual to issue fatwa in matter of religion except when he has sound knowledge of the book of Allah, abrogating and abrogated verses, causes of revelation, Makki and Madani verses, themes of the Quran; in-depth knowledge of Sunnah and its sciences; Arabic language, its grammar, poetry, besides having knowledge of different practices and traditions of different societies. If he possesses profound knowledge of all these disciplines and fields of knowledge, only then he is eligible to practice fatwa and issue Shariah rulings on halal and haram.'
>
> (Khatib al-Baghdadi, 2/157, p. 582)

About a century after Imam Ghazali significant change took place in the discourse. It was a shift from a rigid stance to a flexible position on the qualification and eligibility of mufti. A prominent Shafi'i jurist, Saifuddin Amidi (d. 1234), for the first time relaxed the condition of Ijtihad, for mufti. He allowed a non-mujtahid individual, but specialist in Islamic law, to issue fatwa according to principles of the school to which he belonged. After Amidi, it was generally recognized that a mufti, who is not an absolute mujtahid (mujtahid mustaqil), but a mujtahid within school (mujtahid fi al-madhab), has the right to practise fatwa according to the methodology and opinions of his school. The jurists like Ibn al-Salah (d. 1245), Ibn Abd al-Salam and other prominent Fuqahah and Usuliyyun (theorists), endorsed this position in their verdicts on qualifications of mufti. In subsequent periods, the condition of *mujtahid fi al-Madhab* was further relaxed. Any mufti having mastery over fiqh manuals especially the fatwa manuals of his school, conversant with the hierarchy of jurists of his school, possessing required skill to make distinction between the preferred and less preferable opinions of his school, and choose the most preferred and recognized opinions of his school, and conversant with art of interpretation and derivation of ahkam (usul fiqh), besides being proficient in the Quran and its allied sciences (ulum); Sunnah and its allied sciences (ulum), Arabic language, was held eligible to practise fatwa. It appears that now the focus of Muslim jurists was on Mujtahid al-Tarjih, i.e., mujtahid with ability to choose preferred opinions of his school. Such mujtahid is considered inferior to Mujtahid fi al-madhab in ranking. This means that nothing short of Mujtahid Tarjih was considered eligible for fatwa.

It would be instructive to introduce the position of two celebrated fatwa manuals of premodern period, that is fataawa i Alamgiri and al-Matana fi Maramma al-khazanah (1568). These two manuals explain the qualification and condition of mufti. Fatawa Alamgiri maintains that a mufti must fulfil the following conditions: good character, knowledge of the Quran and Sunnah, and a capacity of independent reasoning. Fatawa Alamgiri maintains that all the jurists are convinced that a mufti must be a mujtahid and hence a non-mujtahid who has only memorized the statements of mujtahid cannot be a mufti but he also makes it clear that what is called a fatwa these days, is not in fact so. It is rather quoting the statement of mufti, for the benefit of a petitioner so this mufti is only a transmitter, as such he is obliged to cite the statement and the authorities of his masters. He should clearly mention the verse of his early jurists of his school (Khalid Masud, p. 176).

Al-Matanah fi Marammah al-Khazanah, a celebrated Hanafi manual on fatwa, prescribes following requirements for a mufti: 'He should have knowledge of the Arabic language, grammar, legal hadith (ahadith having legal content and import), abrogated verses in the Quran, statement of earlier jurists, history, biographies of the companions of the Prophet (S.A.W.S), mastery of the doctrines of the school of law to which the mufti adheres, and principles and theories of Islamic law' (Khalid, p. 135). All the Muslim jurists of later ages are unanimous that since the mufti of this last category is inferior to the first two types, i.e. Mufti mustaqil and mufti fi al-madhab, he must quote in his fatwa the authorities upon which he has relied in his fatwa. Thus, to give his verdict that this transaction or act is permissible or impermissible is not sufficient compliance of the requirement of adab al-mufti and fatwa manuals.

Fatawa Alamgiri maintains as a matter of principle that a mufti must be mujtahid, but immediately relaxes the condition, and makes it clear that what is called a fatwa in days is not in fact so. It is rather statement of mufti for the benefit of petitioners. So he must quote the authority in his fatwa.

3.3.2 Specialization in a Particular Field of Fatwa

Another condition and requirement for mufti is that he should be specialist in a particular field of Islamic law, such as specialist in Fiqh ul Muamlat (Islamic Commercial law) or Fiqh al Munakahat (Islamic Law of Marriage and Divorce) or Fiqh Jinai (Islamic Criminal Law) or Fiqh Dawli (Islamic International Law), etc. This specialization in Fiqh is known as Tjazzu al Fatwa in classical Islamic jurisprudence. The concept of Tajazzu al–Fatwa wal-ijtihad or compartmentalization of fatwa derives its legitimacy from the opinions of some classical jurists (Fuqaha) and theorists (Usuliyyun) who allow ijtihad, fatwa and legal reasoning in a particular branch of Islamic law to the exclusion of other branches. It is pertinent to note that the Fuqaha allowing field-specific fatwa have not practised this fatwa in their own period. But their opinions certainly paved way for the development of specializations in fatwa.

Here are some views of classical jurists on Tajazzi al–fatwa or wal-ijtihad. According to Ibn-al-Qayyim (751H) if mujtahid does not fulfil all conditions of ijtihad in different fields, but he is specialized in one particular field, he is eligible to undertake ijtihad in that field. This goes without saying that specialization in fatwa and ijtihad (tajazzi fi al-fatwa wal-ijtihad) is a solution to the problems of this age. According to Amdi (631H), if mujtahid has enough knowledge regarding certain matter (subject) and does not know about other fields of knowledge is allowed to undertake ijtihad and that his ignorance of other fields will not affect his ability of ijtihad, because it is not necessary for a mufti to know about all the fields. Imam Razi (606H) says that if one fulfils the stipulated qualification of a mujtahid, he is mujtahid, but if he fulfils qualification of ijtihad in a specific subject, it is permissible for him to make ijtihad in that specific subject. AAOIFI Shariah standard in this regard mentions that issuing fatwa to institutions does not require competence in all areas of fiqh. Fatwa can be issued by a scholar who is competent only in the area of financial transactions performed by institutions.

Concept of specializations in different branches of Fiqh implies that a mufti in the field of Islamic finance should have an academic degree in that field, with sound and serious research in the area of Fiqh al-Muamlat, besides having good experience of issuing fatawa in Islamic finance. He should be known among ulama and Shariah scholars as specialist in fiqh al-Muamlat. It seems unconceivable that a person in one year's time acquires specialization in all branches of Islamic law, i.e., Ibadat, family matters, inheritance, Islamic criminal law, Islamic administrative law (siyasah Shariah), Islamic law of international relations, Islamic medical jurisprudence, etc., and in the same year he learns how to issue fatwa and then in the same year he becomes eligible and competent fatwa even in complex issues of Islamic finance which he has never studied during his 8 years of studies. How can such a person claim to be specialist in Fiqh al-Muamlat with one year of specialization in fatwa in all fields of Fiqh (Takhassus fi al-fiqh)? This appears to be just repetition of what he has already studied, not specialization in all fields of fiqh, and cannot be termed as specialization.

3.3.3 Qualities and Characteristics of Mufti

In addition to elaborating qualifications of mufti, the Adab al-Mufti or fatwa manuals also provide guidance on the required qualities and characteristics of mufti. These qualities include: freedom from greediness and ambition; self-reliance; generosity; humility; abstinence from the forbidden; a smiling and untiring nature; strong will; freedom from prejudice and from vanity (Khalid Masud 1984). Fatawa Deoband also describes characteristics and moral qualities of a mufti. It mentions a number of qualities including good intentions, magnanimity, staidness, perception, freedom from greediness, modesty piety, and intelligence, balance of mind, self-reliance, cheerfulness, and sense of responsibility (1984).

Fatwa manuals also suggest that a Mufti must not accept the appointment for the office of Ifta, if it is offered by Kings or nobles. He should rather accept this office in the name of the King of Kings (Allah), the Exalted, he should ask his wages from Him, he should trust Him. He should trust Him alone, in order that He may guide him in accuracy and uprightness. The companions of the Holy Prophet (S.A.W.S) and their successors never accepted any office from the nobles and the sultans (1984, p. 140). The classical Muslim jurists are unanimous on the point that a Mufti is not allowed to receive remuneration for his fatwa. The renowned Maliki jurist Barzali, in his commentary on al-Mudawwana al-Kubra, a classical Maliki text in Islamic law, writes: 'There is Ijma i.e. (consensus opinion) among Muslim jurist that services of a mufti cannot be hired for giving fatwa. It is a kind of bribe. However, another Maliki jurist Ibn Arafa on the chapter of Ijarah allows a Mufti to take remuneration for this service from Bait ul Mal (Al-Sheikh Hussain al-Mallah, 2009, p. 654).

The position of Shafi and Hambli jurist is that if he has dedicated himself for fatwa and he does not earn income from any other source then he is entitled to remuneration from Bait ul Mal. The Bait ul Mal should give him that much remuneration which is sufficient to meet his needs. However, if in certain towns there is no other Mufti except him and he has some economic resources to meet his needs then no remuneration is allowed for him (Ibn al-Salah, Adab al-Mufti wa al-Mustafti, p. 114; Nawawi, Adab al-Fatwa wa al-Mufti, p. 39).

Imam Ibn al Qayyim is of the view that if he is in need of livelihood then it is permissible for him to receive remunerations, but if he is not a needy person then some jurists have allowed this, equating mufti with collector of Zakat. Some jurists have disallowed it, drawing an analogy between the mufti and the guardian of orphan who is not allowed to take any amount from the property of the orphan for his personal expenses when the guardian is a rich and resourceful person (Ibn al Qayyim; Ilam al Muwaqqien, 4:232). The Hambali Jurists generally do not allow remuneration for fatwa because a mufti is an heir of Prophet in transmitting his message. So just it is prohibited for a Aalim to abstain from teaching Islam or praying except against some material consideration, in the same way it is not allowed for a Mufti to demand compensation for this service. It is absolutely *Haram* and if someone gives him some compensation he should return it to the giver. If he receives it, he does not become lawful owner of this money (Ibn al Qayyim: Ilam al Muwaqqien, 4:231). Renowned Hanafi jurist Ibn Aabidin maintains that in our school, it is not lawful to accept remuneration for explaining some Shariah Hukm to the people. However, accepting remuneration for the writing of fatwa is permissible (Ibn Aabidin: Radd al Mukhtar, 4:311). This means that Ibn Aabidin allows receiving expenses incurred on the issuance of fatwa such as expenses of paper, ink, postal charges, etc.

Fatawa Alamgiri also allows receiving remuneration for the charges incurred on the writing of fatwa. However, in his view even this is reprehensible. Fatawa alamgiri suggests that it is obligatory for the Imam to fix an amount for the needs of a teacher (Teacher of Islam). All the jurists are in agreement that to take any gift from the Mustafti, i.e. petitioner, questioner, is prohibited.

3.4 Methods and Principles of Fatwa

A mufti while issuing fatwa is required to observe certain established principles of Islamic jurisprudence and methods of interpretation and derivation. Some of such principles are as follows:

3.4.1 Method of Using Sources and Evidence

A mufti, while undertaking the task of fatwa must observe hierarchy of sources. Thus, he must resort first to the revealed sources, i.e. the Quran and Sunnah, and if he does not find answer to the question presented to him for fatwa in these two sources, then he may have resource to rational or reason-based sources such as Qiyas, Istihsan, Maslahah Mursalah, Sadd al-Darai, etc.

AAOIFI's Shariah standard on fatwa explains this hierarchy of sources and evidences in the following words:

> Fatwa should basically be founded on what has been explicitly stated in the Quran and the Sunnah along with what has been supported by Ijma (consensus of fuqaha) or proved by Qiyas (analogical deduction). After resorting to the preceding sources, the judgment of the mufti (issuer of the fatwa) with regard to the different viewpoints of the Fuqaha (scholars of fiqh); i.e, Istihsan (Shariah approbation) and Maslahah Mursalah (public interest) may be considered as the basis for issuance of Fatwa.
> (Shariah Standard No. 29, Article 7/1)

> Fatwa should not be based on a personal viewpoint that does not cater for the sources referred to in item (1/7) above, or contradict with the general texts of the Quran and the Sunnah that have explicit indication. Moreover, fatwa shall also not fall in disparity with well-established Ijma' or the general rules derived from the Quran and the Sunnah.
> (Shariah Standard No. 29, Article 7/2)

A mufti should not construct or base his fatwa on presumptive or conjectural indications or remote interpretations of text which are contrary to established jurisprudential principles (usul fiqh) and rules of interpretation and derivation (Qawid al-Istinbat). He should not rely in his fatwa on ahadith of Holy Prophet (S.A.W.S) which are proved to be weak and unauthentic. AAOIFI's Shariah standard also stipulates that mufti should cite the source of his fatwa such as established Ijma, i.e. consensus of Muslim jurists and the opinions and verdicts of renowned fuqahah. While relying on opinion of fuqahah, the mufti should select only that opinion which is considered as acknowledged and preferred opinion in that school.

3.4.2 Treatment of Shariah Concessions

AAOIFI's standard does not allow a mufti to heavily rely on Shariah concessions and relaxations in his fatwa with the aim to make things easier for the petitioner (Islamic banks, for instance). Shariah concession may be made the basis of fatwa when it is based on some strong Shariah evidence. Use of Shariah concession and relaxation is prohibited when it leads to prohibited eclecticism (talfiq), i.e. borrowing from different schools and forming a new opinion with this abrupt combination to satisfy desires of the petitioner. Examples of prohibited talfiq (undesirable combination of opinion to create new opinion) are as follows:

a. In Shafii school, when a person sells a house, his neighbour cannot invoke his right to first buy or refuse (pre-emption right) because Shafii school does not acknowledge this right (pre–emption right) for neighbours. The Hanafi school, on the other hand, gives right of pre-emption to neighbours. Now it would not be lawful for a person to invoke pre-emption right when a house is sold in his neighbourhood acting upon Hanafi opinion, and refuse this right to his neighbour when he himself sells house acting upon Shafii law. Hence we observe that he has taken two contradictory positions on the same issue. In the first case, he acts upon Hanafi opinion and in the second case, he acts upon Shafii School. This is clearly a case of personal whims and caprice.
b. A person divorces his wife thrice in one session, and treats it as single repudiation. He divorces his other wife in the same manner, but treats it as irrevocable divorce of major degree. This is not allowed. He is under obligation to treat both the cases in similar manner. The lenient rule adopted by him in the first case, should also be applied to the second case.

Some Ulama have laid down some extra conditions for validity of eclecticism and moving between schools for the purpose of selecting a lenient view:

1. The purpose of adopting the lenient view of another school should be to remove severe hardship.
2. The permission to adopt the lenient view and concessionary rule of another school should issue forth from the experts of Shariah, and the people of upright character. They should have done this through collective Ijtihad.

3.4.3 *Avoidance of Hiyal in Fatwa*

A mufti is also not allowed to relay on stratagems and subterfuges (Hiyal) in his fatwa. Hilah literally means an artifice, device and stratagem. Technically, it may be described as the use of legal means for extra-legal ends that could not, whether by themselves legal or illegal, be achieved directly within the means provided by the Shariah. Thus, hiyal (legal artifices) constitute legal means, by which one can arrive at judicial results otherwise prohibited by the law.

Unlawful hilah is used either to circumvent a prohibition, or to evade an obligation. An example of hilah intended to circumvent Shariah prohibition on riba is Bay al-Inah. Bay' al Inah is to sell a property on credit for a certain price, and then to buy it back at a price less than the sale price on prompt payment basis; both transactions take place simultaneously, in the same session of the contract. The majority of Muslim Jurists consider this transaction invalid, because the intended objective of the transaction opposes the objective laid down by the Lawgiver. This form of transaction, in their view, is nothing more than a legal device, aimed at circumventing the obstacle posed by the prohibition of riba. It is a fictitious deal in usurious loan transaction, as it ensures a predetermined profit, without actually dealing in goods, or in sharing any risk.

A hilah affected on a debt transaction is generally treated as unlawful hilah, because it intends to give some extra benefit to the creditor. Buy-Back Agreement (Bay' al-Inah) and sale with right of redemption (bay bi al-wafa), belong to this category. A famous maxim states: 'hilah affected on debt is a hilah for Riba'. Some examples of hiyal on debt transaction are: to mortgage a house with the creditor and allow him to stay in it, or to sell an object to the prospective debtor for an exaggerated price and then immediately lending him some money, or to buy from him certain commodity at a lower price, or to lease to him some asset, at a rental higher than its prevailing market rate.

Despite the fact that the word bilah is a value-neutral word and it does not necessarily mean subterfuge, playing around law, vile tricks, deception, circumvention of prohibitions, etc.; nonetheless, this meaning and nuance is prominent, both in the classical and modern Islamic legal usages of the term. Ibn Taymiyyah explains that when the word hilah is used unqualified, then it conveys the meaning of subversive hiyal, i.e. the legal devices whereby Shariah prohibitions are circumvented, like the legal devices used by Jews. Ibn al-Qayyim holds the view that in the common usage of Fuqaha', *hilah* means unlawful and reprehensible tricks. Though not declared explicitly in its fatwa standard, AAOIFI in its rulings frequently warns against use of Hiyal in fatwa and legal reasoning.

3.4.4 Eclecticism or Borrowing between Schools

The classical fatwa manuals generally do not allow a mufti to deviate from his school, while giving fatwa. Fatawa Alamgiri requires from Hanafi mufti: 'to adhere to Hanafi authorities in which Imam Abu Hanifa comes first then his disciples. This order is expounded in reference not only to jurists but also to their books. The adab al-Mufti manuals insist on adherence to the Hanafi school to the extent that even if the petitioner specifically asks the view of other schools, the mufti is to state only the Hanafi view' (Khalid Masud: Adab, al-Mufti, p. 138).

Ibn Abidin, a renowned Hanafi jurist, like his predecessors, is also inclined towards prohibition of departure from Hanafi school to another school for Hanafi mufti. He says: 'It is our considered opinion that when Abu Hanifah and his two disciples agree on an opinion, it is not permissible to deviate from it. He, however, allows it with certain conditions that include: that (i) there is dire necessity for this departure, (ii) there is no solution to the problem is Hanafi texts, (iii) the available solution causes severe hardship for the society, (iv) the view of other school best serves the general welfare.'

3.4.4.1 Is Borrowing between Schools Prohibited?

A close examination of classical and modern texts of fiqh reveals that many prominent jurists have allowed deviation from one school to another school.

Renowned Hanafi jurist Ibn al-Humam in al-Tahrir writes: 'A muqallid (non-mujtahid) has the right to follow any opinion he wishes. To follow easy view from different views is permissible. No evidence from revealed sources or reason is available to prohibit such practice.' Prominent Maliki jurists Imam Qarafi writes: 'It is permissible to practice the concessions of different schools, because no Shariah evidence proscribes it. Every person wants to practice what is easier for him to practice.'

Prominent modern Shariah scholar Dr. Wahbah Zuhaili writes: 'In the field of muamlat (civil transactions), it is imperative to borrow from each school and adopt the opinion that serves most the interest of people and their well-being even if this practice entails talfiq, i.e. eclecticism.'

Zuhayli does not find any Shariah justification for prohibition of borrowing between schools. He writes: 'The assertion that Shariah forbids talfiq and eclecticism' is against the Shariah principle that suggests that 'Difference of opinion among Ummah is mercy'. It also contradicts the principles of ease, and removal of hardship on which Shariah Ahkam are built.

Moulana Rashid Ahmad Gangohi, a renowned religious scholar of subcontinent observed: 'contemporary legal issues have become complex. As a result faith sensitive and God fearing people are in difficulty. I suggest that in the field of civil transactions and sale and purchase transactions Fatwa may be issued on the easiest opinion of Fiqhi schools.'

Moulana Khalid Saifullah Rahmani, another leading scholar of the sub-continent says: 'If the Muslim society in certain period suffers from difficulty by acting upon a particular opinion of a school, such society is allowed to act upon the ruling of other school that may remove hardship from them and bring ease and facilitation for them.'

In the past we observe that a mufti of a particular school gave fatwa according to the opinion of another school when he observed that his school was deficient on that point and that the competing view was more practical and served best the interest of public. The later Hanafi jurists, for instance, allowed charging fees for teaching Quran, leading prayer keeping in view of the larger interest of Shariah in the recent past, the Hanafi jurists of sub-continent endorsed the position of Maliki school on dissolution of Muslim marriage and adopted a law based on Maliki opinion. In Hanafi Law a woman cannot apply for judicial separation on grounds of non-payment of maintenance by the husband, while according to Maliki law, she is admitted for dissolution of marriage through the court of Law. The Dissolution of Muslim Marriage Act 1939, originally proposed by the Hanafi scholars, contains many such grounds which were not recognized as valid grounds of dissolution of marriage in the Hanafi Law. This is evidence of the fact that jurists do not prohibit from moving between the schools.

The Hanafi jurists have, however, laid down certain conditions for eclecticism and moving between schools:

1. It should not go against some established ijma, i.e. consensus of Jurists.
2. It should serve the public interest.

It should not be the result of one's whims and caprice.

AAOIFI's Shariah standard on fatwa does not allow a mufti to base his fatwa on a particular school. It states:

3.4.5 Consideration of Maqasid al-Shariah in Fatwa

Muslim jurists strongly advocate the use of Maqasid al-Shariah, Hikmah and Maslahah in fatwa. Imam Ghazali, Imam ibn-Taymiyyah and Imam Shatibi have frequently emphasized the significance of Maqasid for fatwa and legal reasoning (Ghazali, 1993; Ibn Taymiyyah, 2005; Shatibi, 1994). The modern Muslim jurists like Tahir ibn Ashur, Yususf al-Qaradawi, Allal al-Fasi, Ahmad al-Raysuni, Hamid al-Alam and many other prominent Shariah scholars have also emphasized the centrality of Maqasid al-Shariah in Ijtihad and legal reasoning (Ibn Ashur, 1978). Dr. Wahba Zuhaili (1986), a renowned contemporary Shariah scholar of Islamic law, also endorses the above view that Maqasid al-Shariah is a valid paradigm for *fatwa*. In his view a particular Maqasid al-Shariah is suitable for legal reasoning when it meets the following three conditions:

1. It is established by the Shariah evidence such as Quran and Sunnah.
2. It is clear and manifest in its meaning in such a way that its meaning and contours could easily be determined.
3. That it is a constant and stable objective (Zuhaili, 1986).

On certain issues, renowned Shariah scholar Mufti Muhammad Taqi Usmani, has also taken a maqasid-based position for evaluating Islamic finance products. In a working paper presented before the Shariah Board of AAOIFI, Mufti Taqi Usmani describes many current Sukuk inimical to objectives of Shariah. He observes:

> If we consider the matter from the perspective of the higher objectives of Islamic law, or the objectives of Islamic economics, then Sukuk in which they are to be found nearly all of the characteristics of conventional bonds, are inimical in every way to these purposes and objectives. The whole objective for which riba was prohibited is the equitable distribution among partners of revenues from commercial and industrial enterprise. The mechanism used in Sukuk today, however, strikes at the foundations of these objectives, and renders the Sukuk exactly the same as conventional bonds in terms of their economic results.
>
> (usmani: alqalam.org.uk)

The passage clearly establishes that Mufti Taqi Usmani endorses maqasid-based evaluation of Islamic banking products and transactions. It also implies that he acknowledges maqasid as basis of fatwa.

In early Islamic legal history, we find that in many cases, fatawa and rulings were issued exclusively on the basis of ḥikmah, maqasid and general propositions of Shariah. For instance, Hadrat 'Umer (RA) decided to kill a large number of persons by way of relation who participated in the killing of a single person in Yemen. His ruling was based on *'Preservation of life'*, which is an objective and purpose of Islamic law. The companions (Sahabah) decided to hold the artisans such as tailors, cobblers, carpenters, etc. liable for the goods of people destroyed in their custody. This decision was based on *'preservation of the wealth* of community' which is a purpose of Islamic law. Hadrat Umar (RA) abolished the share of *mu'allfah al-Qulub* considering the ḥikmah, i.e., rationale and wisdom behind the law of Zakat for *Mu'allafah al-Qulub*.

The early Hanafi jurists ruled that sadaqa al-fitr can be given in monetary equivalence. The other scholars were of the view that it should be given in kind in form of dates, wheat etc. as required in the Haidth. The position of Hanafi jurists is based on the consideration of the rationale of Zakat al-fitr. Since the purpose of this Zakat is to satisfy the needs of the poor, the issue of payment in kind becomes irrelevant. The purpose can be achieved by payment in any form. We observe here that this fatwa is based on the consideration of ḥikmah and purpose for which zakat al-fitr is instituted.

Prophet Muhammad (PBUH) has prohibited *tas'ir* (price fixation), but the latest jurists ruled for its fixation when they saw that the traders are exploiting the rule of non-fixation of price for reaping exorbitant profit. Imam Ibn al-Qayyim says 'Tasi'r or price fixation sometime amounts to injustice and sometime it is just. If the purpose of price fixation is to force traders to sell their goods at an unjust price, which does not suit them, then *tasi'r* is unlawful. But if it promotes justice like forcing them to sell at a just market value then such price fixation is permissible.' We observe here that the main consideration in this ruling of Imam Ibn al-Qayyim is the ḥikmah or rationale and the purpose behind the law.

From the above discussion it can be easily concluded that the classical Muslim jurists and the prominent modern Shariah scholars have given prime consideration to *ḥikmah*, *maslahah*, general proposition of the law giver and *Maqasid al-Shariah* in legal reasoning. They have generally opposed the form-based approach in the formulation of opinion on Shariah matters. The Maliki and Hanafi jurists even goes one step further and suggest that a *Mujtahid* (person who does ijtihad or legal reasoning) while interpreting a text, should interpret in the light of the wisdom and rationale underlying the text, instead of following the outward meaning of the text. It is worthy to mention here that jurisprudential principle: "Ruling is based on *'illah* and not on *Ḥikmah*" is confined only to the cases of *Qiyas* and analogical deduction. The discourse on *Ḥikmah* in our study, is not confined to the cases of *Qiyas* where ruling is generally based on 'illah, being a manifest, stable and constant attribute of the text. It extends to all cases of rule-making, whether it is a new rule or it is an interpretation of the existing rule. The study argues, that while formulating any ruling the purposes of the Shariah and motivating causes of the *ahkām* should always be taken into consideration.

3.4.6 Consideration of end-results of juridical act (Ma'ālāt al-Af'āl)

'Consideration of consequences and end-results of act' (*I'tibār ma'ālāt al-Af'āl*) is an important Maliki principle for fatwa. It suggests that while giving ruling on certain matter by a mufti, he should give consideration to the magnitude of benefit to be drawn and the harm to be averted from it. Thus, it requires that the *mufti* should possess high level of judgmental ability to weigh with accuracy the benefit and harm. The principle also implies that he should constantly watch the end-results and consequences of his ruling. Principle of *ma'ālāt al-Af'āl* in Shariah opinions, has been strongly advocated by Imam Shatibi: He says: 'The consideration of end-results of act is an acknowledged and approved rule in Shariah, regardless of whether the act is that of commission or omission' (Shatibi, 1994) vol. 4, p. 194). He suggests that a mujtahid and a mufti, while forming Shariah opinion on certain acts (certain banking products, for instance) should see what are its possible consequences. Will it bring benefit and will it give rise to *mafsadah*. In the opinion of Imam Shatibi, the investigation of future consequences of act, is a difficult task for mujtahid, but it is very much desired in Shariah since such activity is the best way to protect *Maqasid al-Shariah* (Shatibi, 1994).

The implication of this principle in Islamic finance is that a mufti, after giving the Shariah opinion on certain products or operations, should constantly monitor its effects and consequences. For instance, if he had allowed, for the purpose of Shariah screening, interest-based borrowing up to 37% for a company 15 years back, he should now revisit it, to see whether this has strengthened interest-based system, or the borrowing companies have used this ruling only for transitional period when these companies did not have access to Islamic banks or other financial institutions, for financing. Similarly, if he has allowed for the subscription to sukuk by conventional banks on the plea that sale to both Muslim and non-Muslim is permissible, now, on the basis of above principle, he should revisit his ruling. He should examine the harm this act of sale of sukuk to conventional banks, has caused to the prestige of Islamic banks. He may ask himself: has this product strengthened the riba-based conventional financial system? Whether or not, this is an act of cooperation in sin.

The above principle also requires that consequences and end-results of Running Musharakah (RM) should also be checked in the light of end-results. In case of bancatakaful, high commissions have been paid to the banks selling bancatakaful product to the customers even without making necessary disclosures, thus leading to exploitation of the clients (Ayub, 2016). The above principle requires a Mufti to issue Shariah ruling and putting a ban on such commissions.

Thus, the consideration consequences of act are an obligation of Mufti. He is not absolved of his duty by mere issuing of a Shariah opinion.

3.4.7 *Change of Fatwa Due to Some Error or Change of Circumstances*

The Muslim jurists maintain that when a fatwa is proved to be wrong, the mufti must not insist on his verdict and ruling. He should rather review it and issue a new ruling which is based on sound Shariah evidence. Rectification of a wrong fatwa is Shariah, has roots in the practice of mufti Sahabah (r.t.a) of Holy Prophet (S.A.W.S). It is narrated that Hadrat Umar (r.t.a) issued a fatwa that denied some of the brothers of deceased right of inheritance, later on he changed his position and issued a new fatwa granting them the inheritance right. Having done so, he said: 'The former case was subject to my previous fatwa, and the new one is subject to the new fatwa. The fatwa may also be changed with the change of time and space as well as the change in customs and traditions on which the fatwa was based. The custom and usage has a force of law in Shariah.'

Thus, if a fatwa is based on certain custom and usage, and that custom and usage has changed in subsequent periods, then the mufti must change his fatwa. On this basis, the later Hanafi jurists deviated from many verdicts of early jurists of their school. Thus, they allowed charging fees for teaching Quran, and leading obligatory prayers.

The above principles and methods of fatwa, may be summarized in the following points:

1. Mufti must observe hierarchy of sources. Thus, he should first resort to revelational sources and then to rational or reason-based sources.
2. He should not avoid relying on presumptive indications and remote interpretations of texts.
3. He should rely only on those ahadith which are proved to be authentic.
4. He should not base his fatwa on Hiyal, i.e. stratagems.
5. Excessive reliance on Shariah concessions and relaxations just to make the matters easier for petitioner (Islamic banks, for instance) is not allowed.
6. Qiyas (analogical deduction), Istihsan (juristic preference), maslahah mursalah (consideration of public interest) and Maqasid al-Shariah are valid sources of fatwa, provided these sources are invoked according to established principles of Islamic jurisprudence.
7. Mufti must consider end-results of his fatwa and weigh between the benefit to be drawn and the harm to be averted.
8. Mufti must change his fatwa when the circumstances, custom and usage have changed or some error has appeared in the fatwa.

3.5 Issues of Fatwa and Mufti in Islamic Banks in Pakistan

Fatwa in the sphere of Islamic finance in Pakistan, has been a subject of intense debate among Shariah scholars, and Islamic finance experts. Are Shariah advisors in Pakistan competent to act as mufti as per standards laid down by the prominent Muslim jurists and the authors of fatwa manuals? Are the Shariah pronouncements of Shariah Advisory committee (SAC) of State Bank of Pakistan and Shariah boards of Islamic Banks, qualified to be a fatwa as per conditions and requirements of fatwa in Islamic legal tradition? Do these pronouncements meet required standards of fatwa?

In this section, we will address above questions and discuss important issues of fatwa and muftiship in Islamic finance industry in Pakistan.

3.5.1 *Issues of Eligibility or 'Fit and Proper Criterion' for Shariah Advisor*

The State Bank of Pakistan has prescribed the following criteria for Shariah advisors in the Islamic finance industry.

1. Academic Qualification:
   Shahadat ul Aalamiyyah Degree (Dars e Nizami) from any recognized Board of Madaris with minimum 70% marks and Bachelor's Degree with a minimum of 2nd class OR
   Post Graduate Degree in Kuliyyatush Shariah or Kuliyyah Usooluddin, L.L.M. (Shariah) with a minimum GPA of 3.0 or equivalent from any recognized University.
2. Experience and Exposure:
   (i) The Shariah scholar members must have at least four (4) years' experience of giving Shariah rulings including the period of Takhasus fil Ifta, or at least five (5) years post qualification experience in teaching or Research and Development in Islamic Banking and Finance. Preference will be given to those who have certificate in Takhassus fil Fiqh/Takhassus fil Ifta.
   (ii) Majority of Shariah scholar members of Shariah board of an IBI, including RSBM, shall have at least three (3) years' experience as Shariah Advisor or Member of Shariah Board (SB) of an Islamic Financial Institutions (IFI) or deputy to a Shariah Advisor or member of the Shariah team of an IFI.
   (iii) Each Shariah scholar member of the SB must be able to demonstrate:
      (a) Adequate understanding of banking and finance in general and Islamic finance in particular;
      (b) Strong skills in Islamic jurisprudence (Usul al-fiqh), as he must know the appropriate Fiqh methodologies for deriving juristic opinion.
      (c) Good comprehension of Arabic language.
      (d) Good communication skills in English language.

On a sufficient cause being shown by an IBI and an application made by it to the effect, the SBP may, at its discretion, allow relaxation from one or more of the aforesaid requirements of the FAPC, for such period and on such condition(s), as the SBP may deem appropriate in the specific circumstances of each case. A close examination of this criterion reveals that qualification prescribed in Shariah governance framework of SBP for the appointment of Shariah board members including SAC of SBP, is not appropriate for this position. AAOIFI's Shariah Standard on ethics of fatwa requires that Mufti for Islamic financial institutions should be specialist in Fiqh al-Muamlat and Islamic finance, based on the principle of tajazzi al-fatwa which suggests that a mufti should be specialized in a particular field of Islamic law.

Thus, as a mufti of Islamic bank he should be specialist in the discipline of Fiqh al-Muamlat, Islamic law of banking and finance and related disciplines. If we look into the syllabus of Dars-I-Nizami, we observe that Dars-I-Nizami is basically a bachelor or master program in Islamic studies. The courses of Islamic studies such as Quran, Tafsir, Hadith, Usul-e-Hadith, Ilm al-Kalam, Mantiq (logic), Fiqh, Usul-e-Fiqh, Arabic grammar and literature, etc., are taught during a period of 8 years, after 5 years primary education or 8 years secondary education.

Fiqh content in this program does not exceed 25% of total subjects in the program. This goes without saying that the course of Fiqh covers all the fields of Islamic law such as fiqh relating to Ibadat, fiqh relating to family matters, i.e. marriage, divorce, fiqh al-muamlat, fiqh Jinai, i.e. Islamic law on crimes and punishments, siyasah shariyyah, i.e. administrative law of Islam, and Fiqh relating to Muslim Non-Muslim relations and war and peace. Thus, Fiqh al-Muamlat is a very small part of fiqh studies. On the other hand, Shariah faculties of Malaysia and Arab universities offer an exclusive academic 8 years program in Shariah (Islamic law) to the exclusion of other disciplines of Islamic learning. Fiqh al-Muamlat occupies a pivotal position in this program. If we add to it PhD program of Shariah, then the years spent for Shariah exceed 12 years. Thus, a student of Shariah program in Malaysia or any Arab country spends about 12 years to study Shariah. There is no doubt that this Shariah program in its content, substance and suitability for Islamic finance is much stronger than Dars-e-Nizami of Pakistani Madaris. The program of takhassus fi ifta fi al-fiqh also does not contribute much towards producing required mufti for Islamic finance industry. The student in one-year or two-year programs of takhassus, studies Fiqh in general not the Fiqh relating to commercial transactions. The program is not designed to produce specialist in fiqh al-Muamlat. The fatawa which the student writes in this program, mainly pertain to Ibadaat, and family matters. Perhaps less than 20% of total fatawa belong to the field of fiqh al-Muamlat. Thus, the whole Dars-e-Nizami does not suit the needs of Islamic finance industry. If we look at this program from the perspective of the number of years of schooling, we notice that total period of schooling along with takhassus, a student of madrasah spends in his madrasah until graduation, hardly exceeds 15 years after primary education and 18 years after secondary education. Thus, a student at the age of 22 years, becomes mufti and occupies position of 'heir of Prophet (S.A.W.S)' and 'Signatory of Allah, Al-mighty'. The state bank of Pakistan may verify this fact by examining some takhassus certificates on a test and check basis. In many cases, it was observed that a madrasah student completed his education along with takhassus at the age of 21 years.

In all Shariah faculties of Arabic and Islamic world, fiqh is taught in comparative perspective. This is known as fiqh muqaran or comparative fiqh. Under comparative methodology, a student, at all levels of degree program, studies all the prominent fiqh texts of different schools of Islamic law. In Dars-e-Nizami, a student does not go outside the Hanafi books. He has not even heard the names of important books of other schools. Fatwa in Islamic finance is required to be based on the views of all schools. It should not be school specific. AAOIFI's Shariah standard on ethics of fatwa does not allow a mufti to form his Shariah opinion based on a specific fiqh. This implies that a mufti of Islamic finance industry should be fully conversant with fiqh manuals of all schools. In the absence of this command and mastery over fiqh manuals of different schools how can a mufti choose suitable views from variant schools for his fatwa?

Shariah governance framework requires from a mufti that he should have 3 years' experience of writing of fatwa. However, the SGF does not specify the field of fatwa required by the SBP. Thus, a person who has been trained in giving fatwa in marriage, divorce, maintenance, zakat, Hajj, etc., is eligible, according to SGF to issue fatwa on complex issues of Islamic banking. There is no mechanism in place to verify the content and subject as well as number of fatawa a mufti has issued during 3 years of training in takhassus program. Dar al-Ifta generally issues a certificate that he has completed takhassus in Ifta. It does not indicate the area of fatwa. A general certificate is considered sufficient document to establish that he is competent mufti for Islamic finance industry. The state bank, while approving his appointment for Shariah board, never asks the mufti to provide a list of fatawa indicating their titles, field of fatwa, date of issuance, reference number and their web link. In the absence of any robust mechanism, the whole fatwa system, becomes doubtful. It is worth mentioning that except Jamiah al-Rashid, no madrasah offer Takhassus in Fiqh al-Muamlat.

3.5.2 *Issues of Conflict of Interest/Threats in Sharia Advisory of Islamic Banks*

Sharia Board (SB) of an Islamic Financial Institution (IFI) is the apex body that has the authority to determine what is permissible and what is impermissible ('the Shariah principles and rules') for an IFI in all areas of its operations. Since the fatwa, decisions and rulings of the SB are binding on the institution, this authority needs the highest level of integrity, objectivity, independence and professional excellence. Any threat to these values on the part of Sharia board members may impair the confidence of the general public on the provision of strict Sharia compliance in these institutions, which may hamper their long-term sustainable growth.

However, we are experiencing certain practices in contemporary Islamic financial institutions that are contrary to high moral grounds and globally established principles of ethics and professional excellence. Some of the examples are as follows:

Many Sharia scholars are serving on the Sharia boards of different financial institutions working in the same jurisdiction. Since all these financial institutions (e.g., banks) are competitors by way of scope of the business and target market, there is a possibility that any member may disclose, inadvertently or deliberately, the information of one bank to another bank. This creates the issue of confidentiality.

Moreover, in case of any syndicate financing/investment, Sukuk structuring or any joint market-based operations it may affect the transparency and independence to carry out arms-length transactions.

Similarly, many Sharia scholars are serving on the Sharia boards of different commercial banks and simultaneously appointed as member of Sharia committee of the central bank. It may lead to a number of violations on the part of ethics and professional behaviour. For example, any product approved by Sharia board member in the commercial bank is then presented to Sharia board of the central bank for approval. Similarly, any conflict on any Sharia matter issue between Sharia board of commercial bank and Sharia inspection team of the central bank will be presented to Sharia committee of the central bank. It is clear violation of independence, threat of self-review and leads to conflict of interest.

Many of the Sharia board members have established personal Sharia advisory, consultancy and training firms. The target markets of these firms are the same financial institutions and markets. Establishing Sharia advisory firms and serving on the boards of Islamic financial institutions is an obvious conflict of interest. Some of the Sharia board members are working on the board of bank's Sharia advisory services and simultaneously running their own Sharia advisory firm besides serving on the Sharia board of the same bank. Other instances in this regard may include outsourcing the training services to own Sharia advisory of training firm or to the firms of other colleagues against getting the training requirements from their banks.

In some instances, it is seen that family members are on the same board, while their other family members are on the boards of other banks. Similarly, there are instances where any Sharia board member on the board of a commercial bank is also serving on the board of Takaful operator and bank is taking Takaful services from the same Takaful operator.

People also think that a 'familiarity threat' exists between Sharia scholars and boards/management of the bank. Sharia scholars are sympathetic to their

Fatwa in Legal Tradition and Its Implications for Islamic Banks 55

interests or accepting of their work which leads to the issue of integrity and objectivity. Sharia scholars are also facing the criticism of 'advocacy threat' whereby they are promoting employing the bank to the point that the Sharia board members' objectivity is compromised, e.g. promoting particular bank's products in public seminars, bank's advertising campaigns, etc. Another potential threat is 'intimidation' where Sharia scholars are deterred from acting objectively because of actual or perceived pressures, including attempts to exercise undue influence over the Sharia board members. Last but not the least is the threat of professional competence, i.e. serving on the Sharia boards without proper professional competence required for the position. It includes related knowledge and skills at the level required to ensure provision of competent service.

3.5.3 Issues in Fatwa: Analysis of Some Selected Fatawa

Here we will discuss some prominent fatawa of Islamic finance industry. We will examine these fatawa on the touchstone of principles discussed in the preceding sections. A reader may observe that these fatawa have either ignored Maqasid al-Shariah and end-results of transaction or have been based on stratagems and subterfuges (Hiyal).

3.5.3.1 Fatwa on Mudarabah Sukuk

A few years back, three leading Islamic banks – Meezan Bank, Dubai Islamic Bank and Bank Islami – in order to comply with the regulatory requirements in respect of Capital Adequacy Ratio (CAR) issued Additional Tier 1 Sukuk on the basis of Mudarabah. The Sukuk were approved by the respective Shariah boards of these banks. The fatwa approving the structure of Sukuk, is a type of approval and certification rather than fatwa in strict legal sense as per classical meaning of fatwa. In the fatwa, the structure has been first explained and then at the end, Shariah board members have approved the transaction. The structure of Additional Tier 1 Sukuk or Mudarabah Sukuk in all the above three cases is almost identical. Here we outline the structure of Mudarabah Sukuk without specifying the issuing bank and identify Shariah issues in the fatwa. Following are the characteristics of Sukuk.

1. Sukuk is structured on the basis of Mudarabah.
2. The Sukuk is perpetual in nature. The Sukuk holders are Rab-ul-Maal and the Bank is the Mudarib.
3. The proceeds of the Sukuk are commingled with other depositors' funds, i.e. invested on unrestricted basis into the Pool of the Bank and are classified as Special LCY Sukuk. On the date of the commencement of the Mudarabah, the Pool shall comprise of: (i) the Bank's shareholder's equity; (ii) proceeds of all current, savings and investment deposit accounts with

the Bank (iii) any other source(s) of funds to be included in the Pool by the Bank from time to time.
4. The Sukuk holders are partners with other members of the Pool.
5. The profits and loss emanating from the Pool is managed in accordance with the Shariah principles applicable to the Mudarabah and the SBP 'Instructions for Profit & Loss Distribution and Pool Management for Islamic Banking Institutions (IBIs)', unless otherwise waived or relaxed.
6. The Mudarib assigns weightages to the Special LCY Sukuk on monthly basis before the start of each month along with the announcement of weightages for remunerative deposit categories. The weightages are set by keeping in view the expected profit rate as per the term sheet, however, actual result depends upon the actual performance of the pool.
7. The Bank can exercise a call option after 5 years of the issuance with prior approval of the State Bank of Pakistan (SBP) and such redemption is made as per the NAV of the Pool that is the outstanding value of the Sukuk subject to attributable profit or loss of the Pool and thus no call premium will be paid. Sukuk holders do not have any put option to exit from the Sukuk but they can sell the Sukuk to any other party at any agreed price if they want to exit.
8. In case of events where (a) payment of profit results in breach of the regulatory MCR, CAR and Leverage Ratio (LR) requirements set by SBP or (b) SBP determines that bar on profit distribution is necessary to protect the Bank from non-viability, the ban has an upfront right to reduce the monthly profit weightages of the Sukuk holders to a minimal level (say 0.01 resulting in expected profit of up to 0.005% p.a.) till the month in which such condition is withdrawn by SBP.
9. The Mudarabah between the Sukuk holder and the Bank is be subject to the following conditions (in order to comply with the requirements of Additional Tier 1 Capital under the State Bank of Pakistan's Basel III Capital Rules):
  (a) Upon the occurrence of a Point of Non-Viability, the Sukuk will be converted into common shares of the Bank and shall not be written off. The Sukuk holders, for the purpose of mandatory conversion of the Sukuk into the common shares of the Bank (as determined by the State Bank of Pakistan), shall, pursuant to subscription undertaking issued by the Sukuk holders in favor of the Bank, subscribe to a pro-rata pre-agreed number of common shares of the Bank. The Bank, for such conversion, will inform the Sukuk holders within due time.
  (b) Such conversion will be the termination of Mudarabah relationship and issuance of common shares will be treated as payment of Mudarabah capital back to the Rab-ul-Maal. The conversion into common shares will be done after consideration of the outstanding value (Face Value plus/minus attributable profit and loss of the Sukuk) and the Fair Value per share (i.e. market price of share on the day

Fatwa in Legal Tradition and Its Implications for Islamic Banks 57

preceding the date of declaration of PONV, or, in case market price is not available, the break-up value of share duly certified by the independent auditor) of the Bank's common equity upon trigger of the non-viability event as declared by SBP, subject to a cap of 210,398,801 shares of the Bank.

(c) Following the conversion of the Sukuk into common shares of the Bank in the event of PONV, the Mudarabah Agreement between the Bank (as Mudarib) and Sukuk holders (as Rab-ul-Maal) shall stand terminated.

10. After conversion into common shares, the Sukuk rank equal to equity and will be subordinate to all other indebtedness of the issuer including liabilities towards depositors.

Issues in Fatwa:

1. The contract heavily tilts in favour of Sukuk issuing bank, thus, it frustrates the values of justice, fairness, and equity in transactions. It is perpetual for investor, who does not have option to exit from the transaction, whereas this option is available for the issuer. In Islamic law Mudarabah is basically a terminable contract. Any party can exit from it. But, if the parties decide otherwise, then it is binding for both the parties. The classical structure of Mudarabah does not allow preferential treatment to one party. In Islamic law, a condition that gives benefit to one party to the transaction is irregular condition (shart fasid). In case of Mudarabah, and Musharakah, inclusion of such condition, makes the contract, invalid.

2. The transaction provides that in case, breach of regulatory requirement is caused by the mudarib, the issuing bank of Sukuk, the rabb-ul-mal (investors), will bear the loss and their profit ratio will be reduced as low as 0.005% p.a. It means that during the period of occurrence of event of default, an investor will get Rs. 50 annually for every one lac rupees on his capital. What Shariah basis of this arbitrary change in profit sharing ratio? Can reduction of profit and fixing new ratio of profit distribution, be made contingent upon happening of an uncertain event in future? How can this Gharar be justified? Can mudarib stipulate in the contract that if such and such event (unknown event) happens, then rabb ul-maal will get profit with a new ratio? Why should rabbul mal be held responsible for an act of mudarib? Why should rabb ul-mal, investor bear the liability for loss? Where is PSR in this arrangement?

3. These Mudarabah Sukuk are in fact Mudarabah certificates. They are put in general pool. The profit generated from this general pool, is distributed between the Sukuk holders and other ordinary depositors. If this is the case, then why Mudarabah Sukuk holders be treated like other depositors and Mudarabah Sukuk holders? If deposit of Sukuk holder is one billion, and deposit of another depositor is also one billion, why should the former

get, say 13% and the other depositor get 8% or 9%? On what basis, we can differentiate between one rabb ul-mal and the other rabb ul-Mal? These and similar other issues need to thoroughly investigated.

3.5.3.2 Fatwa on Bay' Mu'ajjah of Sukuk

A controversial fatwa of Islamic finance is fatwa that has legitimized Bay'Mu'ajjah of Sukuk. The fatwa is clearly based on *heelah* not any solid Shariah ground. Bay'Mu'ajjah of Sukuk is a popular treasury product whereby Islamic banks provide their excess liquidity to conventional banks and earn profit on it. It is practised in the following way. 'A' an Islamic bank sells its Sukuk on credit on musawama or Murabahah basis to 'B', a conventional bank. A, sells Sukuk worth Rs. 10 million for Rs. 11 million on credit of 3 months. 'B' immediately sells these Sukuk to 'C' a conventional bank for Rs. 10 million on cash, and delivers 10 million to B. 'C' then immediately sells these Sukuk to A on cash for 10 million. Sukuk now have returned to A. B now owes 11 million to A. the whole transaction is completed in two minutes. Islamic banks call it a sale transaction. They claim that 'A' has sold commodity with its free will to 'B' but, in fact, A has lent Rs. 10 million to B, with the mark up of one million. A, is lender, B is borrower. C, is router, and facilitator for this transaction. It generally receives service charge and commission for this facilitation role (generally one lac to two lac rupees). We may look at this transaction form two perspectives: perspective of Form of contract and perspective of intention, purpose and motivating cause of transaction. From first perspective, it is a valid contract, because apparently it is a sale not loan. B, with his free consent sells it to C. C, with his free will sells it to A. It is not technically prohibited bay'al-Inah, because B is not selling again to A, but to C. Thus, by the inclusion of C in the deal, transaction is apparently saved from bilateral bay'al-Inah .Now from the perspective of substance of contract, it is lending, not sale because conventional bank never intended to buy Sukuk. It only needed money which he obtained thorough cash sale to C. C, never wanted to be owner of Sukuk. It only facilitates the transaction between A and B, and takes commission for this service. From the perspective of maqasid, and substance, it is only a *heelah* transaction to circumvent the prohibition of riba. The notion of general propositions of Shariah requires from us to investigate that what are the dispositions and treatment of Shariah in other similar matters. We know that Shariah cursed *ashab al-Sabt*. Shariah cursed the facilitator (muhallil) in *halaalah* marriage and termed him a 'borrowed bull', because he facilitates remarriage between a divorced couple by entering an intervening marriage with a divorced woman and establishing sexual relations with her for a short period. Shariah has prohibited every trick intended to evade obligations and to commit prohibition, avoiding zakat by gifting it or to undertake bay'al-Inah to obtain or give usurious loan from back door. Shariah has prohibited cooperation in act of sin. In the instant case, Islamic banks cooperate with the conventional bank and strengthen it through providing required funds. State Bank of Pakistan, after many years, has taken notice of this transaction and asked the Islamic banks to ensure that the money given by the Islamic banks to conventional banks is not used in Shariah-non-compliant business. Islamic banks are busy now to explore Shariah compliant business avenues in conventional banks. There is strong likelihood that they will succeed in this mission.

Now the question is: should the above transaction be judged from the perspective of contract mechanics of from the perspective of substance? On what basis should its permissibility be examined?

3.5.3.3 PMEX Murabahah Transaction

In 2017, a product 'PMEX Murabahah Transaction' approved by the Shariah board of a leading Islamic bank, was introduced by SBP and SECP in the market. The purpose of the product was to manage interbank liquidity. Through PMEX Murabahah transaction, high-speed diesel worth 8 million PKR was sold by the lender bank (the bank with excess liquidity) to the borrower bank (the bank short of liquidity) on the basis of cost-plus profit basis. The product still exists but not in practice for the time being. Following is the process of transaction:

1. HASCOL, oil marketing company sells diesel say, worth million on cash to A, an Islamic bank on cash.
2. A sells it immediately to B, an Islamic bank for 1.1 million on credit, say for 6 months.
3. B sells it immediately on cash for 1 million to HASCOL, acting as agent of hundreds of dealers and distributors.
4. Neither A nor B is allowed to take physical possession of oil and dispose it of at its free will.
5. HASCOL and PMEX receive commission from A for this service, as they have facilitated this transaction.

From the perspective of contract mechanics, or form of transaction, PMEX Murabahah transaction meets requirement of a valid contract, but it certainly frustrates the substance and spirit of Shariah. Some maqasid-based issues involved in the transaction are as follows:

1. It is a fictitious sale transaction. No party involved in the transaction is interested in the high speed diesel. Oil is irrelevant for banks. Banks are not users of oil.
2. It is in substance a lending transaction in which A has earned interest profit of one lac rupees.
3. The transaction does not generate any economic activity.
4. From the perspective of end-results of transaction, it is just a *heelah* for interest-based lending.
5. Purchase of oil by HASCOL as agent of dealers, is only a *heelah* to avoid apparent indulgence in bay'al-Inah.

60 *Muhammad Tahir Mansoori*

It seems illogical that a party created for sale of oil (OMC), after 15 minutes of first sale to primary bank, becomes buyer or buyer's agent without any reason. It is pertinent to note that whole transaction (sale of oil worth one million by HASCOL to primary bank 'A' (lender) and from A to B, secondary bank (borrower) and from B to HASCOL, is completed in 15 to 18 minutes). Can a real sale of a commodity of this size be undertaken in 18 minutes?

3.5.3.4 Fatwa on Running Musharakah

Another fatwa of Islamic finance industry is fatwa that approved RM as a Shariah-compliant product. It is a prominent product in which substance and spirit of Shariah has been compromised. No Islamic country except Pakistan has adopted this product. RM was approved by the Shariah board of a leading Islamic bank as an alternative to interest-based product running finance and then other boards followed it. Now it is a popular Pakistan specific banking product. In RM, an Islamic bank joins the business of client as sleeping partner through contractual partnership (*Shirkah al 'aqd*). Islamic bank specifies a credit limit that is considered Islamic bank's investment. Two-stage profit rates are determined in RM. For the first stage, Islamic bank gives the client its target rate/profit ceiling that is usually equal to the KIBOR rate. It is mutually agreed that up to the profit ceiling, profit would be distributed according to investment shares of bank. For second stage, Islamic bank agrees to reduce its profit share as low as .0001% in over and above profit of target profit and 99.9999% will be given to the client. Usually, this remaining profit is more than the total profit that is distributed between Islamic bank and corporate client at first stage.

It appears that Islamic bank wants to give the remaining profit as *hibah* (gift) to corporate client but since Shariah does not allow pre-agreed *hibah* in favour of any partner, it does not resort to this solution. To circumvent such prohibition, Islamic bank adopts *heelah*. The *heelah* is that it distributes remaining profit according to .0001% and 99.9999% between Islamic bank and client. In *form* it is profit sharing ratio but in *substance* it is *hibah*.

Here we observe that RM, in its meaning, purpose, effect and end-results is not substantially different from running finance of conventional bank, where the bank gets a fixed return, i.e. interest on its investment, which is 7 million rupees on the capital of Rs. 100 million provided by the bank, in the above example. The only difference is that Islamic bank, under RM receives additional amount of Rs. 230 which is insignificant for the bank. This goes without saying that Musharakah in Islamic law is a partnership to share real returns of business to the partners. If this purpose is frustrated by some fictitious profit-sharing ratio such as 99.9999% and 0.0001% then in substance it is not real Musharakah but a transaction close to running finance.

As mentioned earlier, the primary objective Musharakah in Shariah is to give opportunity to the partners to share real returns of business in a just and fair manner. The *fuqahā* are so sensitive about this objective that some of them do not allow a profit ratio which is not strictly in proportion to the investment. According to Maliki and Shāfiī jurists, both the profit and loss should follow the investment of the parties. In the instant case, a large portion of profit goes to the corporate client without any counter value, defeating the purpose of Shariah behind instituting Musharakah. This arrangement clearly frustrates the objective of fair distribution of returns. So, from the perspective of form, it is Musharakah, but by substance and meaning it is not the Musharakah or more specifically *shirkah al-'inan*, as contemplated by early jurists.

The proponents of RM generally place their reliance on the clause of Shariah Standard on Musharakah which allows Islamic bank to allocate its share of profit to the client, if the profit of bank is beyond the desired rate. The desired rate has been interpreted as KIBOR-linked fixed return on capital. It means if the bank wants 7% of its capital, then whatever profit is above this rate, may be allocated to the other partner.

The above argument may not be accepted on the ground that here the bank has entered into partnership with corporate client as *muarib* for *rabb al-mal*. So, all the rules relevant to *mdarib* are applicable to the transaction. One of such rules is that *mudarib* cannot withdraw or surrender any financial right belonging to *rabb al mal*. How Islamic bank deprives depositors of their due right in profit, may be judged from a RM transaction of an Islamic bank which earned a profit of Rs.10 billion above desired rate, i.e. KIBOR related rate (9% of bank's capital). The bank received from this amount Rs.2000 only. All remaining profit went to the client in line with the profit distribution ratio of 99.9999% for client and 0.0001% for bank. This means that Islamic bank received one paisa on every one million rupees of extra profit i.e. above target profit. A negligible amount of Rs.2000 out of one billion is only a deception and '*ilah* intended to prove that there was a real profit sharing and that it was a Musharakah, but the fact of the matter is that it is just a running finance arrangement. The client at the inception of contract knows clearly that he has to pay 9% of the bank's financing. This is how the parties agree at the time of contract. If the client has paid Rs.2000, it does not change the nature and reality of transaction.

PMEX Murabahah transaction is also a *heelah* to lend money by the primary bank to the secondary bank. Oil is irrelevant for both the banks, because neither primary bank nor secondary bank are users of oil. HASCOL act only as facilitator for this lending and borrowing. Again, this is a type of earning money on money. It also involves violation of law of land. Oil is a regulated commodity. It can be sold and purchased only by licenced dealers. Banks are not authorized to deal in oil. Besides, oil cannot be sold at a price different from the regulated price. This is not a fit case for Murabahah. We should bear in mind that violation of law of land is violation of Shariah, if the law is not against the Shariah. Salam in currency ignores the hikmah (wisdom, rationale) for which currency, dirham and dinar have been created. The illah of dinar (gold) dirham (silver) is thamaniyyah, 'price worthness', not the weighability. To equate modern paper currency with fulus practically relegates this currency to commodity. According to Shariah, dirham and dinar, and for that purpose modern paper currency is money not commodity. This treatment of modern paper currency paves the way for undue benefit for one of the two parties exchanging money with delay.

RM is valid in external form but not in substance an unreasonable profit-sharing ratio of 99.9999% is only a *heelah* to give corporate client a fixed return like running finance. It frustrates the spirit for which Musharakah has been instituted in Shariah. Musharakah and Sharikah in Shariah aim that both partners share the real returns of business. The above treatment of Musharakah frustrates the substance and very purpose of Musharakah in Shariah. Besides, this causes concentration of wealth in the hands of a rich segment of society. The Quran prohibits concentration of wealth in the hands of the rich. It is injustice to the depositors who are given return like returns on Murabahah and Ijarah. Had it been a real Musharakah, they would have received much higher profit.

3.6 Conclusion

Fatwa occupies a very significant position in Islamic legal tradition. A mufti is 'heir of Prophet (S.A.W.S)' and thus he expounds and explains the hukm of Shariah to those who ask him for hukm ShIr'i on certain issues of Islamic law. Thus, he performs a very sensitive task which requires from him honestly, moral probity, objectivity, due diligence and in-depth knowledge of Shariah, freedom from greed and running after monetary benefits. Keeping in view the sensitivity of the task of muftiship, the Muslim jurists (fuqaha) have prescribed high ethical standards and eligibility criteria for mufti which cover both the qualifications and qualities. A mufti is required to have mastery over Quran and its allied sciences, Sunnah and its allied disciplines, Usul Fiqh and the rules of interpretation and modes of derivation of ahkam, celebrated fiqh works of early Muslim jurists, Arabic language and thorough knowledge of disciplines associated with the field of fatwa.

The concept of tajazzi al-fatwa additionally requires from mufti that he should be specialist in a particular field of Islamic law. On this ground, a Shariah advisor of Islamic bank must be specialist in fiqh ul muamlat, Islamic law of banking and finance. He should have command over the whole spectrum of Islamic finance, that includes knowledge of finance, banking, business law, basics of accounting, economics, besides knowledge of Shariah.

The current fatwa and muftiship in the field of Islamic finance in Pakistan has many issues. These issues pertain to eligibility of mufti, curriculum for production of Islamic finance mufti, structure and format of fatwa, conflict of interest issues, multiple memberships of mufti, and flaws in the fatawa. It has been observed in the study that the syllabus of Dars-e-Nizami is not appropriate and suitable for Islamic finance industry. Dars-e-Nizami is basically general Islamic studies program. The content of fiqh al-Muamlat in the whole syllabus may not exceed 5% of the total program. On the other hand, Shariah faculties on Arab and Muslim countries offer exclusive Islamic law program at BS, MS and PhD levels. Thus, this is a comprehensive Islamic law specialization program in which commercial law occupies prominent position. In Malaysia, Indonesia and Arab countries, generally the graduates of Shariah faculties serve on Shariah boards of Islamic finance industry. The senior professors of universities from Shariah programs are members of Shariah boards. In no case do the graduates of madrassah perform this role.

Apart from issues pertaining to eligibility and qualification of mufti, issues have also been observed in the fatawa. Many controversial fatawa have been issued that have badly frustrated the true spirit of Islamic law and have consequently adversely affected the originality and legitimacy of Islamic banking and finance.

Fatwa and muftiship in Islamic finance industry need radical reform. Curriculum to produce Islamic finance mufti needs to be revised. Pre-service training program in finance, banking, economics, business law may be arranged on the pattern of training for newly selected civil judges by the Judicial Academy. Multiple memberships of Shariah boards must be banned. In all the Islamic financial institutions in the Muslim world, except Pakistan, multiple memberships are prohibited. Fatwa should be accompanied by evidence. Shariah verdicts should be available on websites for the public. Shariah Advisory Committee (SAC) of State Bank of Pakistan should play its leading role in matters of Shariah. It should lead the industry, bring uniformity in the products and translations, and resolve conflicts arising from different verdicts of Shariah boards. In order to avoid conflict of interest and to maintain their independence, the Shariah board members should not receive their remuneration directly from the bank, like any employee. The remuneration should be rather disbursed by the State Bank of Pakistan.

References

AAOIFI (2019). *Accounting and Auditing Organization for Islamic Financial Institutions. Shari'ah Standards*. Dar al Maiman for Publishing and Distribution.

Amidi, S. D. (1968). *al-Ihkam fi Usul al-Ahkam*. Matba'ah Muhammad Ali Shuaib.

Ayub, M. (2016). Running Musharkah– Running from Musharakah (Editorial). *Journal of Islamic Business and Management*, 6(1), 7–18.

Bubkani, S. (1999). *al –Mtatanah fi Marammah al-Kkizanah*.

Ghazali, A. H. M. (1980). *al-Mankhul min T'aliqat al-Usul. Ed. Muhammad Hasan Hayto*. Dar al-Fikr.

Ibn, A. (1810). *Radd al-Muhtar ala al-Durr al-Mukhtar, Hashiyah Ibn Abidin*. Ihya al-Turath al-Arabiyyah.

Ibn Salah (1986). *Adab al-Mufti wa al-Mustafti* (Ed.) Abd al-Mu'ti Qal'aji. Dar al-Ma'rifah.

Ibn al-Qayyim (1983). *I'lam al-Muwaqqa'in a Rabb al-A'lamin*. Dar al-Kutub al-Hadithah.

Juwayni, A., & Imam, H. (1979). *al-Burhan fi Usul al-Fiqh*. Dar al-Ansar.
Khalid, M. (1984). Adab al-Mufti: The Muslim Understanding of Values, Characteristics, and Role of Mufti in Barbara Daly Metcalf (Ed.) *Moral Conduct and Authority: The Place of Adab in South Asian Islam*.
Khalid, M., & Brinkley, D. (1996). *Islamic Legal Interpretation*. Harvard College.
Mallah, S., & Hussaun, M. (2009). *al-Fatwa, Nash;atuha wa Tatawwuraha , Usuluha wa Tatbiqatuha*. al-Maktabah al-Asriyyah.
Qarafi, A. (1926). *al-Furuq*. Dar Ihya al-Lutub al-Arabiyyah.
Shatibi, A. I. (1994). *al-Muwafaqat fi Usul al-Ahkam*. Matba'ah Ali Subaih.

4 Central Advisory Board and the New Shariah Governance Framework for Islamic Banks in Turkey

A Qualitative Approach

Murat Yaş and Ahmet Faruk Aysan

4.1 Introduction

Turkey has a long history of Islamic banking where Islamic banking operations have started in 1984 with the establishment of AlBaraka Turk (Yas, Aslan, & Ozdemir, 2018). According to the report of Banking Regulation and Supervision Agency (BRSA), 53 banks are currently operating in Turkey, six of which are fully-fledged Islamic banks (IBs) (Banking Regulation and Supervision Agency, 2021). The market share of Turkish Islamic banks, known as Participation Banks (PBs), has grown from 2.4% in 2005 (US$6.8 billion) to 7.7% (US$50 billion) in 2021. The establishment of three state-owned PBs and improving regulatory framework has been a catalyst for the expansion of the Islamic banking industry over the last decade. The BRSA regulates both participation and conventional banks under the same Banking Law and associated regulations. Although there is no dedicated legislation for Islamic banking, the Banking Law recognizes the distinctiveness of Shariah-compliant transactions. However, using Arabic and Shariah/Islamic terms for Islamic financial products and services is often avoided due to secular constitutions.

In terms of Shariah governance practices, Turkey has been embracing a decentralized or laissez-faire approach for decades. However, on 22 February 2018, BRSA allowed Participation Bank Association of Turkey (PBAT) to establish a Shariah Supervisory Board, namely the Advisory Board (AB) for ensuring that the activities of PBs comply with Islamic rules and principles. Even though BRSA required Advisory Committees (AC) of PBs to follow standards, guidelines, and decisions issued by AB, PBAT is independent in terms of determining AB's responsibilities, qualifications, and composition of AB members, procedures of appointment and cessation for AB members, working procedures and organizational structure, and interaction of AB with ACs.

Even if BRSA recognized the independence of PBAT's AB, on 14 September 2019, 'The Communiqué on Compliance to the Principles and

Standards of Interest-Free Banking' was issued for regulating ACs of PBs to improve Shariah governance framework (SGF). The Communiqué contains articles about the structure, working principles, and independence of advisory committees and Shariah compliance and Internal Shariah audit functions within banks. Furthermore, by specifying the tasks and activities of PBs' advisory committees, this Communiqué offered a Shariah governance structure for PBs.

The centralized Shariah governance framework (CSGF) in Turkey differs from the rest of the world in terms of the composition and qualifications of AB members, organizational structure, working procedures, and interaction with ACs of PBs. Therefore, it is significant to improve a robust and comprehensive SGF for IBs in Turkey because the lack of a solid corporate governance structure and a full-fledged legal framework for managing Islamic banking operations impede the development of the Islamic finance industry (Alam et al., 2020a; Ahmad et al., 2014; Perves, 2015). Therefore, this study aims to elaborate on and revisit the new SGF for the IBs in Turkey by investigating current issues, challenges, and expectations regarding the implementation of SGF. The study uses a semi-structured interview to accomplish the research objectives. The data was collected from nine respondents with a combination of regulators, members of PBAT's AB, PBs' ACs, and experts from regulatory authorities and PBs in Turkey. Our empirical results suggest that central AB needs to redefine the boundaries of Shariah standards, issue harmonized standards, and strengthen the organizational structure. Moreover, necessary policies should be implemented to improve legal infrastructure, ensure the independence of AB, improve appointment and composition criteria, emphasize the role of the Board of Directors (BoDs), and ensure the effectiveness of Shariah auditing for improving new SGF in Turkey.

There is a rapidly growing literature focusing on SGF in various countries such as Bangladesh (Alam, 2022; Alam & Thakur, 2022), Malaysia (Aziz, Abdul-Rahman, & Markom, 2019; Masruki, Hanefah, & Dhar, 2020), Pakistan (Farooq, Jan Wasim, & Othman Bin, 2021), and Gulf countries (Grassa, 2015; Hamza, 2013). Moreover, there is a recent debate on the SGF in Turkey after AB's three years of activities to improve Shariah governance mechanism in Turkey (Bektaş & Yenice, 2022; Yılmaz & Şencal, 2022). However, the literature on CSGF in Turkey is very limited.

This study aims to contribute to the existing literature in several ways. To the best of our knowledge, this is the first study that investigates issues, challenges, and expectations about the CSGF in Turkey by employing a qualitative analysis. Second, the research extends the literature on Islamic banking and SG mechanisms in the context of Turkey by presenting insights and policy recommendations to ensure a robust and comprehensive SGF. The paper is structured as follows: Section 2 provides the literature review. In Section 3, data and methodology will be presented. Section 4 describes the empirical evidence, and section 5 illustrates the conclusions and policy recommendations.

4.2 Literature Review

With the rapid growth of Islamic finance industry on a global scale for two decades, especially Muslim-majority countries have taken important initiatives to improve Shariah governance mechanisms for effective management of Shariah non-compliance risk. However, there is no common structure for the implementation of a Shariah governance framework at the national level because each country tries to establish a Shariah governance framework based on its own social, political, and economic realities (Grassa & Gazdar, 2014; Hassan et al., 2011). While some nations take an interventionist approach to institutions for creating a Shariah governance framework, others prefer to leave the decision-making process to market dynamics and voluntary efforts (Grassa, 2013; Yılmaz & Şencal, 2022). In that sense, there are three categories of approaches in the global Shariah governance practices for IBs: centralized approach, decentralized approach, and hybrid approach.

In decentralized practices, the IBs have their own Shariah boards (SBs) to monitor their activities and operations because they are independent of the Central Bank. As a result, according to AAOIFI guidelines, IBs must establish distinct SBs to guarantee and assess Shariah compliance within the IBs. The practice of decentralization is prevalent in Gulf Cooperation Countries (GCC) and Middle East countries (Alam et al., 2020). SBs decide whether the contracts and financial products of IBs are in compliance with Islamic rules and principles in this approach.

Turkey had been embracing a decentralized Shariah governance mechanism for decades to such an extent that even members of SBs and their rulings regarding the financial products of PBs in Turkey were not disclosed publicly due to concerns about secularism in the constitution (Yas et al., 2018). However, the IBs should have fully revealed information on Shariah enforcement processes and procedures since such information gives insights into the procedures used by IBs to guarantee that their goods and activities are Shariah compliant (Besar et al., 2009).

The centralized approach to Shariah governance requires a centralized Shariah Supervisory Board (SSB) at the central banks. Each IB must have its own SSB, but it must follow the regulations and standards established by the central SSB. Therefore, the presence of a central SSB in the Central Bank will diminish interpretation disputes. A CSGF is used in the United Arab Emirates, Malaysia, Pakistan, and Oman. The central SSB encourages the preliminary framework of the country's overall Islamic financial system and plays a supportive role in the establishment of an SGF (Alam, 2022; Farooq et al., 2021; Fatmawati et al., 2022). Even though regulatory bodies in Turkey have understood the critical role of setting up a more centralized SGF for minimizing Shariah non-compliance and reputational risk of PBs, there was an ongoing concern of secularism by avoiding determining Islamic rules and principles that PBs must follow.

The hybrid approach is common in countries where regulatory bodies recognize the necessity of a CSGF but do not want to be directly involved in announcing Islamic rules and principles regarding contracts and financial products of IBs. Yılmaz and Şencal (2022) argue that national authorities might put pressure on central SSBs positioned in regulatory bodies to issue lax Shariah standards and decisions to facilitate operations and activities of IBs. However, implementation of such a centralized approach might give rise to Shariah non-comliance risk and damage the global reputation and credibility of the Islamic banking industry in the country. Currently, Indonesia, Bangladesh, and Turkey implement the hybrid approach through the establishment of a central SSB as a non-governmental organization by the approval or order of regulatory bodies (Alam et al., 2021; Alam et al., 2020; Hamza, 2013).

4.3 Data and Methodology

The study aims to investigate the function and duties of CSGF and central AB for PBs in Turkey. We used a qualitative case study to achieve the research objective. The qualitative method enables researchers to understand people's motivations, reasons, and actions that quantified data fails to capture (Myers, 2019). In this study, using a qualitative method is justified by its potential to generate comprehensive explanations and discussions about the expected and performed duties and functions of the PBAT's Advisory Board and CSGF in Turkey.

A similar method is also employed by Bektaş and Yenice (2022), Yasoa' et al. (2020), and Alam (2022). The study by Alam (2022) proposed a CSGF for Islamic banking industry in the case of Bangladesh. Additionally, Bektaş and Yenice (2022) also conducted qualitative research for understanding the importance and expected roles of PBs' advisory committees in the case of Turkey. Similarly, Wan Abdullah and Endut (2020) used qualitative method for investigating Shariah audit and Shariah review in IBs in Malaysia based on the structure of reporting, independence, the scope of activities, the technology utilized, guidelines and methodology, coverage period, and qualification of officers.

This study utilizes semi-structured questions during interview sessions so that we can explore more detailed information regarding the central AB and SGF in Turkey. Semi-structured questions related to the working procedure, composition, key responsibilities, and appointment of PBAT's AB members have been prepared to produce a comprehensive discussion on the new face of SGF in Turkey. Utilizing semi-structured questions during the interview sessions opens up free discussion between the researcher and participants in order to understand issues, and challenges and produce recommendations about central AB and the new SGF in Turkey.

In terms of selecting interviewees, we chose purposive sampling in the initial stage because it enables researchers to choose the most relevant items depending on their knowledge and capacity to attain research objectives (Palinkas et al.,

Table 4.1 Background of Interviewees

SL	Participants ID	Position	Organization	Experience (Years)
1	SP#1	Member of Central Advisory Board and Ex-Executive Vice President	PBAT and Participation Bank	36
2	SP#2	Member of Advisory Committee and Professor	Participation Bank and University	18
3	SP#3	Member of Advisory Committee and Ex-Manager	Participation Bank	28
4	RA#1	Head of Department	Regulatory Body	18
5	RA#2	Head of Department	Regulatory Body	12
6	RA#3	Head of Department	Regulatory Body	18
7	M#1	Executive and Ex-Executive Vice President	PBAT and Participation Bank	25
8	M#2	Chief Executive Officer	Participation Bank	12
9	M#3	Board of Director	Participation Bank	20

2015). However, few interviewees have been included in the sample by snowball sampling tactics later. The semi-structured interviews were conducted with nine members of the Advisory Board and Advisory Committees, executives of PBs, and key regulators. The interviewees were directly connected to PBs, Advisory Boards and Advisory Committees, SG functions, policy, and regulations. Table 4.1 shows the list of interviewees in detail.

The interviews lasted between 45 and 65 minutes. The respondents were notified about the recording before the interviews, and they agreed to it. Furthermore, we pledged that their identity would not be made public and would be kept anonymous. Thus, to protect the privacy of the interviewees, their names were used in code, i.e. 'RA' (regulatory aspects) for regulators, 'SP' (Shariah practitioners) for Advisory Committees and central Advisory Board members and 'M' (Managers) for managers of PBs.

4.4 Findings and Discussions

This study aimed to evaluate new CSGF and central AB for the PBs in Turkey. As this study focuses on analysing the functions and roles of SGF and PBAT's AB, it discusses issues and challenges as well as offers solutions and recommendations to ensure proper Shariah governance mechanism for the IBs in Turkey.

PBs in Turkey had been operating by decentralized Shariah governance practices for more than three decades. Therefore, it is important to elaborate on respondents' views on the implementation of a CSGF and the establishment of a central AB in Turkey. Several respondents (SP#3, M#1) argue that the presence of a CSGF and central AB ensures fair competition among PBs and decreases Shariah non-compliance risk. Therefore, it was necessary to establish a CSGF and a central AB in Turkey.

> Considering 40-year of experience until today, Participation banks had operated by their own approaches to Islamic rules and principles. However, they faced many problems (regarding Shari'ah non-compliance risk). Decentralized SG practices enabled flexibility in the activities of Participation banks, but it also eventually increased the reputational risk of the industry. Especially, lack of a CSGF and central AB led to unfair competition and unfavorable marketing practices. As a result, the public image of Participation banks was gradually being harmed. [M#1]

> Compulsory Shari'ah standards are possible and necessary. Otherwise, we have an environment of unfair competition. [SP#3]

4.4.1 Roles and Functions of Central Advisory Board

4.4.1.1 Boundaries of Shariah Standards

Many respondents highlighted the importance of defining the boundaries of Shariah standards that central advisory board issues. To begin with, there are several schools of Islamic law. Due to the cultural diversity and differences in Islamic law schools throughout the Muslim world, there is a wide range of Islamic financial practices today (Laldin, Khir, & Parid, 2012). Along this line, participants (RA#2, SP#2, RA#1) stated that determining essential principles for financial transactions on which diverse schools of law may agree is preferable to inferring strict rules on contentious issues.

> It is possible to create standards that draw the general framework, but detailed standards are not possible. Extremely detailed procedures are neither helpful nor correct. There are strict rules and there are judgments that vary according to the school of Islamic law. In such cases, creating a space for different forms of application can be good and comforting. It may not be right to apply only a strict fatwa to the industry. [RA#2]

> There are different sects and cultures, but Islamic finance should be 100% standardized. Finance is a technical field. It is a mathematical field. It has no sect. Just as international standards and formulas are the same in conventional finance, so should the standards in Islamic banking. The sectarian debate is an excuse for the wolf to eat the lamb. We don't have to stick to sects. [SP#2]

> There must be universal principles. It is necessary to develop standards that meet the global and everyone's needs at a minimum level. [RA#1]

4.4.1.2 Harmonization of Shariah Standards

The role of harmonized Shariah standards for the integration of Participation banking into the global Islamic banking industry is another crucial discussion.

New Shariah Governance Framework for Islamic Banks in Turkey 71

AAOIFI Shariah standards were translated into Turkish by PBAT and Istanbul Sabahattin Zaim University in collaboration with BRSA. The book was released in December 2018 to contribute to the Islamic banking industry (BRSA, 2018). However, AB of PBAT decided to release its own Shariah standards. The importance and need for harmonization of international Islamic financial contracts have been highlighted and emphasized in interviews as well.

> Usually, Board of Directors in a company represents different opinions. Similarly, AB should be composed of people with diverse opinions to find a balance in their decision-making. However, they all have a similar mindset in the case of Turkey. This leads to a lack of harmonization of Islamic financial contracts and services. If Turkey is keen to become a hub of Islamic finance industry, harmonization of Islamic financial standards is essential. [M#3]

> If it were me, I would use AAOIFI Shariah standards. I would scan quickly. We'd approve or patch it up and go with it. there is no need to spend effort from zero in vain. Many people want the Turkey model. Malaysian gulf and turkey model. We have Ottoman traditions etc. But there is a no different model of fiqh. [SP#2]

> AAOIFI and IFSB standards should be the reference points. Then we can make some adjustments to it. In order for Istanbul to become a financial hub, we must either be a playmaker, or we have to become a compatible player in the game. [RA#3]

However, one participant (RA#1) argued that the adoption of international Shariah standards without making any change can cause unexpected problems.

> Adopting international standards directly may pose a problem, as there may be conflicts with culture, constitution, and legislation. [RA#1]

One response from interviews was also highlighting the lack of collaboration and effort by central AB to influence global Shariah standards.

> Turkish is not good enough to introduce themselves. We do not explain ourselves to international institutions. We are not good enough at lobbying. Let's create the Turkey model (for Shari'ah standards), but let's explain ourselves to others as well. [M#2]

4.4.1.3 Organizational Structure and Working Procedure of Advisory Board

Currently, there is one manager and three experts in addition to seven members of the Advisory Board. After the issue of standardization is determined by central AB, experts conduct research and prepare a Shariah research report for the relevant product or service. After the first draft is prepared by experts through the supervision of an AB member, all members of AB share their opinions on the draft. After the draft is finalized, it is shared with stakeholders, especially Participant Banks. After feedback from stakeholders is evaluated by AB members, a workshop is conducted to finalize the standard. After the final version is shared with stakeholders, it is released on PBAT's website.

Initially, members of AB were gathering once a month. Then, the frequency of meetings rose to twice a month and then finally, four times a month. Similarly, some experts work full-time while some experts work part-time. Most respondents claim that there are many challenges and issues related to AB's organization and working procedure. In Turkey, the AB is still relatively new, with only a few standards produced thus far. The respondents (M#1, SP#2, SP#1) believe the AB needs a more robust organizational structure and longer working hours to publish guidelines faster and reduce Shariah non-compliance risk in the Islamic financial business.

> Preparing Shari'ah standards can take a long time and the AB has produced and published 4 standards so far. Members of AB must work full-time to issue standards rapidly. [M#1]

> Employees should work every day, not once a week. There had to be a strong research center underneath. Scholarship staff etc. is not enough. With the current experience in Turkey, there is no need for someone from abroad. We have the potential to produce better standards, but the current organizational structure is bad. AB has been established like a *gecekondu*, a slum house constructed overnight secretly. The working procedure develops with some trial and error. [SP#2]

> In normal management practices, how many employees should work under one manager? At least two or three, right? But here we are seven members of AB who have four or five experts working with us. The number should be much greater. [SP1]

One respondent (SP#1) highlighted the importance and need for more experts to work with AB to speed up standardization efforts in Turkey.

> Rights of employees in PBAT are not sufficient enough. They would have better rights probably if AB is positioned within BRSA or the Central Bank. Thus, experts would easily leave the position and it affects standardization procedure negatively. [SP1]

4.4.1.4 Certificate Programs

Currently, there are several certificate programs about standardizations in Islamic finance that some of the professionals in IFIs are required to obtain as requested by regulatory bodies. The Advisory Board of PBAT conducts a 61-hour certificate program on 'Compliance with Interest-free Banking' over five weeks. The certificate program is run by industry professionals and prominent academic staff. This certificate is compulsory for a limited number of participating bank employees, especially those who work in the auditing and Shariah auditing departments.

One interviewee (RA#2) argues that this certificate program can be compulsory for a larger number of employees in different departments of PBs to decrease Shariah non-compliance risk and increase awareness about Islamic rules and principles for Islamic banking activities. While another respondent (M#1) highlighted the importance of offering more sophisticated training for key staff of Shariah auditing.

> Participation Compliance Certificate is nice for Participation banks. There are 45–50 hours of PBAT training. Surely, it is positive news for the industry but insufficient. Shari'ah non-compliance risk is high for Participation banks. That's why staff training is very important ... Examination and training should be done from the top-level managers to the bottom-level employees of Participation banks. [RA#2]

> BRSA employees are also invited to this training for conducting the external audit, but this training does not provide enough education for conducting a comprehensive external audit. [M#1]

Several interviews highlighted the need for accreditation of certificate programs and enabling independent training programs by accredited institutions to improve the quality of certificate programs.

> Democratization is also needed in education. Supervisory and regulatory institutions should be able to provide their own training and certification, but the important thing is to do accreditation. This job gets cumbersome when only one institution issues the compulsory certificate. [M#2]

> This certificate program must be accredited. [RA#3]

> BRSA made this certificate program compulsory. If you scrutinize the educational content and the names of trainers, you can notice that organizers invite their friend circles as a trainer and are not open to trainers with different views. It misses the main purpose of the certificate program. [SP2]

4.4.2 Centralized Shariah Governance Framework

4.4.2.1 Legal Infrastructure and Shariah Governance Framework

The hierarchy of norms and building a comprehensive and robust regulatory framework are key for the effective implementation of Shariah governance mechanism in Turkey. Many interviewees stated that there are weak or no connections among regulations, communiqué, decrees, and acts regarding the IFSI. Thus, even if regulatory bodies issue communiqué and regulations for IFIs, they may not comply with superior norms. Contradictions between Islamic finance regulations and communiqué and superior norms, in particular, can generate significant obstacles to implementing Shariah governance framework. Many respondents (M#1, SP#2, M#2, SP#3) argue that IFIs are subject to the same acts as their conventional counterparts, and those acts are not designed to meet the needs of IFIs. Therefore, those acts often cause challenges in using suitable Islamic financial products, transactions, accounting entries, and taxation because regulatory bodies usually try to match those products/transactions with a conventional product/transaction in relevant acts as a temporary solution.

> There are deficiencies in the legislation at many points. A great burden falls on supervisory and regulatory bodies. [M#1]

> The legislation in Turkey is not compatible with the needs of Participation banks. Regulations do not provide a comprehensive legal infrastructure for the operations of Participation banks. However, there is a great effort to issue an act for the Participation finance industry at the moment ... BRSA tells AB's Shari'ah standards are binding, but the law does not say so. [SP#2]

> The needs of Participation banking have no real place under the banking law. Certain steps must and are being taken for producing an Act for Participation Finance. Now, there are many issues such as the issuance of Sukuk by private companies or management and ownership of Islamic funds by conventional asset managers. It is necessary to prepare a very comprehensive act. Supervisory and regulatory bodies claim that the industry is still not very differentiated. This prevents the enactment of the new law. [M#2]

> There should be no 'interest' word in an act for Participation banking, but there is 'late payment interest' etc. in the act and you do not have the power to change them. It is necessary to make corrections in places that intersect with every field of the act and where Shari'ah law touches the act. There should be a separate act for IFIs. When omnibus bills are issued, everything becomes messy and disorganized like a ragbag. [SP#3]

4.4.2.2 Independence of Advisory Board

To improve independence, members of AB cannot serve on the committees of PBs, which helps to avoid conflicts of interest. On the other hand, our interviews with respondents show that there is still a crucial debate on the independence of AB. Most interviewees point out that the independence of the advisory board is essential for preventing a conflict of interest and minimizing Shariah non-compliance risk in PBs.

> There should be a central advisory board, but a place with legal personality. It should be a completely separate institution. [RA#2]

> The activities of AB started fast, but it started late. The establishment of an autonomous institution within BRSA or the central bank might be more

New Shariah Governance Framework for Islamic Banks in Turkey   75

suitable. It is like a subsidiary of Participation banks now. It is important to increase the immunity of the AB in terms of issuing fatwas and Shari'ah standards. [SP#1]

However, one respondent highlighted that lack of legal infrastructure for PBs is a challenge to set up AB within regulatory bodies. Therefore, it was necessary and convenient to establish AB within PBAT to speed up issuing Shariah standards and implement an effective CSGF for PBs.

Some are worried about the independence of central AB because it has been established within PBAT. However, AB is fully independent of Participation banks since the appointment of members is approved by BRSA. Moreover, it has been positioned under PBAT because the legal infrastructure was not ready to establish AB in a governmental institution and it was essential to speed up the preparation of Shari'ah standards to minimize Shari'ah non-compliance risk in Turkey. [M#1]

4.4.2.3 Appointment and Composition of Advisory Board Members

Currently, BRSA allowed PBAT to determine the composition and appointment procedure of AB members. The communiqué of PBAT (2018) about the criteria for appointment for AB members is as follows:

- At least four members of AB must have a PhD in Islamic studies.
- At least one member of AB must be a member of the Supreme Council for Religious Affairs.
- At least one member must have a degree in economics, management, banking, law, or participation banking and at least seven-year experience in the industry.

Currently, there are seven members of PBAT's AB. Two members are picked from the Supreme Council for Religious Affairs, with an additional three members chosen from the Divinity Faculty of Universities. One member from the Islamic banking industry and one from the Law Faculty of Universities are also selected. Following the determination of a list of candidates for the Advisory Board by PBAT, the list is forwarded to BRSA for approval. The BRSA has the right to modify names on the list and may insist on the selection of certain individuals. After conducting interviews with participants, many respondents expressed that AB's appointment mechanism is contentious. Several respondents (M#1, SP#3, SP#2) argued that many members of AB are from academia, and AB lacks professionals to undertake study and write studies on Shariah concerns to expedite the release of new standards.

What the academy lacks is their distance from industry practice. Sometimes ijtihad can be made without knowing the established commercial rules. [M#1]

> There should be people from the industry. Even if you are a professor in the field of fiqh, you may not know how the business works, and the fatwa may not be correct. Half of the members must have industry experience. [SP#3]

> The professors there are experts in their field, but they do not understand finance well. They say 'let's talk about products more' when they see new Islamic products. Thus, the industry reacted negatively. Since a senior expert from the industry started to work therein recently, the deficiency there has decreased. [SP#2]

One interviewee argued that it will be beneficial for the industry if AB members have diverse opinions.

> AB should be composed of people with various opinions to find a balance in their decision-making. However, they all have a similar mindset in the case of Turkey. This leads to a lack of harmonization of Islamic financial contracts and services as well. [M#3]

There is another important discussion that AB members should have an international reputation.

> We need international names. [RA#3]

4.4.2.4 Board of Directors (BOD)

The board executive committee is responsible for implementing the Board of Directors' decisions and directions. If BODs exhibit negative conduct on occasion, they prefer to prioritize bank profitability and business risks instead of Shariah issues. Similarly, one regulator (RA#1) expressed a similar concern regarding BODs of PBs.

> Participation banks must be sincere. Executives and board members who have not any experience in Islamic banking come in and can interfere with the functions that advisory committees should perform. Before the advisory board was established, no one saw their decisions and it was possible to act with the instructions from above. [RA#1]

4.4.2.5 Shariah Audit

Shariah audit is a key element of CSGF for PBs in Turkey. Current regulations highlight that internal Shariah auditors and external Shariah auditors, namely BRSA auditors and independent auditing agencies need to ensure operations of PBs are in compliance with Islamic rules and principles. However, several interviews (M#1, RA#1) claimed that the external Shariah auditing mechanism is not functioning well at the moment, and it poses Shariah non-compliance risk in the activities of PBs.

The audit and Advisory committee within the bank has to ensure compliance of activities with Islamic rules and principles. In case of non-compliance with the produced Shari'ah standards, the responsibility belongs to the board of directors. The BRSA can also impose penalties up to license cancellation. Independent external auditors are required. This part is still in the stage of infancy. BRSA employees receive external audit training from the PBAT, but they do not have comprehensive training to conduct an audit in terms of Islamic law. [M#1]

For example, when the BRSA requests a zakat chart, Participation banks are revolting, saying, 'We are already preparing a lot of tables, and are we going to prepare a zakat table as well?' Many do not know how to prepare it. [RA#1]

4.5 Conclusions and Policy Recommendations

Despite four-decade Islamic banking experience in Turkey, regulatory authorities initiated the establishment of central AB and CSGF only four years ago. Our study shows that central AB and CSGF recently played an important role to decrease Shariah violations by PBs. However, there are ongoing debates about the expectations of stakeholders from central AB and the effectiveness of current SG practices in Turkey. Therefore, this study employed a qualitative method to revisit the roles and functions of PBAT's AB and new SGF and to understand current SG issues and challenges deeper. We find that there is still more room for improvement of CSGF in Turkey.

This study offers important policy recommendations for PBAT's AB, regulators, and PBs to improve CSG practices. First, the boundaries of Shariah standards can be defined carefully to comply with local regulations and international standards. Second, members of the AB can gather more frequently, and there can be more Shariah and Islamic finance experts to research Islamic rulings on financial products and services. Third, certificate programs can be conducted by independent and accredited institutions while different certificate programs can be organized depending on the need of regulators and PBs. Fourth, establishing the AB as a Juridical person under the government can increase its independence and prevent conflict of interests. Fifth, it is critical to include more experienced Shariah scholars from industry instead of preferring only Shariah scholars from universities and the Supreme Council for Religious Affairs. Sixth, the representation of experienced participation bankers in executive and BoD positions can prevent Shariah violations and be included in regulations. Finally, external Shariah auditors from BRSA and independent auditing agencies can play a more active role to ensure activities of participations banks are in compliance with Islamic rules and principles.

References

Alam, M. K. (2022). A proposed centralized Shari'ah governance framework for Islamic banks in Bangladesh. *Journal of Islamic Accounting and Business Research*, *13*(2), 364–389. https://doi.org/10.1108/JIABR-03-2021-0106

Alam, M. K., Mustafa, H., Uddin, M. S., Islam, M. J., Mohua, M. J., & Hassan, M. F. (2020a). Problems of Shari'ah governance framework and different bodies: An empirical investigation of Islamic Banks in Bangladesh. *Journal of Asian Finance, Economics and Business*, *7*(3), 265–276. https://doi.org/10.13106/jafeb.2020.vol7.no3.265

Alam, M. K., Tabash, M. I., Thakur, O. A., Sahabuddin, M., Hosen, S., & Hassan, M. F. (2020b). A central Shari'ah regulatory authority for the islamic banks in Bangladesh: Legalization or formation. *Journal of Asian Finance, Economics and Business*, *7*(1), 91–100. https://doi.org/10.13106/jafeb.2020.vol7.no1.91

Alam, M. K., Ab Rahman, S., Tabash, M. I., Thakur, O. A., & Hosen, S. (2021). Shari'ah supervisory boards of Islamic banks in Bangladesh: Expected duties and performed roles and functions. *Journal of Islamic Accounting and Business Research*, *12*(2), 258–275. https://doi.org/10.1108/JIABR-02-2020-0035

Alam, M. K., & Thakur, O. A. (2022). Why does Bangladesh require a centralized Shari'ah governance framework for Islamic banks? *Journal of Nusantara Studies (JONUS)*, *7*(1), 24–42. https://doi.org/10.24200/jonus.vol7iss1pp24-42

Aziz, R. A., Abdul-Rahman, A., & Markom, R. (2019). Best practices for internal Shari'ah governance framework: Lessons from Malaysian Islamic banks. *Asian Journal of Accounting and Governance*, *12*(1), 1–14. https://doi.org/10.17576/AJAG-2019-12-15

Banking Regulation and Supervision Agency (2021). *Annual Report 2021*.

Bektaş, İ., & Yenice, A. C. (2022). Shari'ah governance in Turkey: A case study on in-bank advisory committees. *Sakarya Üniversitesi İlahiyat Fakültesi Dergisi (SAUIFD)*, *22*, 29–60. https://doi.org/10.17335/sakaifd.1067325

Besar, M. H. A. H., Sukor, M. E. A., Muthalib, N. A., & Gunawa, A. Y. (2009). The practice of Shari'ah review as undertaken by Islamic banking sector in Malaysia. *International Review of Business Research Papers*, *5*(1), 294–306.

BRSA (2018). *BRSA Annual Report 2018*.

Farooq, W., Jan Wasim, S. M., & Othman Bin, A. A. (2021). Regulatory arrangement for Shari'ah governance practice of Islamic banking institutions in Pakistan: Issues and challenges. *Hitit İlahiyat Dergisi*, (June), 167–194. https://doi.org/10.14395/hid.947530

Fatmawati, D., Ariffin, N. M., Abidin, N. H. Z., & Osman, A. Z. (2022). Shari'ah governance in Islamic banks: Practices, practitioners and praxis. *Global Finance Journal*, *51*, 100555. https://doi.org/10.1016/j.gfj.2020.100555

Grassa, R. (2013). Shari'ah supervisory system in Islamic financial institutions: New issues and challenges: A comparative analysis between Southeast Asia models and GCC models. *Humanomics*, *29*(4), 333–348. https://doi.org/10.1108/H-01-2013-0001

Grassa, R. (2015). Shari'ah supervisory systems in Islamic finance institutions across the OIC member countries. *Journal of Financial Regulation and Compliance*, *23*(2), 135–160. https://doi.org/10.1108/jfrc-02-2014-0011

Grassa, R., & Gazdar, K. (2014). Borsa – Istanbul Review Law and Islamic finance: How legal origins affect Islamic finance development? *Borsa Istanbul Review*, *14*(3), 158–166. https://doi.org/10.1016/j.bir.2014.05.001

Hamza, H. (2013). Sharia governance in Islamic banks: Effectiveness and supervision model. *International Journal of Islamic and Middle Eastern Finance and Management*, 6(3), 226–237. https://doi.org/10.1108/IMEFM-02-2013-0021

Hassan, R., Abdullah, N.I., Hassan, A., Ibrahim, U., Sawari, M.F.M., Abd. Aziz, A., & Triyanta, A. (2011). A comparative analysis of Shari'ah governance in Islamic banking institutions across jurisdictions, international Shari'ah Research Academy for Islamic Finance. Retrieved from https://ifikr.isra.my/library/pub/1601/a-comparative-analysis-of-Shari'ah-governance-in-islamic-banking-institutions-across-jurisdictions

Laldin, M. A., Khir, M. F. A., & Parid, N. M. (2012). Fatwas in Islamic banking: A comparative study between Malaysia and Gulf Cooperation Council (GCC) countries. *International Shari'ah Reseach Academy for Islamic Finance ISRA @ INCEIF* (Vol. 31).

Masruki, R., Hanefah, M. M., & Dhar, B. K. (2020). Shari'ah governance practices of Malaysian Islamic banks in the light of Shari'ah compliance. *Asian Journal of Accounting and Governance*, 13, 91–97. https://doi.org/10.17576/AJAG-2020-13-08

Myers, M. D. (2019). *Qualitatve Research in Business & Management*. SAGE Publications.

Palinkas, L. A., Horwitz, S. M., Green, C. A., Wisdom, J. P., Duan, N., & Hoagwood, K. (2015). Purposeful sampling for qualitative data collection and analysis in mixed method implementation research. *Administration and Policy in Mental Health and Mental Health Services Research*, 42(5), 533–544. https://doi.org/10.1007/s10488-013-0528-y

PBAT (2018). Communiqué on the formation, duties, working procedures and principles of the advisory board. Retrieved from https://tkbbdanismakurulu.org.tr/uploads/belgeler/Danisma-kurulunun-olusumu-gorev-calisma-usul-ve-esaslari-hakkinda-teblig-1.pdf

Perves, M. M. (2015). Legal and Regulatory Framework in Islamic Banking System: Bangladesh Perspective. *European Journal of Business and Management*, 7(21), 179–188.

Yas, M., Aslan, H., & Ozdemir, M. (2018). Modern History of Islamic Finance and a Strategic Roadmap for Its Development in Turkey. In A. F. Aysan, M. Babacan, N. Gur, & H. Karahan (Eds.), *Turkish Economy* (pp. 213–238). Cham: Springer International Publishing. https://doi.org/10.1007/978-3-319-70380-0_10

Yasoa', M. R., Wan Abdullah, W. A., & Endut, W. A. (2020). A Comparative Analysis between Shari'ah Audit and Shari'ah Review in Islamic Banks in Malaysia: Practitioners' Perspective. *Environment-Behaviour Proceedings Journal*, 5(14), 195–200. https://doi.org/10.21834/ebpj.v5i14.2208

Yılmaz, H. S., & Şencal, H. (2022). İslam Politik Ekonomisi Açısından Merkezi Fetva Kurullarının Yapısına Dair Bir Değerlendirme. *Journal of Islamic Economics*, 47–66. Retrieved from https://dergipark.org.tr/en/pub/jie/issue/68091/1010986%0Ahttps://dergipark.org.tr/en/download/article-file/2031579

5 From Confidentiality to Concealment

An Issue of Shariah Governance in Islamic Banking Institutions

Mansoor Khan

5.1 Introduction

Islamic finance has become one of the fastest-growing sources of financing all over the world. Islamic finance provides options to those investors who want to make sure their investments are in Shariah-compliant businesses. There is a need for such standards under which operations of Islamic banking institutions can be ensured. These sets of rules are called the Shariah governance system. The goal of Shariah governance is to protect the interests of every stakeholder of the society. There are two Shariah governance models. The first one is *Shura* and *Tawhid* model and second one is stakeholder model (Hasan, 2008). Islamic banks are quite different from their conventional counterparts. Islamic banks are required to provide products and services that are Shariah compliant. The governance structure of Islamic banks is quite different from conventional banks. There are two types of governance arrangements in Islamic banks, internal and external (Grais & Pellegrini, 2006). Internal arrangements include the Shariah board, product development department, Shariah compliance department, Shariah review department and Shariah audit department. The Shariah board is considered as a central pillar of Shariah governance. There are several issues that are associated with the functioning of Shariah board (Grais & Pellegrini, 2006). These issues are independence, confidentiality, disclosure, competence and consistency (Ginene & Hamid, 2015). There is another aspect of these issues that needs to be addressed. In this chapter the issue of confidentiality is discussed and another aspect of confidentiality is explained, that is concealment of information. This chapter contains six sections. The Introduction section is followed by Shariah governance. Section 3 explains Shariah governance in Islamic banking institutions followed by the Shariah board in Islamic banking institutions in Section 4. Section 5 discusses issues of Shariah governance followed by the Conclusion in the last section.

5.2 Shariah Governance

Literature discusses several different approaches on models of Shariah governance. Iqbal and Mirakhor (2004) divide corporate governance into two

DOI: 10.4324/9781003324836-5

different models. The first one is shareholder model and second one is stakeholder model. They argue that under shareholder model the focus of set of rules and regulations are investors. Under this model the investors have complete control of the firm and the managers of the firm works for the protection of interests of the shareholders only. Under this model the goal of the organization is only limited to the profit maximization. On the other hand, they discussed stakeholder model as it focuses upon the protection of the interests of all stakeholders. These stakeholders include but are not limited to customers, investors, staff of the firm and the society as a whole. Under stakeholder model all the stakeholders have the right to take part in the decision-making process. Similarly, the managers of the firm will have to protect the interests of all the stakeholders rather than only investors.

Islamic finance has witnessed huge growth in the last three to four decades. With this growth the need of adequate governance system for Islamic financial institutions also increased (Uddin, 2015; Minhas, 2012). Iqbal and Mirakhor (2004) argues that the term corporate has two different concepts. It starts from a set of rules for protection of interests of investors to the set of rules for protection of interests of all stakeholders. Governance is considered as a set of rules which needs to be followed by each component of an organization for its smooth operations. On the other hand, when we talk about Shariah governance, it is considered as a set of organizational arrangements that guides an organization to follow the set of rules defined by the Shariah. Shariah governance is necessary for institutions providing Islamic financial services (Minhas, 2012). Similarly, Alam et al. (2021) argue that Shariah governance is quite different from conventional corporate governance. These differences can be seen in terms of roles, objectives and rules that need to be followed by the institutions. These rules, objectives and roles are based upon the teaching of Quran and Sunnah. Obaid and Naysary (2014) also discuss the difference of corporate governance and Shariah governance by arguing that Shariah governance is quite different from conventional corporate governance whose ultimate goal is to protect the interests of shareholders and management. While the Shariah governance focuses upon the protection of the interests of all stakeholders and to achieve Maqasid al-Shariah which is a tool defined by the Shariah for the protection of interests of whole society (Obaid & Naysary, 2014).

In Islam the governance system is based upon principles and rights of individuals, state and society. In Islam there are three types of rights: rights of individuals; rights of state; and rights of community and society as a whole. Similarly, Hasan (2008) argues that the corporate governance from perspective of Islam focuses upon protection of interests of all stakeholders. This focus is beyond the financial interest and profit maximization. Under Islam the corporate governance is based upon the principles of Shariah. In addition to this it also includes the components of ethics and is based upon the concept of Tawhid.

Hasan (2008) discussed two basic Shariah governance models. The first one is *Tawhid* and *Shura* based model and second one is stakeholder's model. Foundation of corporate governance is based upon concept of *Tawhid* that is oneness of Allah. Allah is the ultimate ownership of everything under this principle and human beings are vicegerent of Allah (S.W.T). Under this model the Shariah board and *Shura* that consists of all stakeholders play an important role. On the other hand, Hasan (2008) also discusses stakeholder model of Shariah governance. Under this model the governance structure of an organization focuses upon the protection of interests of all the stakeholders rather than the shareholders only. Under this model the Islamic banking institution will have to protect the rights of all the stakeholders irrespective of their equity in the institution. This model is based upon two main principles. These are the principles of property rights and the agreements that enforce these rights of individuals, society and the state. Based upon these principles this particular model is classified into stakeholder model. Islam does recognize the concept of private ownership but this right is subject to the fulfillment of balance with other stakeholders of the society which includes individuals, state and society as a whole. The second pillar deals with fulfillment of legal contracts, rights and responsibilities by all the pledging parties. All the parties – either an individual, any corporation, state and society as a whole – will have to fulfil their pledging responsibilities under these contracts (Hasan 2008).

Similarly, Kausar Alam et al. (2019) argue that the ultimate ownership of the property is with Allah (S.W.T). Human beings are vicegerent of Allah (S.W.T) and will act as a custodian of the property. Under this principle every individual of the society is stakeholder of that property and every stakeholder will have to be included in the decision-making process and eventually every individual of the society will be accountable for that property. The human being has the right to manage the property in such a manner that he is a custodian of that property. They further argue that Shariah governance focuses upon the right of all stakeholders and to bring economic and social fairness among the individuals and society as a whole. Under the stakeholder model of Shariah governance all stakeholders will take part in the decision-making process of the firm for protection of their interest. In addition to this, Shariah governance ensures social justice by setting rules and regulation for the organizations based upon the principles of Shariah (Alam et al., 2019). Whenever we talk about Islamic banking institutions the corporate structure of these institutions is not only based upon fundamental principles of Islam but it also focuses upon the lawful and unlawful transaction under the teachings of Quran and Sunnah.

5.3 Shariah Governance in Islamic Banking Institutions

Islamic banks are quite different from their conventional counterparts. These differences can be witnessed in terms of the structure of Islamic banks, their functioning and most importantly their objectives. Whenever we talk about Islamic banks one of the major differences between Islamic banking institutions and their counterparts is prohibition of Riba. It is necessary for Islamic banks to provide products and services to the customers that are Shariah compliant. In case of non-Shariah compliance, the banks will be exposed to several risks including reputational risk and Shariah noncompliance risk which can result in losing investments from the clients and it can also result in losing confidence of the customer. Effective Shariah governance is necessary for Islamic banking institutions to strengthen the trust of customers. Similarly, when it comes to Islamic banks, it includes multiple stakeholders. These stakeholders are shareholders of Islamic banks, investors of Islamic banks, employees of Islamic banks and most importantly account holders of Islamic banks whether they are current account holders or savings account holders. Last but not least the society as a whole. It is the responsibility of the board of directors to ensure Shariah compliance. Islamic banks have a multi-layer governance structure. It includes board of directors and Shariah board (Nomran & Haron 2020). Similarly, Farag et al. (2018) and Shibani and Fuentes (2017) also have a similar understanding, they argue that Islamic banks have a unique governance structure. There are two boards in Islamic banking institutions: the first one is the board of directors; and second one is the Shariah board.

Alnofli and Ali (2020) divide Shariah governance models into three types. The first one is centralized model; second one is self-regulated model; and the third one is hybrid model. Similarly, Alam et al. (2021) also divide Shariah governance models into three types: centralized; laissez fair; and hybrid model. In centralized model of Shariah governance for Islamic banking institutions the central Shariah board have ultimate decision power in case of disagreement between the decision of Shariah board and central Shariah board. Furthermore, the decision of central Shariah board will be binding for Islamic banking institutions. This particular model is being adopted in Pakistan and Malaysia. In self-regulated model or laissez faire model the Islamic banking institutions adopt self-regulation due to non-availability of regulations for the Islamic financial industry. Under this model there is no central authority. This model is being adopted by the GCC countries except Bahrain (Alam et al., 2021). Under the hybrid model of Shariah governance there is a central Shariah board but its role is advisory, to supervise and ensure compliance of the products with the Shariah. This model is being adopted by Bahrain (Alnofli & Ali, 2020; Hasan & Sabirzyanov, 2015).

On the other hand, Hussein (2014) classifies Shariah governance models into five different models. His classification is based upon regulatory perspective. He classifies Shariah governance models as reactive approach, passive approach, pro-active approach, interventionist approach and minimalist approach. Reactive approach is adopted in those countries where the legal environment is not Islamic. The regulator in such countries only reacts when there is an issue that might affect Islamic banking or Islamic financial institutions. There is no proper Shariah governance framework in such countries. Next one is passive approach. Under this approach the regulator does not have any specific requirements for Islamic financial institutions or Islamic banking institutions. The regulator will deal with both Islamic and non-Islamic bank or financial institution equally. Under this approach Shariah governance system will be self-regulated. The next one is proactive approach. Under this approach the regulator actively engages in regulations for Islamic banking institutions. Malaysia is a particle example of this approach. The Malaysian parliament passed several acts over the last few decades for institutions providing Islamic financial services. The next one is interventionist approach. Under this approach any Shariah-related issue is referred to the third party. This model is being practised in Pakistan currently. In Pakistan federal Shariah court is the highest authority in matters related to Shariah. Although there is also a central Shariah board of State Bank of Pakistan. The last approach is minimalist approach. Under this approach the regulators expect that Islamic banking institutions or Islamic financial institutions will have their own Shariah governance system. The regulator does not specify any requirements under this approach and believes in less intervention from the regulator.

Islamic financial service board (IFSB) defines Shariah governance as a 'set of institutional arrangements through Islamic financial institutions that ensures Shariah compliance upon the issuance of Shariah pronouncements by Shariah board and its implementation by the management, and internal and external Shariah review and Shariah audit' (Fatmawati et al., 2022, p. 2). Similarly, IFSB identifies Shariah governance process as issuance of Shariah pronouncements on products and services, implementation of these Shariah pronouncements, their internal Shariah review and internal Shariah audit (Fatmawati et al., 2022). Similarly, Saba and Lahsasna (2013) also identified the process of Shariah governance. They argue that Shariah governance process includes composition and appointment of Shariah board, approval of products by Shariah board, observance of Shariah compliance of the products, Shariah review and Shariah audit of the transactions that has been done by the Islamic banking institutions. It also includes the reporting of all the process and findings by the above-mentioned process in the annual reports of the Islamic banks. Furthermore, the decision of the Shariah board will be binding for Islamic banking institutions and in case of any dispute the issue will be referred to the central Shariah board. Bahari and Baharudin (2016) also identify somewhat similar process of Shariah governance. They argue that Shariah governance system contains effective board of directors and higher management. It includes independent Shariah board, effective Shariah review, Shariah audit and risk management system. They argue that for effective Shariah governance system the above-mentioned pillars need to be align with each other. Furthermore, they argue that a comprehensive Shariah governance system depends upon effective management and supervision, strong Shariah board, Shariah compliance, independent Shariah audit and transparency and disclosure.

On the other hand, Minhas (2012) identifies four basic pillars of Shariah governance. He argues that management and supervision; Shariah advisory; Shariah compliance and review; and transparency and disclosure are the main four pillars of Shariah governance. The first and main pillar of Shariah governance is management. He argues that for effective Shariah compliance, willingness of management, i.e. board of directors and higher management is necessary. Without willingness of higher management and board of directors Shariah compliance cannot be achieved. The second pillar of Shariah governance includes independent Shariah board. Shariah board is advisory board that helps board of directors in the matters that are related to Shariah. Similarly, the third most important pillar of Shariah governance is Shariah compliance and Shariah review. For effective Shariah compliance there is Shariah compliance department in banks and for effective Shariah review there is Shariah review and Shariah audit department. To strengthen the trust of the customer with Islamic banking institutions the external Shariah audit is also conducted. The fourth main pillar of Shariah governance is disclosure and transparency. These two factors have an effect on the reputation of Islamic banking institutions, perceptions of public about the Islamic banking institutions and decisions made by the investors.

Similarly, Shahzad et al. (2020) argues that there are four basic components of Shariah governance. These components are board of directors, executive management, Shariah board and Shariah audit. Furthermore, they argue that as far as functions of these components are concerned, the function of board of directors in Islamic bank is oversight and control. It is considered as a first and vital pillar of Shariah governance in Islamic banks. The success of any Islamic bank is based upon the board of directors and it plays a crucial role in Shariah compliance of Islamic banks. Similarly, the executive management is considered as a second important pillar of Islamic banks and success of Islamic banks depends upon the tendency of executive management towards Shariah compliance. Similarly, the third and most critical pillar of Islamic banks is Shariah board and it is considered as backbone of Shariah governance process in Islamic banks. For ideal Shariah compliance in Islamic banks the independent and competent Shariah board is critical. The last pillar of Shariah governance is Shariah audit. Shariah audit looks into the transactions of Islamic banks and evaluates those transactions and ensures that the products and services that are provided by Islamic banks are in compliance with Shariah.

On the other hand, Grais and Pellegrini (2006b) identify two types of governance arrangements for Islamic banking institutions. The first one is internal arrangements and the second one is external arrangements. The internal arrangements include board of directors, Shariah board, product development department, Shariah review units and Shariah audit department. Similarly, the external governance arrangements for Islamic banking institutions include regulatory framework, legal framework and framework for conflict resolution. The above discussion identified several dimensions of Shariah governance that are covered in literature. It is evident from above discussion that for perfect Shariah compliance all the pillars of Shariah governance process need to work in parallel to ensure Shariah compliance in the Islamic banking industry.

5.4 Shariah Board in Islamic Banking Institutions

In Islamic banking institutions Shariah board is considered as one of the important components of Shariah governance. Similarly, Shariah board is considered as one of the main attributes that differentiate Islamic banks from its conventional counterparts. Accounting and auditing organization for Islamic financial institutions (AAOIFI) define Shariah board as a group of jurists with specialization in *Fiq Al Muamlat*. Shariah board may include people other than experts of *Fiq Al-Muamlat* but they need to be an expert of Islamic finance with a sound knowledge of *Fiq Al-Muamlat* (AAOIFI, 1999, p. 885). Similarly, Malkawi (2013) also defines Shariah board as an independent group of jurists with expertise *in Fiq Al-Muamlat*. AlAbbad et al. (2019) argues that Shariah board is considered as one of the major components of Islamic banks that differentiates Islamic banks from its counterparts. It works directly with board of directors and ensures that the matter of Islamic banking institutions is in compliance with Shariah. Chowdhury and Fahim (2015) also have a similar stance on Shariah board. They argue that Islamic banks have different structure than conventional banks and one of the major differences is Shariah board. Similarly, Rashwan (2012) also argues that Islamic banks have to follow the law defined by the Shariah and Shariah board is the crucial pillar of Shariah governance that ensures Shariah compliance in Islamic banking institutions.

Malkawi (2013) differentiates Shariah board at three different levels. He divides Shariah boards into Shariah board at international level, central Shariah board and Shariah board at Islamic financial institution or Islamic banking institutions level. Whenever we talk about Shariah board at international level it includes Shariah board of different standard-setting bodies like IFSB and AAOIFI. It also includes Shariah board of International *Fiqh* academy and Shariah board of Islamic development bank. The main role of these Shariah boards is to bring consistency in Shariah pronouncements related to financial issues around the world. These Shariah boards are also involved in the process of development of standards for Islamic banking institutions by the standard-setting bodies like AAOIFI and IFSB. On the other hand, when we talk about central Shariah board, its major function includes resolving the conflict between Shariah board of Islamic banks and management of Islamic banks. It also plays a vital role in bringing harmonization of Shariah pronouncements related to products and services of Islamic banking institutions. It is mandatory for the Islamic banking institution to follow the decisions of the central Shariah board. Lastly, when we talk about Shariah board at Islamic banking institutions level, there are several responsibilities of these Shariah boards. Malkawi (2013) argues that the responsibilities of Shariah board at Islamic banking institution level includes giving Shariah pronouncements on products and services offered by the Islamic banking institutions, and they also review matters related to Shariah. They also issue Shariah compliance certificate in the annual report of the Islamic banks. Similarly, they will be involved in the internal Shariah review process and internal Shariah audit process. It is also the duty of Shariah board to ensure that the investments made by the Islamic banking institutions are in Shariah-complaint businesses.

As far as structure of Shariah board is concerned, Malkawi (2013) discusses the structure Shariah and argues that it Shariah can be of three types. The first one is the Shariah board composed of outside Shariah scholars; second, one that contains an in-house Shariah department that will be composed of in-house Shariah scholars; and the third one is those Shariah board members who are not experts of Shariah. As far as role and responsibilities of Shariah board are concerned several studies have identified these roles and responsibilities. Darwanto and Chariri (2019) argue that roles and responsibilities of Shariah board include provision of advice on matters related to Shariah for Islamic banking institutions. In addition to this Shariah board will also be responsible for developing rules and regulations and provision of Shariah pronouncements on the products and services offered by the Islamic banking institutions. AAOIFI (1999) also discusses the duties of Shariah board. It includes obligation of governing, evaluating and supervising operations of Islamic banking institutions. Shariah board will also have to ensure that the operations of Islamic banking institutions are in compliance with Shariah. In addition to this, the Shariah pronouncements and rulings of the Shariah board are binding for the Islamic banking institutions. Similarly, Darwanto and Chariri (2019) and Rahajeng (2012) argue that the roles and responsibilities of Shariah board include provision of advice to Islamic banking institutions on matters related to Shariah and developing rules and regulations related to the products and services and issuing Shariah pronouncements on those products and services.

Toufik (2015) also identifies roles and responsibilities of Shariah board. He argues that one of the main purposes of Shariah board is to validate the products and services provided by the Islamic banking institution. Shariah board also have an advisory role. It will advise Islamic banking institution on Shariah compliance and Shariah noncompliance on any action taken by the Islamic banking institution. The second role of Shariah board is the role of compliance. It starts with issuing of Shariah pronouncements and ends with the periodic annual Shariah compliance and Shariah review and Shariah audit report. Shariah board is expected to develop a proper mechanism for Islamic banking institutions to follow principles of Shariah. This mechanism should include the product approval process and it should also include the process of product delivery. The third role of Shariah board is role of audit. After the delivery of the product or service to the customer Shariah board is required to confirm that the product or service that has been delivered was in compliance with the rules and regulation of Shariah.

Malkawi (2013) also discussed the roles and responsibilities of Shariah board. He argues that Shariah board has fiduciary duty towards all stakeholders of Islamic banking institutions. The Shariah board plays a vital role in strengthening the integrity of the Islamic banking institution among the general public through proper Shariah compliance. In addition to this, the primary duty of Shariah board is supervision of Islamic banking institutions and ensuring that the activities of the Islamic banking institutions are in compliance with Shariah. It is also the duty of the Shariah board to provide guidance to the management of Islamic banking institutions regarding the products and services provided to the customers. Furthermore, he argues that duties of Shariah board can be found in the article of association of Islamic banking institutions. He also identifies three areas in which Shariah board plays a vital role. The first one is issuance of *fatwa*; the second is supervision of Islamic banking institution; and the third one is audit. At Islamic bank level Shariah board plays a vital role in operations of Islamic banks by ensuring that the operations are in compliance with Shariah. They also provide documentation and manuals for the products and services provided by Islamic banks. Most importantly it is the primary duty of Shariah board to ensure that the decisions of Shariah board related to products and services are implemented in true spirit.

5.5 Issues of Shariah Governance

Shariah board is considered as the basic pillar of Shariah governance. With this responsibility the liability of Shariah board also increases. There are several issues that are associated with Shariah board. Grais and Pellegrini (2006) identify these issues as disclosure, confidentiality, competence of Shariah board members, independence and consistency. On the other hand, Adam and Al-Aid (2020) call these elements of Shariah governance. Similarly, Ginene and Hamid (2015) discuss six key guidelines for Shariah governance. These guidelines are independence, confidentiality, consistency, transparency, objectivity and disclosure. On the other hand, Uddin (2015) also identifies attributes of Shariah board. These attributes are competence, independence, confidentiality and consistency. Although Hussein (2014) only identifies two attributes which are confidentiality and independence of Shariah board members. On the other hand, Hasan (2014) identifies four attributes of Shariah board. He argues that the attributes of Shariah board include confidentiality, competence, independence and transparency. Similarly, Askari et al. (2012) argue that Shariah board members have to follow five principles. These principles are confidentiality, disclosure, consistency, independence and competence. They argue that the Shariah board should be independent and there should not be any conflict of interest. Similarly, a proper mechanism should be in place to minimize the breach of confidentiality by the Shariah board members that are representing multiple boards. Furthermore, the Shariah pronouncements of Shariah board members should be consistent with their previous ones. In addition to this the Shariah board members should be competent and should be able to understand the issues that are presenting in front of them. Similarly, Garas (2012) argues that one of the reasons for multiple board representation is shortage of Shariah scholars within the Islamic banking industry. This multiple representation causes conflict of interest and breach of confidentiality.

Grais and Pellegrini (2006) argue that for effective Shariah governance process Shari'ah board members need to be independent from the higher management and board of directors. As the Shariah board members are appointed by the board of directors and their remuneration is also decided by the board of directors, additionally they are also being paid by the Islamic banking institution. This creates a situation of conflict of interest. Similarly, it is often observed that Shariah board members are sitting on multiple boards. This multiple board representation triggers an issue of confidentiality. There are chances of breach of confidentiality due to this multiple board representation. Similarly, Ayedh and Echchabi (2015) also discuss that the issue of confidentiality is associated with multiple representation of Shariah board members. This multiple representation is also seen as a strength of Shariah board members but when we look into the multiple representation from the perspective of Islamic banking institution it is also considered a huge threat. Similarly, Adam and Al-Aid (2020) argue that confidentiality is considered a critical element of Shariah governance. Shariah board members have access to every kind of proprietary information and they are required to protect such confidential information. With multiple representation the chances of breach of confidentiality increases. Similarly, the Shariah board members need to be aware which information needs to be kept confidential. Hussein (2014) finds that 29% of their respondents were not fully familiar with the concept of confidentiality. Similarly, he found evidence that Shariah board members with multiple board representation did unintentionally disclose sensitive information to others. Similarly, Garas (2012) also argues that with multiple representation the chances of breach of confidentiality also increases. As Shariah board members have access to several types of sensitive information that includes under process products and services, any information related to violations of Shariah by Islamic banking institutions can be fatal for Islamic banking institutions if shared with competitors. Furthermore, such information can also be used for personal advantage by the Shariah board members.

Grais and Pellegrini (2006) argue that there is another issue that is associated with functioning of Shariah board and that is competence of Shariah board members. Haridan et al. (2018) argue that the effectiveness of Shariah board is associated with the competency of Shariah board members. They argue that Shariah board members play a vital role in ensuring Shariah compliance. Furthermore, Islamic banking institutions prefer those Shariah board members that are flexible and management of Islamic banking institutions influence them. Similarly, they found that Shariah board members also lack in banking and financial knowledge and they consider this as a major incompetency at the end of Shariah board members. Similarly, Grassa (2013) argues that the current financial system is very complicated and requires that Shariah board members should have thorough knowledge of conventional finance and accounting.

In addition to this Hasan (2014) argues that most of the Islamic banking institutions do not have any mechanism to evaluate the decisions taken by the Shariah board. Similarly, Shariah board members do not conduct self-evaluation. In addition to this he found that some Shariah scholars do not perform proper Shariah review and just sign the declaration without proper review. Furthermore, he suggests that the Shariah board members need to improve their understanding and competency level in the area of banking and conventional finance. Lastly, he found that there is no practice of assessment of performance of Shariah board.

Grais and Pellegrini (2006) argue that the issue of disclosure is associated with the credibility of the decisions taken by the Shariah board. Similarly, Askari et al. (2012) argue that there should be a mechanism for proper disclosure of Shariah basis of the decisions taken by the Islamic banking institutions. However, when we look into the disclosure practices of the Islamic banking institutions across different regions the Shariah basis of the products and services provided by the Islamic banking institutions are concealed. Whenever we look into the disclosure practices of Malaysian and Pakistani Islamic banking institutions the Shariah basis of the products and services offered by the Islamic banking institutions are disclosed. On the other hand, the Islamic banking institutions of UAE and Dubai do disclose Shariah basis of their products and services on their websites.

Similarly, Alkhamees (2013) did a comparative study of the Islamic banking institutions of the UK and Saudi Arabia and argues that it is often observed that management of Islamic banking institutions conceal information from Shariah board members due to their multiple board representation to mitigate the risk of breach of confidentiality. As a result, the level of Shariah compliance decreases in the Islamic banking institutions. In addition to this, the disclosure level in the Islamic banking institutions of UK is higher than the Islamic banking institutions of Saudi Arabia despite Saudi Arabia being an Islamic country. Most importantly, it is very beneficial for the general public and all the stakeholders to be aware of the Shariah pronouncements of the Shariah board, but in both countries the Shariah pronouncements of the

Shariah board are concealed. Tabash et al. (2022) also did a study of Islamic banking institutions of Bangladesh and found that there are few things being concealed such as Shariah doubtful income is being concealed in Bangladesh. Islamic banks also conceal information regarding any issue with another bank or especially with the Shariah supervisory board. In addition to this *fatwa* issued by the SSB are also being concealed.

5.6 Conclusion

It is evident from the above discussion that there are several types of information that are being concealed either by the Shariah board members or by management of Islamic banking institutions by trying to mitigate the risk of breach of confidentiality. When we look into the causes of this concealment one can argue that the governance arrangement might play an important role in it. If we follow the division of Shariah governance models of Alnofli and Ali (2020), we can deduce that the countries with self-regulated Shariah governance models disclose more information and conceal less information as compared to the countries with centralized or hybrid Shariah governance models. One of the reasons can be that there is no such requirement by the regulator to disclose Shariah basis of the products and services offered by the Islamic banking institutions. There is a need to explore the causes of this concealment of information further. In future research this particular question can be answered.

References

AAOIFI (1999). *Governance Standard No. (1) Shari'ah Supervisory Board: Appointment, Composition and Report* (Issue 1). http://aaoifi.com/aaoifi-gs-1-sharia-supervisory-board-appointment-composition-and-report/?lang=en

Adam, S. B., & Al-Aid, A.-H. (2020). A Proposed Framework for Shari'ah Supervisory Board (SSB) Practice of Islamic Banks. *Kebbi Journal of Accounting Research, 1*(1), 28–39.

AlAbbad, A., Hassan, M. K., & Saba, I. (2019). Can Shari'ah Board Characteristics Influence Risk-Taking Behavior of Islamic Banks? *International Journal of Islamic and Middle Eastern Finance and Management, 12*(4), 469–488. https://doi.org/10.1108/IMEFM-11-2018-0403

Alam, M. K., Islam, F. T., & Runy, M. K. (2021). Why Does Shari'ah Governance Framework Important for Islamic Banks? *Asian Journal of Economics and Banking, 5*(2), 158–172. https://doi.org/10.1108/ajeb-02-2021-0018

Alam, M. K., Rahman, S. A., Mustafa, H., Shah, S. M., & Rahman, M. M. (2019). An Overview of Corporate Governance Models in Financial Institutions. *International Journal of Management and Sustainability, 8*(4), 181–195. https://doi.org/10.18488/journal.11.2019.84.181.195

Alkhamees, A. A. (2013). The Impact of Shari'ah Governance Practices on Shari'ah Compliance in Contemporary Islamic Finance. *Journal of Banking Regulation, 14*(2), 134–163. https://doi.org/10.1057/jbr.2012.12

Alnofli, A., & Ali, E. R. A. E. (2020). The Role of Key Functions of Shari'ah Governance in Islamic Financial Institutions. *International Journal of Fiqh and Usul Al-Fiqh Studies*, 4(1), 98–107.

Askari, H., Iqbal, Z., Krichene, N., & Mirakhor, A. (2012). *The Stability of Islamic Finance: Creating a Resilient Financial Environment for a Secure Future*. John Wiley & Sons. https://doi.org/10.1002/9781118390450

Ayedh, A. M., & Echchabi, A. (2015). Shari'ah Supervision in the Yemeni Islamic Banks: A Qualitative Survey. *Qualitative Research in Financial Markets*, 7(2), 159–172. https://doi.org/10.1108/QRFM-06-2014-0017

Bahari, N. F., & Baharudin, N. A. (2016). Shari'ah Governance Framework: The Roles of Shari'ah Review and Shari'ah Auditing. *Proceeding of the 3rd International Conference on Management & Muamalah 2016 (3rd ICoMM)*.

Chowdhury, N. T., & Fahim, S. (2015). Shari'ah Governance of Islamic Banks in Malaysia. *International Journal of Management Sciences and Business Research*, 4(10), 115–124.

Darwanto, & Chariri, A. (2019). Corporate Governance and Financial Performance in Islamic Banks: The role of the Sharia Supervisory Board in Multiple-layer Management. *Banks and Bank Systems*, 14(4), 183–191. https://doi.org/10.21511/bbs.14(4).2019.17

Farag, H., Mallin, C., & Ow-Yong, K. (2018). Corporate Governance in Islamic Banks: New Insights for Dual Board Structure and Agency Relationships. *Journal of International Financial Markets, Institutions and Money*, 54, 59–77. https://doi.org/10.1016/j.intfin.2017.08.002

Fatmawati, D., Ariffin, N. M., Abidin, N. H. Z., & Osman, A. Z. (2022). Shari'ah Governance in Islamic Banks: Practices, Practitioners and Praxis. *Global Finance Journal*, 51, 1–20. https://doi.org/10.1016/j.gfj.2020.100555

Garas, S. N. (2012). The Conflicts of Interest Inside the Shari'a Supervisory Board. *International Journal of Islamic and Middle Eastern Finance and Management*, 5(2), 88–105. https://doi.org/10.1108/17538391211233399

Ginene, K., & Hamid, A. (2015). *Foundation of Shari'ah Governance of Islamic Banks*. John Wiley & Sons.

Grais, W., & Pellegrini, M. (2006a). Corporate Governance and Shari'ah Compliance in Institutions Offering Islamic Financial Services. In *World Bank Policy Research Working Paper* (No. 4052; Policy Research Working Paper).

Grais, W., & Pellegrini, M. (2006b). Corporate Governance and Stakeholders Financial Interests in Institutions Offering Islamic Financial Services (No. 4053; World Bank Policy Research Working Paper).

Grassa, R. (2013). Shari'ah Supervisory System in Islamic Financial Institutions New Issues and Challenges: A Comparative Analysis Between Southeast Asia Models and GCC Models. *Humanomics*, 29(4), 333–348. https://doi.org/10.1108/H-01-2013-0001

Haridan, N. M., Hassan, A. F. S., & Karbhari, Y. (2018). Governance, Religious Assurance and Islamic Banks: Do Shari'ah Boards Effectively Serve? *Journal of Management and Governance*, 22, 1015–1043. https://doi.org/10.1007/s10997-018-9418-8

Hasan, A., & Sabirzyanov, R. (2015). Optimal Shari'ah Governance Model in Islamic Finance. *International Journal of Education and Research*, 3(4), 243–258.

Hasan, Z. (2008). Corporate Governance Of Islamic Financial Institutions. Malaysian Study of Islam.

Hasan, Z. (2014). In Search of the Perceptions of the Shari'ah Scholars on Shari'ah Governance System. *International Journal of Islamic and Middle Eastern Finance and Management*, 7(1), 22–36. https://doi.org/10.1108/IMEFM-07-2012-0059

Hussein, E. (2014). *Corporate governance in Islamic Finance: Basic concepts and issues* (No. 56872).

Iqbal, Z., & Mirakhor, A. (2004). Stakeholder Model of Governance in Islamic Economic System. *Islamic Economic Studies*, 11(2), 44–62.

Malkawi, B. H. (2013). Shari'ah Board in the Governance Structure of Islamic Financial Institutions. *The American Journal of Comparative Law*, 61(3), 539–577.

Minhas, I. H. (2012). Shari'ah Governance Model (SGM) and Its Four Basic Pillars. *Journal of Islamic Banking and Finance*, 29(2), 30–34.

Nomran, N. M., & Haron, R. (2020). A Systematic Literature Review on Shari'ah Governance Mechanism and Firm Performance in Islamic Banking. *Islamic Economic Studies*, 27(2), 91–123. https://doi.org/10.1108/IES-06-2019-0013

Obaid, S. N. S., & Naysary, B. (2014). Toward a Comprehensive Theoretical Framework for Shari'ah Governance in Islamic Financial Institutions. *Journal of Financial Services Marketing*, 19, 304–318. https://doi.org/10.1057/fsm.2014.26

Rahajeng, D. K. (2012). The Effectiveness of Shari'ah Supervisory Board Roles in Islamic Banks. https://doi.org/10.2139/ssrn.2357831

Rashwan, M. H. (2012). Corporate Governance in Islamic Banks: A Critical Review. https://ssrn.com/abstract=2955106

Saba, I., & Lahsasna, A. (2013). Corporate Governance in Islamic Banks from an Islamic Perspective. *International Accounting and Business Conference*.

Shahzad, M. A., Khan, A., Mansoori, M. T., & Ehsan, A. (2020). Shari'ah Governance in Islamic Banking Institutions in Pakistan: An Empirical Investigation. *Journal of Islamic Business and Management*, 10(1), 28–42. https://doi.org/10.26501/jibm/2020.1001-003

Shibani, O., & Fuentes, C. De. (2017). Differences and similaritites between corporate governance principles in Islamic banks and Conventional banks. *Research in International Business and Finance*, 1–15. https://doi.org/10.1016/j.ribaf.2017.07.036

Tabash, M. I., Alam, M. K., & Rahman, M. M. (2022). Ethical Legitimacy of Islamic Banks and Shari'ah Governance: Evidence from Bangladesh. *Journal of Public Affairs*, 22(2), 1–10. https://doi.org/10.1002/pa.2487

Toufik, B. B. (2015). The Role of Shari'ah Supervisory Board in Ensuring Good Corporate Governance Practice in Islamic Banks. *AAOFI*, 2(2), 109–118.

Uddin, M. A. (2015). Governance from Islamic Economic Perspective: A Shari'ah Governance Framework. In *Munich Personal RePEc Archive (MPRA)* (No. 67695; MIPRA). https://mpra.ub.uni-muenchen.de/67695/

6 Paradox of Shariah Governance and Price Competitiveness in Islamic Banking

Salman Ahmed Shaikh

6.1 Paradox: Trade-Off between Shariah Compliance and Price Competitiveness

Shariah compliance in Islamic banking is necessary. However, achieving that requires certain additional operations and costs which may lead to Islamic banks incurring some additional costs which conventional banks simply avoid. Then, there are certain opportunity costs which Islamic banks incur, but which conventional banks do not have to. This may make Islamic banks costlier than conventional banks and which will reflect in a weak position in price competitiveness.

Around the world, a large number of people and even experts still have apprehensions about Islamic banking. It is because in their view, they are not even price competitive. In search for ensuring price competitiveness given their inherent internal structural problems and external disadvantageous factors, Islamic banks find it hard to innovate in product design from the point of view of serving the economic and financial needs in a different cashflow pattern.

First, it results in relatively disappointing performance in ensuring financial inclusion of involuntary financially excluded segments of the society, especially on the financing side.

Second, it also results in higher spread where a faith premium is to be paid by financing side clients (high cost of finance), investment depositors (lower return on deposits), shareholders (lower return on capital) or government (by providing subsidies to one of the first two stakeholders).

Third, it also results in losing a distinctive mark in distributional impact. If conventional banking is providing finance and credit to a minority of capitalist elites, Islamic banks provide financing to the same segment even more narrowly with relatively higher cost of intermediation. The next three subsections elaborate these points further.

6.1.1 Financial Inclusion of Involuntary Excluded Segments in Islamic Banks

Naceur et al. (2017) disclose that the share of excluded individuals citing religious reasons for not using bank accounts is noticeably greater in Muslim

DOI: 10.4324/9781003324836-6

majority countries than in other countries. Kumru and Sarntisart (2016) explicate that for financially excluded Muslims, Islamic banking provides an alternative to use banking services. By reducing financial exclusion due to religious reasons, Islamic banking can potentially increase the rate of savings. Since these savings are employed in asset-backed financing, there is increased potential for capital formation and economic growth in the presence of Islamic banking.

Knowledge Attitude and Practices study in Pakistan which was a nationwide survey reveals that out of non-banked respondents, 93% consider conventional interest as Riba (State Bank of Pakistan, 2018). Furthermore, out of non-banked respondents, 98.77% considered this statement as important that Islamic products and services provide religious satisfaction. In this regard, of course, Islamic banking has provided access to banking to those customers who would not bank primarily for the religious reason. Those who consider Riba as prohibited and who want to avoid it would voluntarily exclude themselves from banking. Islamic banks have provided an option of doing banking to those who are voluntarily excluded.

However, it is also interesting to see that Islamic banks have been able to widen their outreach beyond large cities or not so that involuntary financial exclusion due to outreach constraints is also minimized. Like conventional banking, Islamic banks are also majorly financing the corporate sector. A majority of the total financing in Islamic banking goes to the corporate sector. SMEs and agriculture get a small share. Islamic microfinance has only 1% share in global Islamic financing assets. Institutions like Akhuwat have provided Qard-e-Hasan based loans to 5 million people with a recovery rate of around 99%, but Islamic banks or their sponsors have not ventured in providing micro financial services as enthusiastically as they ventured in Islamic commercial banking and asset management.

6.1.2 Price Competitiveness in Islamic Banks

The deposit mobilization picture in Islamic banking in Pakistan suggests that their reliance is majorly on non-remunerative current accounts. Hence, they could have provided subsidized financing to critical sectors of the economy like agriculture and SMEs sector. Even on savings accounts, Islamic banks pay much less returns to the depositors than conventional banks in some jurisdictions like Pakistan, for instance. Not only they have much less cost of deposits than conventional banks, but they also fall short of expectations when it comes to outreach to economic sectors like agriculture and SMEs and even when it comes to pricing. Lebdaoui and Wild (2016) substantiate that the competition of banking sector intensifies in countries with higher Islamic banking shares. However, in the case of Pakistan, Islamic banks have higher spreads implying costly inefficient intermediation with a narrower outreach and inclusiveness.

Even globally, Leon and Weill (2018) show that Islamic banking development has overall no impact on credit constraints. However, their results show that Islamic banking development exerts a positive impact on access to credit when conventional banking development is low. That is why there is increased focus on rent seeking than on ensuring internal efficiency to achieve competitiveness. Interestingly, while conventional banking is demonized and cursed, Islamic banking is not able to penetrate in the agriculture sector, SMEs and microfinance as much as conventional banking. Even where Islamic banking does provide financing solutions to the corporate sector and upper income class urban population, it does so at an equal or higher cost of finance than conventional.

Intermediation function performed by Islamic banks is costlier, yet inferior from the distributional perspective since they have much less exposure to agriculture sector, SME sector and almost nothing when it comes to microfinance sector. From the economics perspective, depositors in Islamic banking obtain much less profits as compared to depositors in conventional banks. Therefore, on the grounds of competitiveness, Islamic banks have still a long way to travel. It is ironic that in marketing campaigns and public discourse, practitioners of Islamic banks project conventional banking as evil while Islamic banks pay much less profit rates despite charging customers higher cost of finance than conventional banks. This relatively high cost of intermediation as compared to conventional banks is paid by the society. Yet, there is no universal agreement on Shariah-compliant nature of contracts like Tawarruq-based personal finance, Tawarruq-based credit cards, and Salam in currency, for instance. Some scholarly circles in Pakistan are even critical of combining a separate Murabaha and Muajjal sale as a mode of financing to closely mimic the cashflow stream of conventional interest-based loans (Jamia Uloom-ul-Islamia, 2008).

Given that outreach is limited majorly in urban areas and market segmentation is concentrated in corporates, Islamic banks have still a lot of work to do in improving their outreach geographically and in diverse and critical sectors of the economy including agriculture, SMEs and microfinance.

6.1.3 Distributional Impact of Islamic Banks

There is literature available on economic assessment of Islamic banking. Asutay (2013) feels that Islamic finance has given more emphasis to commercialization rather than sticking to the moral economy principles. The initial experience of social finance has been engulfed by the proliferation of Islamic commercial financial institutions in banking, asset management and insurance.

Jan and Asutay (2019) think that Islamic banking and finance have been successful in transactional accumulation, but it has not developed any strategy for transformational objectives. Mansour et al. (2015) agree that Islamic banking has not realized its vision to enhance equitability, social well-being and justice. Asutay (2012) thinks that while there is much to show when it comes to growth and penetration of Islamic banking and finance, such remarkable growth has been achieved by overshadowing the social aspirations of the

Islamic moral economy. Hence, if Islamic banks and financial institutions are criticized for their social failure, there is some merit in it.

Cebeci (2012) attributes underachievement on the social front to the product structures, which are primarily debt-based in which cashflows use conventional interest-based benchmarks strictly. Hence, the final outcome from the cashflows and cost perspective is identical or even worse for the client with higher spreads in Islamic banking. On the other hand, Baki and Uthman (2017) think that the reason for social failure lies with an external environment which is not conducive for fostering social goals even if they are deemed to be desirable. Such defence takes cover in the argument that Islamic banks are a small part of a large industry and they cannot be price leaders in a dual banking system dominated by conventional banking.

Islamic principles lay great emphasis on social justice, inclusion, and sharing of resources between the haves and the have-nots (Mohieldin et al., 2011). Scholars who are economists-cum-Shariah advisors explicate three specific ends (Maqasid) which are important in Islamic finance, i.e. (i) wealth circulation, (ii) fair and transparent financial practices and (iii) justice at the micro and macro level (Laldin & Furqani, 2013). Some add equitable income redistribution and circulation of wealth to the list as well (Chapra, 1979; Chaudhury, 1999). Social justice requires that financiers and those which require finance share rewards as well as losses in an equitable fashion (Iqbal, 1997). But, in this regard, Asutay (2008) maintains that Islamic banking fails to fulfil the required higher objectives of Shariah.

Fulfilling only the necessary conditions of Shariah compliance in product structuring is insufficient to make progress towards circulation of wealth and distributive justice (Laldin and Furqani, 2013). Islamic finance industry in essence remains delinked from the real economy in terms of their cashflows, and hence their distributional impact is similar to conventional banking. (Ibrahim et al., 2014).

Due to the overemphasis on the form over substance, Dusuki and Abozaid (2007) argue that Islamic banks are just an exercise in semantics. Khan (2010) also concedes that Islamic banking provides suitable Islamic jargon for de facto conventional banking. Balz (2008) thinks that Islamic finance is experiencing a 'formalist deadlock'. Even Mansoori (2011) who is an academic as well as advisor to some Islamic financial institutions admits that there are certain contracts in which the stratagems used do not conform fully to the strict principles of Shariah. Choudhury (2012) thinks that Islamic banking is good for the rich shareholders and only narrowly avoids financial interest, with no fundamental, epistemological and economic distinction. Haniffa and Hudaib (2010) argue that Maqasid al-Shariah have been unduly used to justify the innovation of financial products to compete and converge with conventional banking. Sharing the same concern, Dusuki and Abozaid (2007) reveal that there are also cases of overstretching Maqasid al-Shariah to validate financial transactions which are not in conformity with the Shariah principles. In financial economics, Diamond (1984) explains banks as financial intermediaries who can centralize costly monitoring. He explains that banks monitor debt (loan) contracts, and issue unmonitored debt (deposit) contracts. In this context, Islamic banks seem to work similar to conventional banks when one compares capital to assets, finance to deposits and deposits to equity and such ratios.

From the distributive justice perspective, the texts in Islamic banking criticize conventional banking on the ground that it is a highly leveraged institution in which most of the funds are contributed by the depositors and from which financing is provided to the large industrialists. However, only a small portion of industrial profits go to the depositors of the bank and in case of default, it is the depositors who suffer. The industrialists add their cost of finance in pricing their products and eventually they recoup all their costs including the financing costs from the pockets of consumers (Usmani, 2004).

Let us see if Islamic banks do work any differently from the economics perspective. Currently, Islamic banks also operate within the same fractional reserve banking system where the capital to assets ratio is smaller and major portion of the financing is provided from the depositor's funds. Onus is also on Islamic banks to ensure more significant distinction from conventional banks. Currently, in the lease and mortgage-based financing, the client is made the legal owner in books right away as per the asset and property registration documents in many cases. In trade finance, this is even harder to avoid. Article 5 of the Uniform Customs and Practices for Documentary Credits (UCP) states: 'Banks deal with documents and not with goods, services or performance to which the documents may relate.'

Again, Islamic banks cite unfavorable tax framework as the reason due to which multiple transfers of asset or property is avoided in legal documentation in order to avoid duplication of taxes. Nonetheless, in non-Muslim majority jurisdictions, Islamic banks themselves plead for tax neutrality by proving their economic substance as similar to conventional banks. Thus, as suggested by the respected scholar, Mufti Muhammad Taqi Usmani, there is a need for paradigm shift in Islamic banking. In his book, 'Introduction to Islamic Finance', the respected scholar, Mufti Muhammad Taqi Usmani (2004) writes: 'It should never be overlooked that, originally, Murabaha is not a mode of financing. It is only a device to escape from "interest" and not an ideal instrument for carrying out the real economic objectives of Islam. Therefore, this instrument should be used as a transitory step taken in the process of the Islamization of the economy, and its use should be restricted only to those cases where Mudarabah or Musharakah are not practicable' (p. 72). In Running Musharakah, the concept of risk-sharing is neutralized through (i) cost sharing in only specific heads, (ii) skewed profit sharing towards the client beyond achievement of target level of return to the bank, and (iii) the target return benchmarks the prevailing interbank rate (Ayub, 2016). Furthermore, calculation of profit on daily product basis and the capital contribution from the aggregate reported numbers in consolidated accounts remain unable to determine true profitability and true level of investment capital.

All Islamic banking financing products are linked with conventional interbank rate. The product structures also have resemblance and precedents in conventional banking. For instance, from the cashflows and finance perspective and not strictly from a Shariah compliance perspective, Diminishing Musharakah in real estate is similar to mortgage, Ijarah is similar to hire purchase, Sovereign Ijarah Sukuk is similar to sale and leaseback structure and Salam Sukuk is similar to zero coupon bills or commercial paper. Without ownership transfer in Ijarah Sukuk to the Sukuk holders genuinely, the structure merely remains asset-backed or asset-light rather than asset-based.

Even then, the payoffs are linked with assets, but accrue not on the basis of how productive the asset turns out to be, but on the basis of prevailing interbank rates. In a pandemic like Covid-19, when lockdown happens, the Ijarah rentals are not going to be affected by the fact that machinery remains idle in lockdown.

Interestingly, most state-owned enterprises are running in losses as they are inefficient and subsidize their services, while Islamic banks demand issuance of more sovereign Sukuk where the rentals or payoffs are going to be linked with policy interest rate rather than actual productivity of assets or projects. In the 'Asset Light' structures, the same inefficient government which is unable to run state-owned public monopolies profitably in industries with inelastic demand or utilize its idle public infrastructure effectively is entrusted as 'investment agent' in Wakalah Sukuk, 'selling agent' in Salam and Istisna Sukuk or working partner in Mudarabah and Musharakah Sukuk to engineer returns equivalent to policy interest rate.

Maududi (1970) writing on the mindset of financial capitalists charging interest states that the financial capitalist wants the cow to give milk to him, but fetch its own food from somewhere else. In current Islamic financing product structures, it is hard to confidently claim that this mindset has been completely transformed.

While derivatives are derided a lot, Wa'ad based sales where Wa'ad (promise) is binding achieve the aims of derivatives contracts. In the infamous commodity Murabaha transaction, multiple asset sales are involved one after the other to achieve transfer of equivalent cashflows as in repo transactions wherein no financial party is interested in buying physical assets genuinely.

In summary, Islamic banks provide Shariah-compliant approved products, but they have to improve in certain areas in the light of these observations which are put forward by critics who envision and expect a lot more out of Islamic banks.

(i) Average financing cost in Islamic banking is generally higher than conventional banks.
(ii) Average return on investment in Islamic banking is generally lower than conventional banks.
(iii) Agriculture and SMEs provide employment to majority of the population in Muslim majority countries, but they only get small share of all financing provided from Islamic banks.

(iv) Regional concentration of Islamic banking branches is restricted mostly to urban areas.
(v) Microfinance, health finance, education finance, start-up finance, agriculture finance and SME finance hardly feature in financing mix in Islamic banking as compared to even conventional banks.
(vi) Apparently, from the economic standpoint, one of the major differences is the higher spread in Islamic banking as compared to conventional. This inefficiency seems to stem from the Shariah compliance cost which includes additional documentation cost, monitoring cost, fees of Shariah compliance officers and advisors and increased labour hours needed in physical assurance of timely identification, delivery, possession and sale of assets in both legs of the transaction.

However, beyond achieving Shariah compliance, it is hard to count too many distinctive economic merits in current practice of Islamic banking as compared to conventional banking. In cases where even the ownership of the asset or property is directly transferred to the client right away in legal documentation by some banks, even this much distinction diminishes further.

6.2 Challenges in Balancing Shariah Governance and Price Competitiveness

6.2.1 Cost in Shariah Product Structuring, Compliance and Auditing

First, the Islamic banking products need to be distinct. They not only shall serve the economic and financial need, but they also have to be Shariah compliant. In order to ensure Shariah-compliant product structuring, Islamic banks use the professional services of Shariah experts. Thus, this additional skilled labour force which Islamic bank employs leads to higher cost for Islamic banks as compared to conventional banks. Conventional banks only need to ensure that their product serves economic and financial need of the client.

Second, it is important to ensure that Islamic finance contracts are executed in a Shariah-compliant way. For instance, in Murabaha, once the price is agreed, it cannot be changed. At the time of the second leg sale between the bank and the client, the asset shall be existing and in constructive possession of the bank. In Salam, price shall be paid in full in advance. Subject matter of Salam sale shall be clearly specified without any ambiguity. These are other details that are necessary to check. Shariah- compliant officer and auditors look after the monitoring of contracts to ensure Shariah compliance. The skilled human resource engaged in this important function is professionally hired. Conventional banks do not incur such additional human resource costs.

Thus, Islamic banks while ensuring Shariah compliance face this challenge that they have certain additional human resource costs which the conventional banks are able to avoid due to their insensitivity to the prohibition of interest. A paradox or challenge for Islamic banks is to make sure that they are able to minimize these additional costs through bringing scale, technology and efficiency.

6.2.2 Documentary Levies in Contracts for Multiple Asset Transfers

In Islamic banking, it is important that if an Islamic bank wants to earn Halal returns linked with asset ownership through sale and lease-based contracts, it shall take ownership, risk and constructive possession of the asset before selling it or leasing it to the client. Thus, Islamic contracts would naturally involve two sale transactions unlike conventional banking where assets can be directly transferred in the name of the client right away. Conventional bank is only interested in the interest amount. It does not want to undertake ownership, risk and constructive possession of the asset. On the other hand, Islamic bank cannot avoid or else it will not be able to earn legitimate returns linked with assets. Islamic bank can manage its risk, but it cannot completely eliminate the risk to begin with.

Thus, in regions where Islamic banks do not have tax neutrality, the Islamic modes of financing involving multiple transfers of asset would be subject to multiple documentary levies. This will not add to additional revenues for the Islamic banks, but it will increase the cost of financing for the clients. Thus, Islamic banks would become uncompetitive in pricing and will face commercial displacement risk.

6.2.3 Greater Benchmark Risk When There Is Slack in Repayments

In Islamic sale-based modes of financing contracts, once the price is agreed, it cannot be changed like in the case of Murabaha. Therefore, even if an Islamic bank offers price schedule keeping in perspective the market rate of return which incorporates time value of economic resources, it will not be able to generate compounded return even when there is delay in payment. Price once agreed cannot be changed unlike in conventional loan where the loan can be easily rescheduled. Hence, if Islamic bank takes cushion for delay in payments and offers a schedule where cashflow commitments for clients are greater than in conventional loan, then Islamic bank may face commercial displacement risk.

6.2.4 Greater Liquidity Risk for Funding Liquidity Shortfall

Conventional banks have access to all money market instruments and lender of last resort facility of central bank to meet their liquidity shortfall. They can use surplus liquidity to invest in government treasury securities. They can use repo contracts and call money loans to fund short-term liquidity shortfall from interbank market or use lender of last resort facility of central bank. Islamic banks do not have access to a lot of options for meeting liquidity shortfall. They cannot use repo transactions as these transactions are like buyback transactions. They do not have access to interest-free loans since call money loans are interest-based. Furthermore, in most jurisdictions, the central bank does not have Shariah-compliant lender of last resort facility. Most governments in Muslim majority regions use interest-based debt in public finance. The share of Sukuk in overall public finance is even much less than the share of Islamic banking in banking sector of different Muslim majority countries. In such a scenario, Islamic banks operate conservatively in their financing operations. If they price additional liquidity risk in pricing, they face the prospect of commercial displacement risk.

6.3 Implication of Challenges on Price Competitiveness of Islamic Banks

6.3.1 Higher Spread in Islamic Banking

The structural issues discussed in Section 2 have the potential to raise the spread in Islamic banking. Generally speaking, Islamic banks are competitive in regions with more flexible product structures and variety of product alternatives. However, some of those alternatives are not unanimously agreed upon. In fact, most scholars do not consider contracts like Tawarruq and Bai Inah as ideal. In some Middle Eastern and South Asian countries where there is more conservative practice of Islamic banking, the challenges in structure result in Islamic banking losing competitiveness. This reflects in higher spread i.e. either higher average cost of financing or lower return on deposits or both together.

This is the faith premium whose cost is borne by the financing side and investing side customers in the form of higher average cost of financing in Islamic banking vis-à-vis conventional banking and/or lower average return in Islamic banking vis-à-vis conventional banking. Therefore, it leaves little strength in the economic arguments against conventional banking when Islamic banking comes second best in price competitiveness or barely able to manage price competitiveness by interestingly becoming more and more like conventional banking in its structure and design. Discussion of Shariah compliance aside, it creates a paradox where the first best alternative turns out to be the mode of banking which Islamic banking proponents are zealous to get rid of.

6.3.2 Greater Operating Expense to Net Spreads

The additional costs incurred in ensuring sound Shariah compliance and governance results in increase in unique costs which are specific to Islamic banks and not to conventional banks. Hence, where these costs cannot be contained, the burden of additional costs is transferred to the stakeholders including financing side and investment side customers. Furthermore, it is being also managed by easing the restraints on managing liquidity risk by giving permission to a variety of instruments in short-term liquidity management regardless of whether they are considered ideal or not, as long as they are permitted by a select few scholars. The next section discusses practices Islamic banks use to manage these challenges.

6.4 Current Best Practices to Manage Price Competitiveness Challenges

6.4.1 Maintaining Higher Asset Quality

Since Islamic banks cannot raise price even when payments are delayed, they ensure that they keep their asset quality high. One negative consequence of this policy is that outreach and access become narrow when it comes to financing from Islamic banking. For instance, conventional banking may have solutions to reschedule financing facilities, rollover loans, provide liquid financing for working capital management, but the solutions toolbox for distressed firms in Islamic banking is quite limited. Distressed firms are not on the lookout for expansion, so providing finance for new asset acquisition is a very rare possibility. Even when asset-based structures are used, they would involve sale and leaseback structure. From the point of view of distributional and productive impact of financing, there is little difference in Islamic banking and conventional banking.

Therefore, Islamic banks try to avert credit crisis by maintaining stricter criteria for creditworthiness. Appreciably, Islamic banks have lower non-performing financing to total financing ratios than conventional banks in most regions. Table 6.1 illustrates the average of major performance indicators of Islamic banking in Muslim-majority countries during the period 2013–2022. It can be seen that the ratio of non-performing financing to total financing is below 10% except in Bahrain where it is marginally above 10%.

Furthermore, at least to the investment depositors of Islamic banks and shareholders, asset-backed financing provide them with the option of foreclosure to recover price. However, for the financing side client, the Islamic mode of financing does not have much distinction from the economic standpoint. Nonetheless, one advantage in Islamic banking is that funds cannot be misused in unapproved ways. While conventional banks simply credit the loan amount in bank account of the customer, Islamic banks do not use Qard based modes of financing in commercial finance. In asset-backed financing like Murabaha and Ijarah, they will use the funds to buy an asset which the client needs. Therefore, there is more effective monitoring and greater cushion to Islamic bank through asset ownership and/or through subsequent option of legal recourse to the asset.

6.4.2 Advocacy for Tax Neutrality

Tax neutrality in the context of tax regulations on financial products refers to providing the same treatment to products where the economic substance,

Table 6.1 Performance Indicators of Islamic Banking in Muslim-Majority Countries

Country	CAR	Gross NPF	ROA	ROE	Net Profit Margin	Cost to Income
Bahrain	18.7	10.8	1.0	7.8	25.6	71.1
Bangladesh	11.5	4.5	1.3	23.5	33.3	43.8
Brunei	20.2	5.0	1.6	12.1	52.0	45.1
Egypt	15.24	7.25	2.62	42.08	58.76	30.91
Indonesia	18.4	4.1	1.3	11.8	13.9	86.1
Jordan	22.3	2.8	1.8	18.3	49.3	50.7
Kuwait	17.8	2.5	1.2	11.0	22.1	32.5
Malaysia	16.7	1.4	1.0	15.0	38.9	39.7
Morocco	20.6	0.2	−3.7	−26.2	−252.8	349.7
Nigeria	30.2	4.3	1.1	12.1	10.5	82.0
Oman	28.5	0.7	−0.8	0.1	−29.6	113.9
Pakistan	15.0	5.0	1.5	24.7	32.2	65.5
Palestine	16.8	2.3	1.0	9.5	24.2	69.6
Qatar	18.0	1.3	1.1	11.0	40.8	13.3
Saudi Arabia	20.1	1.2	2.2	16.4	49.5	49.6
Sudan	15.3	5.1	2.8	41.8	55.9	40.8
Turkey	16.5	4.0	1.3	15.5	21.0	43.3
UAE	17.2	6.3	1.4	11.4	32.0	50.5

Source: Islamic Financial Services Board

effects and implications are the same. Horizontal equity principle demands that individuals and businesses with similar income characteristics and business processes must be treated equally.

As discussed earlier, multiple asset sales between counterparties in Islamic finance structures raise tax issues in Islamic banking products in terms of direct and indirect taxes on asset ownership, multiple instances of transfer and treatment of income and disposal of assets. Islamic banking proponents argue that economic substance in generic Islamic banking products and operations is similar to conventional products even after compliance with Shariah. Thus, Islamic banks deserve to have tax neutral treatment in such cases. If tax neutrality is granted, then the intermediate sale can be exempted from tax. Hence, Islamic banking transactions would not have a disadvantage of higher taxes. Many Muslim majority and non-Muslim majority countries have given tax neutrality to Islamic finance transactions and structures.

In places where tax neutrality is yet to be provided to Islamic banking transactions, Islamic banks avoid legal documentation of intermediate sale and document the sale only in their own records. But the client, while only focusing on legal title, may get the impression that Islamic finance transaction is similar to conventional. For instance, if in Ijarah lease contract, the legal title is straight away transferred to the client and then the client is charged rent on the asset as well, the client may perceive Islamic Ijarah lease contract executed this way to be similar to conventional finance lease. The client may feel that it is not legitimate to ask for rent when the legal title is transferred to the client as well at the same time. Hence, Islamic banks plead and advocate for tax neutrality so that they can keep distinction of Islamic finance contracts and yet not become uncompetitive when it comes to pricing.

6.4.3 Relying on Faith Premium

One dimension of relying on faith premium has been discussed above where Islamic banks afford to pay lower return to the inelastic investment deposits of faith-conscious Muslims and/or charge a greater cost of financing through pricing in Islamic modes of financing.

Another dimension and which is quite popular in countries like Pakistan and Afghanistan is to argue for no fundamental substitution between Islamic banking and conventional banking. Awareness campaigns draw attention of the people towards the fact that one form of banking is Halal (i.e. permissible) and another form of banking is Haram (i.e. prohibited). Hence, it is not a matter of choice where one chooses through economic comparison. Conventional banking is positioned as something which is not a substitute in the preference set of a practising Muslim. In countries like Pakistan, Afghanistan, Sudan and Iran, there is also legal advocacy to get conventional banking banned so that it remains not only Haram, but also illegal. Pakistan is a prime example where this course of action is pursued.

People are made aware of Islamic banking. Concerns about comparison are answered through examples of choosing Halal and Haram in other routines of life. Just like a person may travel a long distance and incur additional transaction cost to get Halal cooked food or Halal meat, Islamic banking is just like that. 'Halal' product or service need not be cheap. Moreover, 'cheap' does not make something 'Halal' necessarily.

6.4.4 Organic and Inorganic Growth

Organic growth in certain financing segments reduces scale disadvantages gradually. As a result, larger Islamic banks or financing segments where Islamic banks have greater market share tend to reflect price convergence, competitiveness or even superiority. Organic growth is slow-paced growth achieved through and within the competition. Inorganic growth happens through legal changes, mergers and acquisitions and conversion. For instance, in Pakistan, after the great financial crisis, a lot of foreign banks which were only interested in consumer finance in big cities decided not to continue and beef up capital as required by the central bank. Meezan Bank's acquisition of stake in HSBC, Bank Islami's acquisition of Citibank's mortgage portfolio and recent transformation of Faysal Bank into a full-fledged Islamic bank have contributed to the expedited growth of Islamic banking in the country. Mutations also happen. For instance, a banking group establishes a separate Islamic bank when it sees growth in its Islamic banking segment. MCB Islamic is an example of that in Pakistan.

In Iran, Sudan and lately in Afghanistan, the government itself gets involved and wants to have interest-free banking. In Pakistan, legal battle is won in banning interest, but, ruling governments, hesitate in folding the dual banking system on the premise that Islamic banking solutions for central banking, domestic public finance and external public finance are not that comprehensive to afford an abrupt closure of dual banking system. This organic and inorganic growth helps in achieving price competitiveness through removing scale disadvantage and by making Islamic banking a viable source of financing even in large projects and public financing.

6.4.5 Development of Asset Light Structures

One last practice that we see in managing price competitiveness challenges is the use of structures which are asset-light. They have much less additional documentary levies and ownership related costs. Hence, they help in managing the additional costs which are incurred in asset-based structures. However, in countries with high Muslim majority population, this could turn against Islamic banking by creating negative perception among Muslims, who are the major target market. But, in countries where this flexibility is allowed in the Shariah legal framework and where there are significant non-Muslim and faith neutral customers, this strategy helps in bringing price competitiveness. Malaysia is an example of a country where Islamic banks are price competitive and hence, they attract Muslims as well as non-Muslims towards Islamic banking.

6.5 Conclusion and Way Forward

This chapter has discussed the paradox of how there may arise a trade-off between sound Shariah governance and price competitiveness. Islamic banks need both. They need to have sound Shariah governance to ensure Shariah compliance and retain trust of faith-conscious investors that Islamic banking is Shariah compliant. On the other hand, Islamic banking needs to have price competitiveness to ensure that it is not perceived similar to conventional banking by those who use cashflows, price and cost as benchmark for comparison. Going forward, some suggestions are outlined for ensuring that both Shariah governance and price competitiveness can be achieved together.

- Use of Fintech to Bring Efficiency

Major hurdles in penetration of Islamic banking to low-income groups and small and medium enterprises include scale inefficiency and high outreach costs. Fintech provides an opportunity to improve efficiency through digitization of processes and operations and thereby enabling provision of finance to small-scale microenterprises. Fintech can help in increasing outreach, reducing the cost of administration and monitoring the financing side clients.

There are examples of Robo-Advisors which provide intelligent support to ensure Shariah compliance. Definitely, the human factor cannot be completely eliminated. However, the costs can be minimized. Once the costs are minimized, it could become possible that the central bank take up these costs and banks are relieved from at least paying to the Shariah advisors for product structuring. This can also improve neutral and more objective Shariah compliance and advisory practices. The existing human resource in compliance and audit can be trained in Islamic finance to do this additional task of Shariah compliance if the task itself can be made simpler and efficient through the use of technology.

- Balance in Redistribution of Payoffs to Depositors and Shareholders

Islamic banks need to provide competitive returns to their loyal depositors rather than relying on the 'faith premium' alone. On smaller deposits of individuals, the government can provide incentive by decreasing the withholding tax rate on returns. This would not eliminate the additional costs incurred in the overall delivery of Islamic banking products, but, it will ease the pressure on Islamic banks where they have scale disadvantages and limited structures to place their deposits and funds to earn Halal returns.

- Not Compromising on Distinction

Islamic banks shall change the mimicking strategy and position themselves as distinct financial institutions with distinctive product structures. More distinct the structure, more distinct shall be the payoffs and the distributional impact of financial services. They can mobilize impact investments and use them in Islamic microfinance to show their potential in socio-economic mobility. Akhuwat in Pakistan has proved that Qard-e-Hasan based Islamic microfinance can contribute in socio-economic mobility. But such programs require donor or government support to cover the operational costs. By embedding technology in operations and by utilizing the gradual and accelerated financing approach wherein clients are supported through social finance first and then through accelerated commercial finance, Islamic banks can create cost synergies and complementarity between social and commercial finance.

- Strict Shariah Compliance to Restrict Opportunity Costs

Since the non-payment and late payment in Islamic finance contracts results in a halt in profit for the Islamic bank during the period of delay, it is important for Islamic banks to manage their credit and liquidity risk pre-emptively.

Another reason of opportunity cost losses is where a structure is deemed Shariah non-compliant in auditing and the profits are donated to charity. Hence, it is important to have vigilant monitoring of execution of Islamic finance contracts in order to ensure that the structure does not become Shariah non-compliant due to missing a necessary step in transaction.

References

Asutay, M. (2008). Islamic Banking and Finance: Social Failure. *New Horizon*, 1–4.
Asutay, M. (2012). Conceptualising and Locating the Social Failure of Islamic Finance: Aspirations of Islamic Moral Economy versus the Realities of Islamic Finance. *Asian and African Area Studies, 11*(2), 93–113.
Asutay, M. (2013). Islamic Moral Economy as the Foundation of Islamic Finance. In V. Cattelan (Ed.) *Islamic Finance in Europe*. Edward Elgar Publishing.
Ayub, M. (2016). Running Musharakah-Running from Musharakah. *Journal of Islamic Business and Management, 6*(1), 7–18.
Baki, Z. A., & Uthman, A. B. (2017). Exploring the 'Social Failures' of Islamic Banks: A Historical Dialectics Analysis. *Journal of Islamic Accounting and Business Research, 8*(3), 250–271.
Balz, K. (2008). *Sharia Risk? How Islamic Finance Has Transformed Islamic Contract Law, Islamic Legal Studies Program*. Harvard Law School.
Cebeci, I. (2012). Integrating the Social Maslaha into Islamic Finance. *Accounting Research Journal, 25*(3), 166–184.
Chapra, M. U. (1979). *Objectives of the Islamic Economic Order*. The Islamic Foundation, Leicester.
Choudhury, M. A. (2012). The 'Impossibility' Theorems of Islamic Economics. *International Journal of Islamic and Middle Eastern Finance and Management, 5*(3), 179–202.
Choudhury, M. S. (1999). *Fundamentals of Islamic Economic System*. Burhan Education and Welfare Trust Lahore.
Diamond, D. W. (1984). Financial Intermediation as Delegated Monitoring: A Simple Example. *Review of Economic Studies, 51*(3), 393–414.
Dusuki, A. W. & Abozaid, A. (2007). A Critical Appraisal on the Challenges of Realizing Maqasid Al-Shari'ah in Islamic Banking and Finance. *IIUM Journal of Economics and Management, 15*(2), 143–165.
Haniffa, R. & Hudaib, M. (2010). Islamic Finance: From Sacred Intentions to Secular Goals? *Journal of Islamic Accounting and Business Research, 1*(2), 85–91.
Ibrahim, A. A., Elatrash, R. J., & Farooq, M. O. (2014). Hoarding Versus Circulation of Wealth from the Perspective of Maqasid al-Shari'ah. *International Journal of Islamic and Middle Eastern Finance and Management, 7*(1), 6–21.
Iqbal, Z. (1997). Islamic Financial Systems. *World Bank Publications*, 42–43.
Jamia Uloom-ul-Islamia (2008). *Marwajja Islami Bankari [Contemporary Islamic Banking]*. Maktaba-e-Bayyinat.
Jan, S., & Asutay, M. (2019). *A Model for Islamic Development: An Approach in Islamic Moral Economy*. Edward Elgar Publishing.
Khan, F. (2010). How 'Islamic' is Islamic Banking? *Journal of Economic Behavior and Organization, 76*(3), 805–820.

Kumru, C. S., & Sarntisart, S. (2016). Banking for those Unwilling to Bank: Implications of Islamic Banking Systems. *Economic Modelling*, *54*, 1–12.

Laldin, M. A. & Furqani, H. (2013). Developing Islamic Finance in the Framework of Maqasid al-Shari'ah: Understanding the Ends (Maqasid) and the Means (Wasa'il). *International Journal of Islamic and Middle Eastern Finance and Management*, *6*(4), 278–289.

Lebdaoui, H., & Wild, J. (2016). Islamic Banking and Financial Development. *Review of Middle East Economics and Finance*, *12*(2), 201–224.

Leon, F., & Weill, L. (2018). Islamic Banking Development and Access to Credit. *Pacific-Basin Finance Journal*, *52*, 54–69.

Mansoori, M. T. (2011). Use of Hiyal in Islamic Finance and its Shari'ah Legitimacy. *Islamic Studies*, *50*(3/4), 383–411.

Mansour, W., Ben Jedidia, K., & Majdoub, J. (2015). How Ethical is Islamic Banking in the Light of the Objectives of Islamic Law? *Journal of Religious Ethics*, *43*(1), 51–77

Maududi, S. A. A. (1970). *Ma'ashiyat-e Islam [Economic System of Islam]*. Islamic Publications.

Mohieldin, M., Iqbal, Z., Rostom, A. M., & Fu, X. (2011). The Role of Islamic Finance in Enhancing Financial Inclusion in Organization of Islamic Cooperation (OIC) Countries, Policy Research Working Paper 5920.

Naceur, S. B., Barajas, A., & Massara, A. (2017). Can Islamic Banking Increase Financial Inclusion?. In M. K. Hassan (Ed.) *Handbook of Empirical Research on Islam and Economic Life*. Edward Elgar Publishing.

State Bank of Pakistan (2018). *KAP Study on Islamic Banking in Pakistan, State Bank of Pakistan and Department for International Development (DFID)*.

Usmani, M. T. (2004). *An Introduction to Islamic Finance*. Maktaba Ma'ariful Quran.

7 Issues in Shariah Governance Framework of Islamic Banking Institutions

Abdul Basit

Introduction

The concept of Islamic banking first developed in the late 1940s but the pioneering effort in bringing Islamic banking principles into practice only became reality in 1963 with the development of the Mit Ghamer Savings Bank and the Nasser Social Bank in Egypt (Haridan, Hassan, & Karbhari, 2018; Razak, 2015). In a few years, the Ummah is much more obsessive and passionate about the Islamic banking system; however, the question of compliance to Shariah rule from Islamic banks is bound to arise. Do the Islamic banks follow the guidelines that are directed by the legislative sources, Quran and Sunnah? Can the Ummah trust Islamic banks to have good compliance and integrity (Wardhani & Arshad, 2012)? The Shariah Supervisory board is answerable to all these questions without any hesitancy.

The products, services, and operations offered by the Islamic financial institutions are completely certified from the Shariah board; however, conventional institutions don't require any such endorsements. The root source of Islamic finance is irrefutable and should not have any room for doubt. Furthermore, the Islamic financial institutions cover the moral, societal, ethical, and spiritual virtues to improve the justice system of the society, while the conventional financial system just depends upon financial and economical transactions for the maximization of profits. Either in a conventional system or Islamic, governance practices play a key role in ensuring that businesses are run smoothly and soundly. A well-established Shariah governance framework plays a significant role in the regulatory and supervisory arrangements of Islamic banking institutions and implements the Shariah principles and guidelines in all aspects of their products, instruments, operations, practices, and management. Dahir, Osman, & Ali (2015) opined that Islamic banks are institutions derived from the Islamic economic system and the objective of these institutions is to eradicate riba from the economy and to ensure the profit-sharing mechanism. To acquire these objectives, Shariah supervisory board has the responsibility for the governance and implementation of Shariah pronouncement in Islamic banking institutions. Shariah governance in Islamic banking institutions is as essential and significant as corporate governance in modern corporate organizations. A Shariah governance arrangement ensures the compliance of Shariah ruling in Islamic banking transactions. It plays a significant role in the industry to ensure that it meets the objective of the establishment of Islamic banks. When Shariah is involved in the corporate sector and especially in Islamic banks, five fundamental issues arise. These issues are: the independence of Shariah board members and the board as a whole; the competency of Shariah board members in all aspects; the consistency of their pronouncements; disclosure of compliance; and the Shariah pronouncements of the Shariah board members. Shariah supervision is a key element in the governance of Islamic banks. As a member of the Shariah board in an Islamic bank, one has to keep oversight of Shariah matters faced by the bank. Members of the Shariah board need to have complete knowledge of Shariah pronouncements on financial matters as well as awareness of contemporary finance. Shariah scholars have thoughtful fears on the issues particularly related to the responsibility and the authority of Shariah Supervisory Board (SSB) members although Shariah governance principles are highlighted and addressed in different forums. SSB is an essential part of the governance structure of Islamic banks for the support and monitoring of the compliance of Shariah rules in bank transactions and product development. In addition to that, SSB is answerable to all the serious concerns, hesitancy, and thirst of the *Ummah* towards Islamic finance. The Islamic banking industry requires a Shariah board to be well established and organized. Furthermore, the Shariah board members are a combination of unique individuals who must have qualified in both Islamic jurisprudence and contemporary finance to perform the supervision and consultation duties in a better way and to advance the quality of services. One of the major rules of SSB is to advise and facilitate the Islamic banks on Shariah matters to ensure the Islamicity of operations of banks. Shariah board members have a strong responsibility of developing the Islamic financial institution within the framework of Shariah. The deficiency of the Islamic finance experts' knowledge and experience is an alarming subject in the rapid growth of the industry. The Islamic finance industry has significant faith in three sets of individuals with complementary skills: financial professionals familiar with conventional financial products as well as the demand for 'Islamic' analogues of those products; Islamic jurists or *Fuqaha*, experts in classical jurisprudence; and lawyers who assist both groups in structuring Islamic financial products while ensuring their compliance with legal and regulative constraints. The performance of a Shariah board is a matter of concern especially for Islamic banking institutions in any country because the regulatory environment varies from one region to another. The basic purpose of conducting this study is to point out the issues regarding the competency of Shariah board members and to figure out better solutions for that problem.

Divine Law and Maqasid al-Shariah

Islamic law is considered a 'system' where the characteristic of determination is recognized through the recognition of Maqasid al-Shariah. Shariah is an approach leading to a certain kind of life that is all about wisdom, justice (adl), kindness, and social welfare for all the community (Margulies et al., 2019). The term Shariah means 'a waterhole where animals gather daily to drink' or 'path to the water source' (Dahir, Osman, & Ali, 2015; Philips, 1990; Quraishi-Landes, 2015; ShiKai, Ali, & Choudhury, 2017). Quran stated the meaning of Shariah as a straight path as mentioned: 'Then we put you on a straight path in your affairs, so follow it and do not follow the desires of those who do not know' (Al-Qur'an 18:45).

Any other ruling that conflicts with Shariah is not the juridical theory of Islamic law (Aude, 2007). Shariah aims at improving and perfecting human life by eradicating biases, easing hardship, and promoting justice (Chapra, 2008). Maqasid al-Shariah relates to everything: laws, views, actions, and services. It summarizes the aims and wisdom (Hikmah) as approved by Shariah in all its rulings to preserve the benefits and interests of society (Vejzagic & Smolo, n.d.). Islam is the religion of diverse cultures and civilizations that crossed over the medieval centuries. Gulam (2016) stated that after the Holy era of Prophet Muhammad (P.B.U.H), his Companions and their first generation relied on how they saw Him practice, but after 600 AD, Islam expands from Hijaz to all over the world and new converts to Islam started. Maqasid of the Islamic law are the intentions behind Islamic declarations and every divine intent has a pearl of wisdom behind the rulings, e.g. civilizing social welfare is the wisdom behind the charity and developing recognition of Almighty is the wisdom behind fasting. The basics of Islamic law cannot be understood without a multidisciplinary approach. It will remain within the boundaries of traditional literature and its scripts.

The objectives of Shariah are not explicitly mentioned in the principal sources of Shariah's set of direct laws, The Quran, and the Prophetic Traditions. When Islam spread out its roots from Makkah, the jurists of the time and region interpreted the extracted laws from primary sources for the consideration of the objectives of Shariah (Ullah & Wafi Al-Karaghouli, 2017). These laws were developed after the first Muslim era by scholars who made efforts to further understand them. According to Islamic theology and jurisprudence, there is a consensus of all the Muslims upon belief (aqidah) in which modification or amendment cannot be accepted while the law accepts modification because of its nature and application for all times, despite globalization and the emergence of new ways of operation in societies. For instance, the teachings of all the Messengers about the faith have been the same but the laws issued by them changed over time (Senturk, 2005). The legal and halal interests of human beings are the absolute objective of the Maqasid al-Shariah and also to protect them from harm. The Quran indicates it, 'O Messenger (P.B.U.H) we have sent you as a mercy for the universe' (Al-Quran 21:107).

Figure 7.1 Dimensions of the Intentions of the Islamic Law in Traditional Classification. Author's Diagram.

However, some Muslim scholars look at it from a different perspective. Traditionally al-Maqasid were studied in the classification of unrestricted interests (Maslaha al Mursalah مصلحة مرسلة) or the suitable feature for the analogy (Qiyas). The concept of custom (Urf) in the theory of Islamic law also originates from 'cognitive culture'. Figure 7.1 visualizes the classification of Maqasid in Islamic law explained by Auda. He mentioned that the traditional taxonomy of Maqasid divides purposes of Islamic law into three rankings which were necessities (daruriyat), needs (hajiyat), and luxuries (tehsiniyyat). Safeguarding necessities is the objective behind any revealed law. In the fifth century the theory of 'levels of necessity' was developed (Auda, 2007).

Core Objectives of Shariah and Islamic Finance

The fundamentals of Islam never change which include aqidah (creed), ibadah (worship), and akhlaq (ethics and morality). While other activities require flexibility and creativity according to space and time, Maqasid al-Shariah refers to the ultimate objectives behind each Islamic ruling given by the lawgiver. According to the majority of Muslim scholars, the objective of Shariah is to ensure human well-being. However, in Shariah, the discussion of Maqasid is quite new compared to the classical Shariah knowledge, i.e. Uloom al Quran, Uloom al-Hadith, Fiqh, Usul al-Fiqh, Asma ul Rijal, etc. Imam Al-Ghazali established the most common theory of Maqasid which stated that the concern of the Shariah is to protect the five objectives by affirming that the ultimate objective of the Shariah is to encourage the well-being and welfare of humankind by safeguarding their religion (din), their lives (nafs), their intellect (aql), their posterity (nasl), and their capital (maal) (Laldin, 2020). According to Chapra (2008), Ghazali's theory of Maqasid depends upon five major categories in Figure 7.2 and these are: Human faith (din), their self (life), intellect (aql), human posterity (nasl), and their wealth (maal). So Al-Ghazali's theory is the expansion of the traditional arrangement (Wajdi & Bouheraoua, 2011). Scholars consider the term 'theory' to be synonymous with the term 'system'. The theory is more comprehensive than a principle, and a theory consists of several principles. In addition, Maqasid al-Shariah was highlighted as a theory

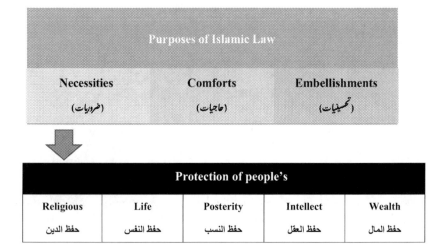

Figure 7.2 Al Ghazali's Maqasid al-Shariah Theory. Author's Diagram.

of objectives (Al-Raysuni, 2005). Afterward, many Shariah scholars worked on that theory and Ghazali's Maqasid theory become broader and broader. This is called evolution or adaptation in Maqasid al-Shariah theory.

The basis of Shariah is achieving human welfare and adherence of all human beings in this life and the hereafter as it is based on wisdom. The rulings of Shariah must not contradict justice, mercy, and wisdom. However, the philosophical foundation of Islamic finance doesn't focus on just the economic and financial aspects of businesses. Rather, it highlights the moral, societal, ethical, and religious dimensions as well to maintain justice and fairness in society. In this regard, Islamic finance falls within the ambit of protection of wealth in Maqasid al-Shariah (Laldin, 2020; Wajdi & Bouheraoua, 2011). The Islamic financial system ensures economic suitability and justice through fair wealth circulation by observing Islamic rules (Ahkam-e Shariah), efficient utilization of resources, and the elimination of poverty and improvement of society in all aspects. Islamic financial institutions including Islamic banks, Takaful companies, Mudarabah companies, and mutual funds play a key role in the efficient resource circulation in the society and consequently uplifting living standards. The Islamic financial system also institutes so many other means of spending in the way of Allah for his sake such as zakat, sadaqah, Infaq, qard, and hisbah (Akram, Laldin, & Furqani, 2013).

The Concept of Banking in Islam

Earlier to the introduction of Islamic banking, Muslims around the globe were hesitant and were limited to enjoying the products and services of the conventional banking system. The Islamic banking system has a unique concept that satisfies the divine law both in form and spirit despite the conventional finance system, the absolute objective being to maximize the profits for the stockholders (Said & Elangkovan, 2014). In other words, the objective and mission of the Islamic banking system are completely dictated by the Quran and the Sunnah as well as the socio-economic features of business activities that value the society at large, Tahqiq al-khidmah al-ijtima' iyah (Ghoul & Karam, 2007; Razak, 2015).

Islamic banking is a financial practice of ensuring the guidelines of Allah on Muamulat. It's not an easy task for a layman to derive Shariah rulings from the Quran and the Sunnah directly. Competent authorities responsible for the interpretation of Shariah rules known as the Ulama, the Mufti, the Ustadz and so many other names, are seen to hold a strong decisive position in pronouncements of halal and haram to achieve the central theme of Islamic banking that is Shariah compliance. In business and financial matters, Islam enforces a high degree of accountability on the shoulders of Shariah boards of Islamic banks principally on Shariah scholars because they are the gatekeepers and responsible to empower the Shariah-compliant products and services of Islamic banks.

Abdullah bin Umar recounted that: 'Prophet Muhammad (peace be upon him) said, "Surely! Every one of you is a guardian and is responsible for his charges; the imam (ruler) of the people is a guardian and is responsible for his subjects; a man is the guardian of his family and is responsible for his subjects; a woman is the guardian of her husband's home and the children and is responsible for them; the slave of a man is a guardian of his master's property and is responsible for it. Surely, every one of you is a guardian and responsible for his charges."'

In another hadith, Prophet Muhammad (peace be upon him) mentioned, 'When two people trade they have the choice (to proceed with or cancel the transaction), so if they are honest and clarify (e.g. the defects in their merchandise) their trade will be blessed, but if they lie and conceal defects, there will be no blessing in their trade.' As a result, any fatwa issued by the Shariah scholar/board in the banking sector must not contradict the Quran and the Sunnah's guidelines of Muamulat.

The Basis for Islamic Corporate Governance: The Institution of Hisbah

In the last few decades, the concept of corporate governance was relatively new to the Islamic banking industry. There is no specific word in Arabic language for the corporate governance. However, the theory of corporate governance is borrowed from the Shariah principle of al-siyasah al-shariyyah which refers to the public policies relevant to the community such as market regulations, taxes, and security (Quraishi-landes, 2015). Several Quranic verses are agreed upon this principle of collaborative efforts among the authorities and the community for the implementation of a good governance system in society

(Al-Qur'an 3:104, 9:71, 5:2). Here, the authority is used in a very broad sense that includes the state, the companies, board of directors of a company, and all other stakeholders. This joint practice is also termed as hisbah in the fiqh perspective which means 'to do good deeds and to avoid forbidden matters mentioned in Islamic law'. This exercise can be practised by an individual or group as Prophet Muhammad (peace be upon him) was the first muhtasib (enforcement officer) of an Islamic state (Al-foul & Soliman, 2010). In simple words, hisbah is the surveillance of muhtasib in all aspects of the community's daily conduct including religious norms, administration, and finance. Later on, muhtasib is also responsible for the execution of a fair market process, and proper usage of weights and measures in the market to protect society from fraud and illegal contracts. Kamali (1989) argues that Abu Bakar and Umar followed the same practice of Prophet Muhammad (peace be upon him) by personally guarding the streets of Madinah at night to know a better picture of the society and prevent crimes. Umar ibn-Khattab was the first one whose practice of hisbah led to the formation of the first police station in the history of Islam to prevent criminal sins in the improvement of fiqh ul-janayat (Islamic criminal law).

As far as the hisbah's relevance to the Islamic banking industry is concerned, the role of the hisbah is supposed to be performed by the Shariah board. Although, there are a lot of opinions on this matter that it is a responsibility of the state to the formation of the hisbah institutions as well as remunerations paid to muhtasibs by the state so that they are independent in their decisions and from the prevention of direct influence from the industry. Vice versa, the Shariah board lies under the jurisdiction of that particular bank which creates several issues in mitigating the Shariah compliance risk. Hence, the Islamic banking industry may consider the formation of a hisbah institution placed under the state's jurisdiction or an independent body like AAOIFI, IFSB, and IFA-OIC.

Issues in Shariah Governance

The higher objectives of Shariah can only be attained through the basis of Islamic corporate governance and these are the ethical and social welfare of a society (Zahid & Khan, 2019). The Shariah scholars, while presenting their concerns on the current Shariah governance system, have also admitted the inconsistencies and flaws in the system that affects the credibility and image of IFIs and highlighted their anxieties on five major issues as shown in Figure 7.3 about the Shariah governance system. Alman (2012) acknowledged that the AAOIFI and IFSB gathered the guiding principles and standards regarding the selection, composition, and responsibilities of the SSB. However, these guiding principles mainly focus on the five concepts as well. These concepts are called components and challenges of the Shariah governance system in IBIs (Grassa, 2013; Z. Hasan, 2014; IFSB-10, 2009). These issues are as follows:

Issues in Shariah Governance Framework of Islamic Banking 117

Figure 7.3 Components of Shariah Governance in IBIs.

Significance of Shariah Advisory/Supervision in Islamic Banking Institutions

The history of Shariah advisory and its importance is backed by many relevant verses from the Holy Quran and Sunnah. The Grand Shariah advisor of the first Islamic state was the Prophet Muhammad himself; however, the presence of Shariah advisory institutes/committees was found in the period of His companions (Sahaba), Tabieen, Taba-Tabieen, Mughal, and Othman dynasties as well (Iqbal & Saqib, 2016). The responsibility of IBIs is to ensure compliance with the Shariah rules and the products they are offering are easy to understand and customers are ready to invest because of its asset-based financing. In this context, the general public has strong beliefs and faith in the opinions of Shariah scholars (Imamuddin, Saeed, & Arain, 2016). Zahid and Khan (2019) indicate its 'Supra Authority'. A competent and effective Shariah board play a key role in the development of the Islamic financial system of any country because they make their policies in the light of Shariah, analyse their present product and services, and structure their new Shariah-based products considering the current financial system and the practice of the society, urf (Iqbal & Saqib, 2018). To reduce the risks in the Islamic banking sector and make them efficient to play a strong role in the economy, a strong and wise supervision mechanism is necessary (Venardos, 2005). Furthermore, Garas and Pierce (2010) argue that in the Islamic banking system, Shariah scholars educate and guide the executive management of a bank by conducting various seminars, workshops, and learning programs where Shariah scholars answer their queries according to Shariah law. Moreover, whenever a new fatwa is issued, Shariah scholars explain its basis and roots to the management and implement it properly and fairly. The way to accomplish the fairness and honesty in governance system can be achieved through a strong transparency and accountability mechanism. Also, it is the social and religious responsibility of Shariah scholars to resolve the legal disputes among the directors and the

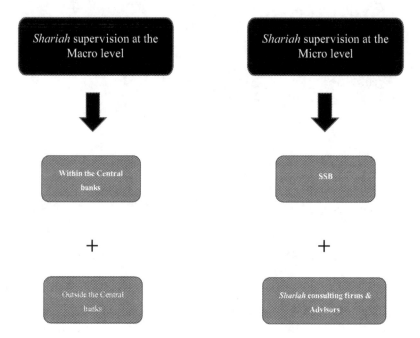

Figure 7.4 The Allocation of Shariah Supervision at the Macro and Micro Levels.

clients. Figure 7.4 indicates that Shariah supervision can be allocated into two forms:

The Principle of Shura in Islam

The term Shura is derived from an Arabic word, 'shawara' which lexical meaning is 'to advice' or 'to consult' (Wehr, 1976). The Prophet Muhammad (peace be upon him) was also ordered by the Almighty that he must consult with his companions on certain issues. However, the Messenger (peace be upon him) does not need to consult with the people concerning the Shariah rulings, several occasions underlined the adoption of shura by the Messenger (peace be upon him). Quran emphasizes that: 'and consult them (the companions) in affairs. Then, when though hast taken a decision put trust in Allah. For Allah loves those who put their trust in him' (Al-Qur'an 3:159).

Al-Razi (1990) and Qurtubi (2004) argue that the principle of shura is not to compromise on divine revelation but to promote the concept of unity and consultation over collective decisions. For instance, after the battle of Badar fought on 17 Ramadan 2AH, the Prophet Muhammad consulted with his companions about the war prisoners. Similarly, the Prophet also discusses the matter of his wife, Ayesha, when she was falsely blamed for lewdness (Nabahani, 1996).

Hasan (2003) mentioned that after the Messenger's journey towards akhirah, his companions also practised this deed of democracy on the appointment of Abu Bakar Siddique as the first caliph of Islam. In the era of Umar Al-Khattab, an advice-giving council was formed for the appointment of later caliphs because there were six intellectuals proposed for the caliph namely, Usman, Ali, Talha, Zubair, Abdul Rahman ibn Awf, and Saeed (Osman, 1997). Nonetheless, it is not necessary that the outcome of every decision of the shura committee will be positive; likewise, the battle of Uhud fought in 3AH imposed a huge loss on Muslims. Abd Razak (2015) pointed out that as long as the decision of a majority is based on the rulings of Shariah, it will be more reliable and beneficial for society. Here, the term cited in the Quran 'ulul amr minkum' is considered as a majority which means those individuals elected by the public themselves and has the power to implement the law (Al-Qur'an 4:59) (Osman, 1997). According to Kurzman (1998), it is said that the concept of shura is similar to the notion of Western democracy in the sense that collective concern is more consistent, inclusive, and sound collectively beneficial for the society rather than decisions made by an individual or minority.

Indeed, consultation on decision-making is appreciated by Islam as it stops the suppression of society's rights in the hands of certain people (Mawdudi, 1988; Shaikh, 1988). Yet, to avoid making the whole shura process a joke, any issue upon which the majority of the shura members agree will be considered binding (El-Awa, 1980; Nabahani, 1996). However, to implement the binding decisions that take place as a result of shura, a strong mechanism of supervision must be practised by Shariah scholars (A. Hasan, 2003; Shaharuddin et al., 2012).

Shariah Supervisory Board: A Shura Committee in Islamic Banking Institutions

The largest sect of Muslims all over the world that compose at least 80% of the world's Muslim population is known as Ahle–Sunnah Wal Jamah (the people of tradition and community), famous among Sunni Muslims (Al-bar & Chamsi-Pasha, 2015). In contrast, Sunni Muslims believe that appointment of the Caliph or Imam who must be a man of integrity and rectitude, is the duty of community leaders through the process of shura consultation.

As far as the Islamic banking system is concerned, the Shariah supervisory board plays the role of the shura committee/council and the Shariah scholars are considered shura members of that particular bank. Consequently, the binding Shariah decisions of shura are practised by several Shariah boards in some Muslim countries, namely:

- Higher Shariah supervisory board (HSSB), Central Board of Bahrain
- Shariah advisory council (SAC), Bank Negara Malaysia
- The Higher Shariah Authority (has), United Arab Emirates
- Fatwa Board of the Ministry of Awqaf, and Islamic affairs, Kuwait

Moving one step forward, few countries implemented binding decisions of the shura council on their parliament and judiciary as well. Likewise, Article 230 (1) of the constitution of Pakistan enlightens that the Islamic council can challenge any bill presented in the parliament that contradicts Islamic law. Also, the decision of the Islamic council must be followed by the parliament and the president.

Furthermore, Muslims all over the globe follow four major schools of Islamic thought whose differences of opinions (ikhtilaf ul-fuqaha) are just on the interpretation of primary sources of fiqh. It is a common phenomenon titled a science of Islamic jurisprudence practices at the time of companions of the Prophet Muhammad (peace be upon him) (Razak, 2018). Therefore, it is slightly difficult for the shura to agree upon all the consensus for a developing industry such as Islamic banking; however, the shura can be regarded to act as a model to bridge the different opinions between these schools of fiqh on business and financial transactions as well as Shariah-compliant products and services offered by Islamic banks.

Role of SSB in Islamic Banking Institutions

Shariah's governance system in the Islamic finance industry is an integral part of the Islamic financial sector to maintain and build reliability among the shareholders and IFIs with the assurance that all the activities, transactions, and practices are on track with Shariah (Musibah et al., 2014). However, the Shariah governance system can be composed of a simple Shariah board or extended to a Shariah system that includes a Shariah board, Shariah audit department, Shariah review department, and Shariah risk management department (Khalil & Taktak, 2020), Hassan et al. (2017) highlighted that the Islamic corporate governance revolves around two models:

(i) The role of SSB is to maximize the benefits for shareholders.
(ii) SSB works not only for the interests of shareholders but for all stakeholders.

Islamic mufti or a Muslim legal expert is an individual who gives his judicial verdict upon a new arising problem or confusion among the community when a question is raised by a mustafti (S. A. Hassan & Wan Mohd Khairul Firdaus Wan Khairuldin, 2020; Khairuldin et al., 2019). The SSB consists of Shariah scholars or ulama specialized in general knowledge of Shariah as well as an expert in fiqh ul muamulat, contemporary finance in general and Islamic finance in particular. In IBIs, SSB has a responsibility to provide objective and effective advice to ensure that the business, products, and services they offered comply with Shariah rulings (BNM, 2019). According to Hamza (2013), the confidence and reliability of the stakeholders on IBs' products and services depend upon the efficient and independent Shariah board. Despite that few Shariah scholars indicate that the majority of the board members focused on

Issues in Shariah Governance Framework of Islamic Banking 121

Figure 7.5 Role of Shariah Supervisory Board in IFIs.

Figure 7.6 Responsibilities of SSB.

the legitimacy of the products and services offered by IBIs from a fiqh perspective rather than the promotion and implementation of the Islamic and ethical values. Shariah Supervisory Board's role can be generally categorized in Figure 7.5 (Hasan, 2014; Toufik, 2015):

According to Wardhani and Arshad (2012), the roles and responsibilities of SSB have been revolving around three main areas (see Figure 7.6).

Characteristics of the Shariah Board

Shariah board should have the following characteristics as shown in Figure 7.7.

Knowledge of Financial Accounting

(Lassoued, 2018; Nomran, Haron, & Hassan, 2018; Ramly & Nordin, 2018) opine that besides knowledge of Shariah law, a Shariah scholar must have a good command of contemporary qualifications (finance/accounting) too. Indeed, Shariah scholars do not have any idea about the complexity of financial products that may lead to poor decision making. In addition to that, a qualified and skilled Shariah scholar confirms the better quality of supervision with the help of bankers and economists which may result in high Shariah compliance and achieve the stakeholders' requirements. Furthermore, a combination of both Shariah knowledge and contemporary education enables a Shariah scholar to communicate with the board of directors in a professional way (Mansoor, Ellahi, & Malik, 2019b). Khalil and Taktak (2020) report that a Shariah scholar with a doctorate in business or finance is well up-to-date on the current implications of Islam in IFIs. Moreover, the method to evaluate the long-term survival of Islamic banks is to have competent Shariah scholars on board having diverse backgrounds in terms of qualification, skill, and understanding (Ajili & Bouri, 2018; Grassa, 2016; Grassa & Matoussi, 2014; Wardhani & Arshad, 2012).

Presence of a Mufti

Al-Qayyam argues that mufti acts as an announcer of Allah's law decision in a certain matter through his ijtihad and fatwa (Khairuldin et al., 2019). Usually, an individual well-versed with fiqh knowledge to explain Islamic laws and problems having a reputable, truthful, and tolerant personality appointed by the government is entitled as a mufti whose responsibility is to interpret the fiqh and issuance of Shariah pronouncements, fatwas (Khalil & Taktak, 2020). So, the financial products of the Islamic banks become more reliable and Shariah-compliant with the presence of a mufti on the Shariah board.

Interlocked Shariah Scholars

The ratio of deficiency of skilled scholars in the industry is very high. To fulfil this requirement, Shariah scholars are often sitting on more than one board (Grassa, 2016; Grassa & Matoussi, 2014). Hasan (2014) indicates that the deficiency of skilled Shariah scholars is not the actual reason behind the sitting of certain Shariah scholars on several boards, it is just because of their good reputation in the industry, and the hiring of these Shariah experts is to publicize and promote their financial products. The expertise and exposure of interlocked Shariah scholars bring more innovative ideas and development of financial products in Islamic banking industry (Farook & Farooq, 2013; Mansoor, Ellahi, & Malik, 2019a). However, Hamza (2013a) predicts that the interlocked Shariah experts may create the problem of confidentiality because they have access to many transactions and information of several Islamic banks. Add to that, this practice affects the credibility of the Shariah board and increases the risk of fatwa shopping (Haridan, Hassan, & Karbhari, 2018; Reuters, 2016).

Foreign Shariah Scholar

It has been perceived that Shariah scholars from different countries having different schools of thought indicates the deviation of legal opinion that creates the nonconformity of Shariah interpretation about a specific issue (Ahmed & Hussainey, 2015). The diverse languages of the Shariah scholars

Issues in Shariah Governance Framework of Islamic Banking 123

on a board increase the problems of communication among them and raise the Shariah risk (Ginena & Hamid, 2015). The negative impact of these issues affects the financial soundness of Islamic banks. However, few researchers believe that the lack of qualified professionals and experts can be resolved by appointing foreign Shariah scholars as already practised by some Islamic banks in different countries (Quttainah & Almutairi, 2017). Mansoor, Ellahi, and Malik (2019) add that Shariah scholars from different regions have different expertise and innovative ideas that boost business growth and reduce the default risk. In addition, it is recommended that at least one of the Shariah board members should be a resident of the country where the Islamic bank is operating.

Shariah Board's Size

The Shariah board is one of the most important elements of Islamic corporate governance consisting of qualified and specialized jurists on the subject of fiqh ul muamulat (AAOIFI, 2010; BNM, 2010; Ramly & Nordin, 2018; Ulussever, 2018). The Shariah board is responsible for the overall financial activities of the Islamic bank to make them Shariah compliant. M. Hassan, Rizwan, and Sohail (2017a) and Khalil and Taktak (2020) show that the board's size highly affects the bank's performance and it decreases the Shariah risk. The theory indicates that a huge board size raises the knowledge and expertise that would lead to the better interpretation of Shariah-compliant transactions and

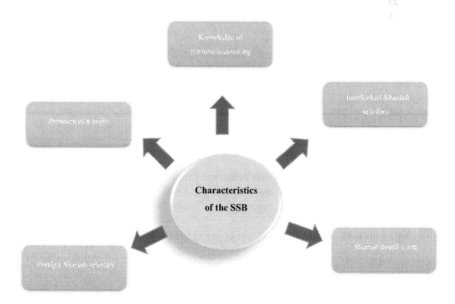

Figure 7.7 Characteristics of the Shariah Supervisory Board.

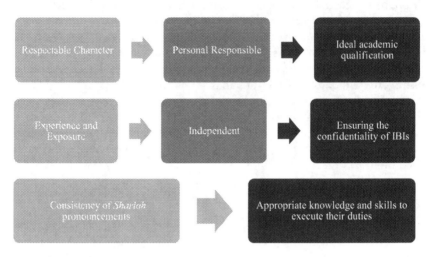

Figure 7.8 Capacities Required for SSB.

reduces agency costs (Mansoor, Ellahi, & Malik, 2019b; Nomran, Haron, & Hassan, 2018; Ramly & Nordin, 2018). Rahman & Bukair (2013) add that the financial soundness of Islamic banks depends upon a large number of Shariah experts. However, some scholars do not agree with the large number of a board's size. Amine (2018) highlighted that unfortunately a high number of Shariah members in a board leads to the conflict of interests, increases agency cost, and creates the communication gap between the scholars. The problem of coordination between board members can easily be solved by minimizing the board size (Lassoued, 2018). Hakimi et al. (2015) conclude that the bank's financial performance is negatively related to the board's size and this result has been confirmed by the researchers.

A competent Shariah board must comprise the following capacities as shown in Figure 7.8.

Conclusion and Recommendations

Shariah supervisory board occupies a unique and essential position in the governance structure of IFIs. The strong governance structure differentiates itself from the conventional corporate governance system. In Islamic banks, the SSB exists as a typical bank board but mainly its purpose is to monitor and certify all the financial transactions and business activities of the bank to sustain Shariah compliance. Sometimes the executives of the Islamic banks just use the Shariah board as a rubber stamp or dummy to serve their purposes and to achieve their ultimate goals by earning profits in the name of Islamic banking. To overcome all these issues, the following recommendations are made by the study:

Issues in Shariah Governance Framework of Islamic Banking 125

- The regulatory bodies should be more concerned and careful about the practices and operational functions of the Shariah board and Shariah executives as they are committed to doing the banking as per Shariah guidelines. In this context, it is recommended that the regulator/central bank has to establish a well-defined and comprehensive Shariah supervisory and regulatory framework for the appointment of qualified Shariah professionals at all levels and also their accountability and transparency to ensure the Shariah compliance in a better way and to mark the barrier on fatwa fishing.
- The management and BODs of the Islamic banks do not have the legislative power and legitimate right to influence the activities and practices of the Shariah board. So, it is recommended that the SSB must be independent and free from biases in decision-making and its implementation and they must not be under the influence of the management of Islamic banks, board of directors, and shareholders directly or indirectly.
- In Muslim societies, Shariah scholars are the most regarded and valuable personalities. To retain their reputation and honour, it is recommended that the salaries of Shariah scholars associated with the Islamic banks must be paid by the central bank. In a few countries like Indonesia and Brunei Darussalam, the Shariah board is funded by the ministry of finance and gets paid by the community contributions as well. Unfortunately, the Shariah board gets the remuneration from the concerned bank which indicates a conflict of interest and shows the negative relationship between the salaries paid and the independence of the Shariah board members. In that case, Islamic banks must release the annual financial remuneration amount of each Shariah scholar.
- Most Islamic banks do not disclose the complete profile of their Shariah scholars in their annual reports. So, it is recommended for Islamic banks to publish and reveal the complete profile of their Shariah board members in terms of educational background and experience.
- In the current scenario, there is a dire need for the robust growth of the Islamic banking sector in the economy. Therefore, it is suggested that the central banks must stop the issuance of a new licenses to the conventional banks for the effective functioning of Islamic banks
- It is recommended that Islamic banks must enhance and improve their R&D department to keep the originality of the Islamic financial products and to avoid focusing on duplicating the conventional products by Islamic financial engineering.
- It is suggested that the regulators and Islamic banks should arrange well-designed seminars for the Shariah scholars and executives of Islamic banks to make them aware of their limitations and future responsibilities. For the employees and lower staff of the bank, training sessions are to be organized so that they become able to answer the questions raised by their customers. Not only for the banking professionals, Islamic banks and central banks also organize such events and awareness programs on Islamic finance for the general public as well.

References

AAOIFI (2010). *Shari'ah Standards for Islamic Financial Institutions*. https://aaoifi.com/shariaa-standards/?lang=en

Abd Razak, A. H. (2015). An inferential reasoning on the centralisation of Islamic BAnks' Sharia' boards towards the advancement of the global Islamic banking industry. *10th International Conference on Islamic Economics and Finance*.

Ahmed, F., & Hussainey, K. (2015). Conversion into Islamic banks: Jurisprudence, EConomic and AAOIFI requirements. *European Journal of Islamic Finance, 3*, 1–9.

Ajili, H., & Bouri, A. (2018). Corporate governance quality of Islamic banks: Measurement and effect on financial performance. *International Journal of Islamic and Middle Eastern Finance and Management, 11*(3). 470–487.https://doi.org/10.1108/IMEFM-05-2017-0131

Akram Laldin, M., & Furqani, H. (2013). Developing Islamic finance in the framework of Maqasid al-Shari'ah: Understanding the ends (Maqasid) and the Means (Wasa'il). *International Journal of Islamic and Middle Eastern Finance and Management, 6*(4), 278–289. https://doi.org/10.1108/IMEFM-05-2013-0057

Al-bar, M. A., & Chamsi-Pasha, H. (2015). *Contemporary Bioethics: Islamic Perspective*. Springer.

Al-foul, B. A., & Soliman, M. (2010). The economic role of the State in the classical Islamic literature: The views of Ibn Taimiyah. *Digest of Middle East Studies, 15*(2), 1–10.

Al-Raysuni, A. (2005). *Imam Al-Shatibi's Theory of the Higher Objectives and Intents of Islamic Law*. The International Institute of Islamic Thought.

Al-Razi, F. A.-D. (1990). *Al-Tafseer Al-Kabir [The Large Commentary]. Dar al-Kutub al-'ilmiyya*. (Original Work Published in 608 AH).

Alman, M. (2012). Shari'ah Supervisory Board composition effects on Islamic banks' risk-taking behavior. *SSRN Electronic Journal*. https://doi.org/10.2139/ssrn.2140042

Amine, B. (2018). Contribution of governance to ensure the stability of Islamic banks: A panel data analysis. *International Journal of Accounting and Financial Reporting, 8*(3), 140–155. https://doi.org/10.5296/ijafr.v8i3.13333

Auda, J. (2007). Maqasid al-Shari'ah as philosophy of Islamic Law: A systems approach. In *Maqasid Al-Shari'ah as Philosophy of Islamic Law*. https://doi.org/10.2307/j.ctvkc67tg.8

BNM (2010). Shari'ah Governance Framework for Islamic Financial Institutions (Vol. 2).

BNM (2019). Shari'ah Governance. In *Bank Negara Malaysia* (Issue 3).

Chapra, M. U. (2008). *The Islamic Vision of Development in the Light of Maqāsid Al-Sharī'ah* (No. 235; Occasional Papers).

Dahir, A., Osman, A., & Ali, A. (2015). Importance of principles of Islamic jurisprudence (Usul Fiqh) in Islamic banking product structuring. *Academia.Edu, May*, 1–11. www.academia.edu/download/37470022/The_Importance_of_Principles_of_Islamic_Jurisprudence_Usul_fiqh_in_Islamic_Banking_Product_Structuring_.pdf

El-Awa, M. S. (1980). *On the Political System of the Islamic State*. American Trust Publications.

Farook, S., & Farooq, M. O. (2013). Sharī'ah governance, expertise and profession: Educational challenges in Islamic finance. *ISRA International Journal of Islamic Finance, 5*(1), 137–160. https://doi.org/10.12816/0002761

Garas, S. N., & Pierce, C. (2010). Shari'a supervision of Islamic financial institutions. *Journal of Financial Regulation and Compliance*, *18*(4), 386–407. https://doi.org/10.1108/13581981011093695

Ghoul, W., & Karam, P. (2007). MRI and SRI Mutual Funds: A comparison of Christian, Islamic (Morally Responsible Investing), and Socially Responsible Investing (SRI) mutual funds. *The Journal of Investing*, *16*(2), 96–102.

Ginena, K., & Hamid, A. (2015). *Foundations of Shari'ah Governance of Islamic Banks*. The Wiley Finance Series.

Grassa, R. (2013). Shari'ah governance system in Islamic financial institutions: New issues and challenges. *Arab Law Quarterly*, *27*, 171–187. https://doi.org/10.1163/15730255-12341254

Grassa, R. (2016). Corporate governance and credit rating in Islamic banks: Does Shari'ah governance matters? In *Journal of Management & Governance* (Vol. 20, Issue 4). Springer US. https://doi.org/10.1007/s10997-015-9322-4

Grassa, R., & Matoussi, H. (2014). Corporate governance of Islamic banks: A comparative study between GCC and Southeast Asia countries. *International Journal of Islamic and Middle Eastern Finance and Management*, *7*(3). https://doi.org/10.1108/IMEFM-01-2013-0001

Gulam, H. (2016). Comparing the legal rules (Ahkam-i Shari'ah) in the Maliki and Shafii schools with the Hanafi School of Thought. *Jurnal Ilmiah Islam Futura*, *16*(1), 1–8.

Hakimi, A., Rachdi, H., Mokni, R. B. S., & Hssini, H. (2015). Do board characteristics affect bank performance? Evidence from the Bahrain Islamic banks. *Journal of Islamic Accounting and Business Research*. https://doi.org/http://doi.org/10.1108/JIABR-06-2015-0029

Hamza, H. (2013a). Sharia governance in Islamic banks: Effectiveness and supervision model. *International Journal of Islamic and Middle Eastern Finance and Management*, *6*(3), 226–237. https://doi.org/10.1108/IMEFM-02-2013-0021

Hamza, H. (2013b). Sharia governance in Islamic banks: Effectiveness and supervision model. *International Journal of Islamic and Middle Eastern Finance and Management*, *6*(3), 226–237. https://doi.org/10.1108/IMEFM-02-2013-0021

Haridan, N. M., Hassan, A. F. S., & Karbhari, Y. (2018). Governance, religious assurance and Islamic banks: Do Shari'ah boards effectively serve? *Journal of Management and Governance*, *22*(4), 1015–1043. https://doi.org/10.1007/s10997-018-9418-8

Hasan, A. (2003). An introduction to Collective Ijtihad (Ijtihad Jama'i): Concept and applications. *The American Journal of Islamic Social Sciences*, *20*(2), 26–49.

Hasan, Z. (2014). In search of the perceptions of the Shari'ah scholars on Shari'ah governance system. *International Journal of Islamic and Middle Eastern Finance and Management*, *7*(1), 22–36. https://doi.org/10.1108/IMEFM-07-2012-0059

Hassan, M., Rizwan, M., & Sohail, H. M. (2017). Corporate governance, Shari'ah advisory boards and Islamic banks' performance. *Pakistan Journal of Islamic Research*, *18*(1), 173–184.

Hassan, S. A., & Wan Mohd Khairul Firdaus Wan Khairuldin (2020). Research design based on fatwa making process: An exploratory study. *International Journal of Higher Education*, *9*(6), 241–246. https://doi.org/10.5430/ijhe.v9n6p241

IFSB-10 (2009). *Guiding Principles on Shari'ah Governance Systems for Institutions Offering Islamic Financial Services*.

Imamuddin, Saeed, A., & Arain, A. W. (2016). Principles of Islamic economics in the light of The Holy Quran and Sunnah. *International Journal of Humanities and Social Science Invention*, 5(5), 48–54.

Iqbal, M., & Saqib, L. (2016). *Maliyati Idaray aur Shari'ah Advisory Board. Zaroorat, Ziimidariyan, Zabtay. Tanqeedi Jaiza (Urdu Edition)*. Centre for Excellence in Islamic Finance, CEIF.

Iqbal, M., & Saqib, L. (2018). Financial institutions and Shari'ah advisory board importance, responsibilities and criterions: A critical review by Muhammad Ismail. In *Journal of Islamic Banking and Finance* (Vol. 35, Issue 2).

Kamali, M. H. (1989). Siyasah Shar'iyah or the policies of Islamic government. *American Journal of Islam and Society*, 6(1), 59–80.

Khairuldin, W. M. K. F. W., Anas, W. N. I. W. N., Embong, A. H., Hassan, S. A., Hanapi, M. S., & Ismail, D. (2019). Ethics of mufti in the declaration of fatwa according to Islam. *Journal of, Legal, Ethical, and Regulatory Issues*, 22(5), 1–7. www.abacademies.org/articles/Ethics-of-mufti-in-the-declaration-of-fatwa-according-to-Islam-1544-0044-22-5-414.pdf

Khalil, A., & Taktak, N. B. (2020). The impact of the Shari'ah board's characteristics on the financial soundness of Islamic banks. *Journal of Islamic Accounting and Business Research*, 11(9), 19. https://doi.org/10.1108/JIABR-08-2018-0127

Kurzman, C. (1998). *Liberal Islam: A Source Book*. Oxford University Press.

Laldin, M. A. (2020). Ethics in the light of Maqasid Al-Shari'ah: A case study of Islamic economics and finance. In A. Mirakhor, Z. Iqbal, & S. K. Sadr (Eds), *Handbook of Ethics of Islamic Economics and Finance* (pp. 21–47). De Gruyter Oldenbourg. https://doi.org/10.1515/9783110593419-002

Lassoued, M. (2018). Corporate governance and financial stability in Islamic banking. *Managerial Finance*, 44(5), 1–15.

Mansoor, M., Ellahi, N., & Malik, Q. A. (2019b). Corporate governance and credit rating: Evidence of Shari'ah governance from Pakistan Islamic banks. *International Transaction Journal of Engineering, Management, & Applied Sciences & Technologies*, 10(18), 1–11. https://doi.org/10.14456/ITJEMAST.2019.251

Mawdudi, A. A. (1988). *Towards Understanding the Qur'an (Tafhim al-Qur'an)*. Islamic Foundation, London.

Mergaliyev, A., Asutay, M., Avdukic, A., & Karbhari, Y. (2019). higher ethical objective (Maqasid al-Shari'ah) augmented framework for Islamic banks: Assessing ethical performance and exploring its determinants. *Journal of Business Ethics*. https://doi.org/10.1007/s10551-019-04331-4

Musibah, A. S., Sulaiman, Wan, B., & Alfattani, Y. (2014). The mediating effect of financial performance on the relationship between Shari'ah Supervisory Board effectiveness, intellectual capital and corporate social responsibility, of Islamic banks in Gulf Cooperation Council countries. *Asian Social Science*, 10(17), 139–164. https://doi.org/10.5539/ass.v10n17p139

Nabahani, T. an. (1996). *The Ruling System in islam*. Khilafah Publications.

Nomran, N. M., Haron, R., & Hassan, R. (2018). Shari'ah supervisory board characteristics effects on Islamic banks' performance: Evidence from Malaysia. *International Journal of Bank Marketing*, 36(2), 290–304. https://doi.org/10.2139/ssrn.3598723

Osman, F. (1997). *Islam in a Modern State: Democracy and the Concept of Shura*. Center for Muslim-Christian Understanding: History and International Affairs, Edmund A. Walsh School of Foreign Service, Georgetown University.

Philips, A. A. B. (1990). *The Evolution of Fiqh (Islamic Law & The Madh-habs)* (4th ed.). International Islamic Publishing House.

Quraishi-landes, A. (2015). The Sharia problem with Sharia legislation. *Ohio Northern UNiversity Law Review*, 4(1), 545–566.

Qurtubi, A. A. Al. (2004). *Al Jami Li-Ahkam Al-Quran*. Dar al-Kutub al-'ilmiyya. (Original Work Published in 671 AH).

Quttainah, M. A., & Almutairi, A. R. (2017). Corporate governance: Evidence from Islamic banks. *Social Responsibility Journal*, 13(2), 601–624.

Rahman, A. A., & Bukair, A. A. (2013). The influence of the Shari'ah supervision board on corporate social responsibility disclosure by Islamic banks of Gulf Co-Operation Council countries. *Asian Journal of Business and Accounting*, 6(2), 65–104.

Ramly, Z., & Nordin, N. D. H. M. (2018). Sharia Supervision Board, board independence, risk committee and risk-taking of Islamic banks in Malaysia. *International Journal of Economics and Financial Issues*, 8(4), 290–300.

Razak, A. H. A. (2015). The fundamentals of Islamic banking and finance: A prologue. *European Journal of Islamic Finance*, 2, 1–12.

Razak, A. H. A. (2018). Centralisation of corporate governance framework for Islamic financial institutions: Is it a worthy cause? *ISRA International Journal of Islamic Finance*, 10(1), 36–51. https://doi.org/10.1108/IJIF-08-2017-0020

Reuters, T. (2016). *Islamic Finance Development Report*. https://ceif.iba.edu.pk/pdf/Thomson%20Reuters%20-%20Islamic%20Finance%20Development%20Report%202016%20Resilient%20Growth.pdf

Said, M. M., & Elangkovan, K. (2014). Prosperity and social justice consequences of applying ethical norms of Islamic finance: Literature review. *Journal of Economics and Sustainable Development*, 5(2), 99–107.

Senturk, R. (2005). Sociology of rights: 'I Am Therefore I Have Rights': Human rights in Islam between universalistic and communalistic perspectives. *Muslim World Journal of Human Rights*, 2(1), 1–32. https://doi.org/10.2202/1554-4419.1030

Shaharuddin, A., Mas'ad, M. A., Safian, Y. H. M., & Shafii, Z. (2012). Fatwas on Islamic Capital Markets: A Comparative Study Between Malaysia and Gulf Co-operation Council (GCC) Countries (No. 2; 40).

Shaikh, M. A. (1988). Ethics of decision-making in Islam and Western environments. *American Journal of Islam and Society*, 5(1), 115–128.

Shinkafi, A. A., Ali, N. A., & Choudhury, M. (2017). Contemporary Islamic economic studies on Maqasid Shari'ah: A systematic literature review. *Humanomics*, 33(3), 315–334.

Toufik, B. B. (2015). The role of Shari'ah Supervisory Board in ensuring good corporate governance practice in Islamic banks. *International Journal of Contemporary Applied Sciences*, 2(2), 10.

Ullah, K., & Wafi Al-Karaghouli. (2017). *Understanding Islamic Financial Services: Theory and Practice*. Kogan Page Publishers.

Ulussever, T. (2018). A comparative analysis of corporate governance and bank performance: Islamic banks versus conventional banks. *Research Journal of Business and Management*, 5(1), 34–50. https://doi.org/10.17261/Pressacademia.2018.815

Vejzagic, M., & Smolo, E. (n.d.). *Maqasid Al–Shar'ah in Islamic Finance: An Overview*. 1–22.

Venardos, A. M. (2005). *Islamic Banking & Finance in South-East Asia: Its Development & Future*. World Scientific Publishing Co. Pte. Ltd.

Wajdi, A., & Bouheraoua, S. (2011). *The Framework of Maqasid Al-Shari'ah and its implication for Islamic Finance*. Islam and Civilizational Renewl ICR Journal.

Wardhani, N., & Arshad, S. (2012). *The Role of Shari'ah Board in Islamic Banks: A Case Study of Malaysia, Indonesia and Brunei Darussalam. 2nd ISRA Colloquium 'Islamic Finance in a Challenging Economy: Moving Forward.'*

Wehr, H. (1976). A Dictionary of Modern Written Arabic (3rd ed.).

Zahid, S. N., & Khan, I. (2019). Islamic corporate governance: The significance and functioning of Shari'ah supervisory board in Islamic banking. *Turkish Journal of Islamic Economics, 6*(1), 87–108. https://doi.org/10.26414/a048

8 Shariah Audit Practices in Islamic Financial Institutions

Yasir Aziz, Muhammad Asif Khan, and Fadillah Mansor

8.1 Background of Shariah Audit

The term 'audit' is derived from the Latin word 'audire', which means 'he hears' (E, 1979). Auditing primarily entailed only a stewardship role. At that time, the function of audit was expanded to include notifying the associates of an organization whether its administration invested their money as intended. Watts and Zimmerman (1983) contend that prior to the eighteenth century, investors may have operated as both directors and auditors. So, the managing directors provide reports to other directors and shareholders of the company. Some of the other directors may also be chosen as an auditor to show how good they are at running the business. These reports demonstrate that no fraud or embezzlement has occurred. In the same way, Napier (1997) says that auditing was traditionally done by the company's auditors (internal and external), directors, and shareholders, who were all responsible for the financial reputation of the company.

The concept of an audit is not new to the Islamic worldview. From the early Islamic period, Islamic literature records the views of Muslim scholars on accounting and auditing, showcasing their eloquent consultations on the financial issues of their times from an Islamic viewpoint based on Al-Quran (divine revelations) and As-Sunnah (prophetic traditions). These documented works attest to the Islamic scholars' obedience to Allah's (SWT) countless commands in the Holy Quran, which emphasize the need to document one's acts and activities. In truth, Allah's (SWT) angels meticulously record every action and deed performed by humans, for which they will be held accountable in the Hereafter. In several places in the Holy Quran, Allah (SWT) tells people to keep accurate records of their transactions. He stresses the need to keep track of acts and deeds in all kinds of transactions, including economic ones.

The institution of Hisbah and the function of the *Muhtasib* to oversee, regulate, and stop fraudulent consumer exploitation in the marketplace date back to the period of Prophet Muhammad (SAW) and the first four Caliphs in Islamic history. The Hisbah institution is in charge of choosing qualified people to fulfil the duty of urging people to do well and prevent them from doing bad. The fundamental goals of the Hisbah institution were to protect the

DOI: 10.4324/9781003324836-8

community's members from wrongdoing, uphold their religious convictions, and guarantee that both their religious practices and worldly affairs properly adhered to the divine rule. The Holy Prophet (SAW) designated a team of managers called '*muhtasib*' to carry out these tasks.

Muhtasib was responsible for ensuring conformity with Shariah standards in the functioning of marketplaces and bazaars (Mirakhor, 2000). Precisely, they were accountable for verifying the weights and measurements of trade commodities to avoid fraud, and they had the authority to examine the notaries who recorded the contracts on behalf of the parties and sale deeds (Abdullah, 2010). The tasks of Hisbah, as shown by its *muhtasib*, resemble those of Shariah audit in many ways. In the end, Hisbah was put into place to help control society and the economy so that all Islamic rules are followed.

In addition, Hisbah was responsible for overseeing ethical commercial and accounting procedures in the community (Gambling & Karim, 1993). Likewise, Rahman (2008) acknowledges the role of Hisbah in the company's governance framework and accountability. In a larger sense, the *muhtasib's* function was to protect the holiness of the community by directing its members to engage in economic pursuits as specified by divine revelation. So, Hisbah's work is similar to Shariah auditing, whose main goal is to make sure that Islamic banking operations are good for society and follow Shariah rules so that *Maqasid al-Shariah* can be reached.

Therefore, auditing in an Islamic context would have a broader scope than conventional auditing. To seek Allah's (SWT) blessings, auditors might use a variety of tactics and aims for the first scenario, such as respecting Shariah standards. In contrast, the functions and methods of traditional auditors in IFI are notably distinct from those of their Islamic counterparts, who have been challenged by a number of Muslim academics. For example, Khan (1985) believes that conventional auditors' responsibility in a capitalist context is to reassure management and shareholders about financial difficulties. On the other hand, in IFI auditors ensure all business transactions are examined based on Islamic standards. This makes sure that the organization's goals are met and that society continues to benefit from what it does.

8.2 Overview of Shariah Audit

Due to recent financial scandals and firm closures, internal auditors are becoming more important in organizations (Belshaw & Nodeland, 2022; Schneider, 2009). For instance, large corporations like WorldCom, Enron, State Street Corporation, and Boeing Company have experienced financial frauds. Effectiveness is a major concern for everyone involved in auditing, like the auditors or the banks' main clients, including (1) the Governance and Audit and Committees and Board of Directors; (2) top management, who make sure that the auditors' tasks cover the most important business risks; and (3) external auditors, who are directly interested in the operations of the internal auditor

(Lenz & Hahn, 2015; Mattei, Grossi, & Am, 2021). Consequently, there is a rise in the need for Shariah auditors to perform the supervisory role and to avoid financial frauds/misuse in IFIs. Auditors are essential in both traditional and Shariah-compliant corporate governance. The auditors are entrusted with maintaining the company's overall financial integrity (Muneeza & Hassan, 2014). According to Aziz et al. (2019), Shariah auditing may be used to assess values that are in conformity with Shariah, hence, it does not reject the entire procedures and processes of traditional auditing. Furthermore, Yahya (2018) said that the socioeconomic framework and culture of Islamic society may benefit from auditing approaches learned from traditional auditing in the financial industry. Internal Shariah auditing has the same goal as auditing in traditional financial firms. The Auditing Standard No. 1 for IFI says that Shariah auditing gives IBs a declaration that their transactions are in line with Shariah laws and principles.

Islamic economic system is an essential component of its jurisprudence, which also addresses the ethical, political, social, and religious facets of life. It is founded on the *fiqh al-muamalat* (law of business), which is influenced by religion. This legislation, according to Allah's divine law and his last prophet, Muhammad (PBUH), stresses the transparency of contractual commitments while also taking into account social justice, fairness, and equality in economic operations. It also promotes entrepreneurship and property rights protection (Salman & Nawaz, 2018). As a consequence, the Shariah audit is crucial to achieving the aforementioned goals and fulfilling Maqasid al-Shariah (Yasoa et al., 2018). As a result, it is important for IBs to improve their Shariah audit structure and make sure that their products and transactions comply with Shariah (Masruki et al., 2020).

A Shariah audit is a procedure that provides an unbiased examination of the IFI's risk management, internal controls, governance procedures, and overall acquiescence with Shariah in its daily operations and activities, (Bank Negara, 2019). Shariah governance says that IFIs must have a Shariah audit function. This function's job is to give stakeholders an independent opinion on whether or not the organization has control on non-compliance risk. It also promotes transparency and accountability and helps to gain the trust of all its stakeholders. This job is also seen as one of the most important parts of good risk management and building a strong foundation for the IFI to follow Shariah rules and principles (Embi & Shafii, 2018). In order to make sure that Shariah is followed, there should be a good Shariah auditing framework that helps to improve the functions of Shariah auditing.

According to 'Accounting and Auditing Organization for Islamic Financial Institutions' (hereafter, AAOIFI, 2015), one of the duties of the Governance and audit Committee is to appraise the auditing process in order to make sure that those banks are adequately supervised. The Audit and Governance Committee (AGC) is also tasked with overseeing the management's adopted strategy. When the AGC makes crucial queries about the internal control system, it is expected that they would be well-informed about the IFI's operations and the monitored environment. It must accept the conclusions reached by both external and internal auditors and evaluate any difficulties or problems that may have arisen. Aside from reviewing the resources, skills, job description, general task, and reporting structure for internal auditors, the AGC is also tasked with evaluating the effectiveness of the internal control mechanisms focusing on audit results, letters from external auditors, other important reports from the management and controlling authorities, and their feedback. The AGC also serves as a reviewer of the audit plan and accounting procedures, paying special attention to the nature and parameters of the audit evaluation. This notably relates to dangerous regions as well as the resources and skills of the auditors; collaboration between the internal auditors of the IFIs and the external auditors; and preservation of the auditors' independence and professional integrity. Additionally, the committee must take into account the appointment, removal, and resignation of the Shariah Supervisory Board (SSB) members, as well as the external auditors and director of the audit department (AAOIFI, 2015).

8.3 Types of Audits

8.3.1 Internal Audit

The role of financial institutions has grown more dynamic, and the industry has adapted creative business strategies in response to the ongoing pressure to operate profitably. The primary goal of internal auditing is the provision of objective consulting services and independent assurance that are meant to improve and advance an organization's operations. Using a multidisciplinary and systematic approach to look at and advance the efficiency of governance structure and risk management practices helps an organization in achieving its targeted goals (International Professional Practices Framework (IPPF), p. 2, IIA-99). To this end, internal auditors are anticipated to perform management and compliance audits in a larger and more proactive capacity, helping financial institutions to accomplish their aims and objectives. Management should use an active auditing mechanism as a resource to pursue their targeted goals. Internal auditors should evaluate the effectiveness of the established policies and processes in addition to the soundness and sufficiency of internal controls. Internal auditors should tell administration if the organization's policies and procedures are enough to protect it from new risks.

Based on the universal auditing standards, there is an explicit connection between external and internal auditors. Rules that tune this connection include the following: meetings between the internal and external auditor should take place often to address issues that they have in common and those that have an impact on the external auditor's position; the performance of internal auditors should be evaluated by the external auditor in light of the assigned scope; the internal auditing processes should be well-known to the external auditor so that they may evaluate the financial statement and check for any potential major misstatements. In order to improve internal auditing plans and procedures, the external auditor should oversee the organization and execution of the internal auditing function. The internal auditor should be notified of the areas that the external auditor should prioritize, and the external auditor should be provided the documentation required to boost the efficacy of the audit efforts (Haron et al., 2004).

8.3.2 Shariah Audit

'Shariah audit is the investigation of the Islamic financial institutions' compliance with Shariah in all of its activities' (Hanif, 2011). Shariah audit is the most recent advancement in the domain of Shariah governance in the international Islamic banking sector. This preserves the legitimacy of the Islamic banks' assertions of Shariah conformity, which are often met with scepticism by detractors. The role of the external Shariah auditors is to determine if an Islamic bank's offerings, agreements, and behaviour are in line with any decisions made by the central bank's Shariah board and the bank's own SSB. The audit's scope may include ensuring adherence to global Shariah norms like those set out by the AAOIFI. The goal of the external Shariah audit is to find out with a fair amount of certainty if the IFI has followed 'Shariah principles and norms' in all important ways when it comes to contracts, financial arrangements, and transactions during the audited period. The AAOIFI rules mandate that IFIs hire an outside auditor to ensure Shariah compliance (Chapra & Habib, 2002). An internal auditor's duties are distinct from those of an external auditor. The job of the external auditor is to give a transparent understanding of the bank's transactions, and the job of the internal Sharia auditor is to evaluate Shariah compliance by looking at the governance, control, and monitoring of IBs (Alama et al., 2020; Chapra, 2014).

8.3.2.1 Objectives of Shariah Audit

(1) The Shariah audit process tries to keep and increase stakeholder trust in Shariah problems by making sure that the product is managed according to the Shariah principles outlined in the Shariah advisory board's initial Shariah compliance fatwa.
(2) The audits must make sure that none of the organization's operations or activities go against what is known as Shariah law.
(3) A Shariah audit provides the product with assurance that it will go on operating without interruption in compliance with Shariah norms.
(4) Because it is obvious to all parties, the Shariah audit procedure as a whole also makes it simpler to sell goods that adhere to Islamic law.
(5) You may save time and money by having an outside Shariah audit done. When something has been checked by an outside Shariah auditor, investors are more likely to believe that it is in line with Shariah.

8.3.2.2 Scope of the Shariah Audit

The socioeconomic framework and culture of Islamic civilization may benefit from auditing methods that evolved from conventional finance sector auditing (Kamaruddin & Hanefah, 2018). It seems sensible that internal Shariah audits have comparable goals to those of conventional financial firms. But if you look at ASIFI No. 1, there are some differences, since it says that Shariah auditing gives assurance that an IB's transactions are in line with national accounting standards, AAOIFI standards, and Shariah principles. Additionally, IFIs have additional goals that call for defining a broader scope. Traditional auditing places a strong emphasis on examining the financial statement and verifying the veracity of transactions and documents (Khalifa et al., 2007). Therefore, the emphasis of auditing in a conventional banking institution is solely from a materialistic standpoint and, as a result, is restricted to policies and processes as well as the financial statement, but Shariah audit has a broader scope in IFIs (Hanif, 2011; Kamaruddin & Hanefah, 2018; Khan, 1985; Sultan, 2007). The Shariah control system takes into account internal Shariah audits as a way to measure how well and how much Shariah is being followed to find out how committed IBs are to achieving their goals (Shafii et al., 2010).

Internal Shariah audits not only have a broader reach, but they also concentrate on the specifics of overall operations to provide a basic assessment of the state of the IB's adherence to the Shariah guidelines and fatwas given by its Shariah committee (Kasim et al., 2013). Anything that could pose a Shariah risk should be audited (Sultan, 2007). This includes IT, people, goods, calculating zakat, operations, financial matters, rules, and processes. The AAOIFI guidelines stipulate that successful auditing should fulfil transparency requirements, which can only be achieved by giving enough evidence to let the auditor suggest that the IB is in conformity with the fundamental tenets of Shariah and the fatwas issued by its SSB. The AAOIFI's governance guidelines for IBs specify that the auditor shall submit their remarks on the yearly financial statement as another crucial aspect (AAOIFI, 1999). Literature from the past (Grais & Pellegrini, 2006; Khalid et al., 2018) says that it's best to hire both internal and external auditors. This could make it easier for internal auditors to give a fair opinion about the final financial statement.

8.3.2.3 Shariah Auditor's Role

From an Islamic perspective, the job of audit is considerably more crucial and necessary since it demonstrates the auditor's responsibility is not limited to the stakeholders but also, in the end, to the Creator, Allah (S.W.T.), Muslims have faith in that Allah is always observing their actions and thoughts (the concept of Muraqabah). These auditors should know what Shariah is and how it affects the products, services, and business operations of Islamic banks.

The traditional or conventional audit framework limits the responsibility of auditors to the certification of financial transactions and the expression of an opinion on a company's financial status (Khan, 1985). However, there is little question that a routine audit has a significant impact on the auditing job in Islamic institutions (Othman & Ameer, 2015). According to the organization's articles of association, the Shariah auditors' tasks and responsibilities at the outset of the construction of the Shariah economic system are divided into three categories (Lewis, 2014). Shariah auditors first present assistance to the administration of the company about whether or not the bank's contractual arrangements and new products are in compliance with Shariah.

The degree to which the bank conducts its business according to Islamic principles is also disclosed in an independent report, which is given to shareholders. Third, a zakat audit is required to make sure that the zakat money is being calculated, managed, and distributed appropriately. Zakat is a unique almsgiving fee. To make sure that the rules and laws of Shariah are followed, a Shariah auditor needs to do an audit of all activities that produce income for the company and ensure all the activities are Shariah-compliant. If there is a non Shariah-compliant case, the role of the Shariah auditor is also to advise the company about the Shariah non-compliance risk, and normally they advise the company to withdraw the activities according to the Shariah purification process. According to a Pricewaterhouse Cooper study from 2010, the majority of the institutions included treasury, credit administration, recovery, operations, legal, disbursements, and Shariah fatwa procedures in their Shariah audit scope. However, just 50% of respondents had included risk management and human resources in their Shariah audit (PwC, 2011).

According to another viewpoint, the major concerns in the financial accounts of Islamic banks are the subject of a comparable audit that should be performed by a Shariah auditor. The funding (debt or equity), investments, risk management, hedging techniques, revenue and cost recognition, distribution of profit, and calculation and payment of zakat may all be attested to in order to accomplish this audit (Mohd Hanefah et al., 2014). Additionally, an audit of Islamic banks' operations is necessary to make sure that they are beneficial to the general public, investors, depositors, and shareholders. Additionally, this audit aims to make sure that they don't endanger the general public (Lahsasna et al., 2013; Yussof, 2013).

Yahya and Mahzan (2012) make the case that Shariah auditors have a very different function in the Islamic economy since they are responsible to the general public and preserve Islamic standards. The Shariah auditor is required to do compliance audits of the organization's structure, personnel, and processes, as well as audit assessments of how well the Shariah governance process works. They must also make suggestions to the Board Audit Committee (Othman & Ameer, 2015). It is also the responsibility of the Shariah auditor to look over contracts, product structures, transaction reports, financial records, marketing data, and other legal documents that relate to how Islamic banking works (Othman & Ameer, 2015).

8.4 The Process of Shariah Audit

An essential step in ensuring corporate accountability and raising stakeholder confidence in management's stewardship is auditing. The following tasks take place in the Shariah audit process as shown in Figure 8.1:

(1) Planning: selecting the appropriate team, time period for executing the Shariah audit, and preparing a suitable audit program and checklists are part of the Shariah audit planning process.

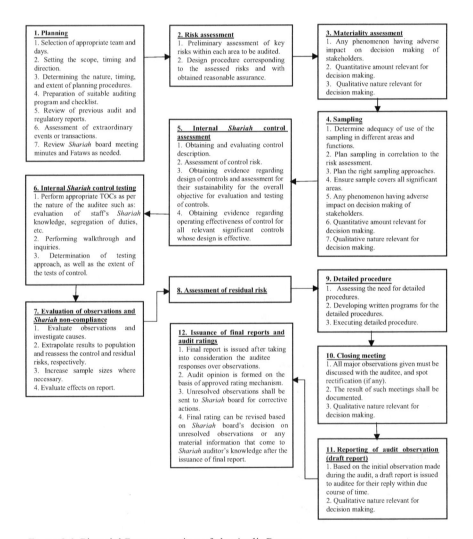

Figure 8.1 Pictorial Representation of the Audit Process.

(2) Risk assessment: during the Shariah audit process, a preliminary assessment of the key risks within each area needs to be audited.
(3) Materiality assessment: the audit team must assess any phenomenon having an adverse impact on decision-making both qualitatively and quantitatively.
(4) Sampling: the audit team should select appropriate sampling approaches for selecting right sample size and to ensure that the sample covers all significant areas.
(5) Internal Shariah control assessment: it is necessary for the audit team to assess the internal Shariah controls by obtaining evidence regarding the design of controls and assessment of their suitability for the overall objective of evaluation and testing controls.
(6) Internal Shariah controls testing: the audit team should use suitable strategies to test the internal Shariah control such as evaluating the staff knowledge regarding their duties, product, and services they offer.
(7) Evaluation of observations and non-Shariah compliance: the Shariah audit team should investigate the non-Shariah compliance events and root out the causes. Extrapolate results to the population and reassess the control and residual risks.
(8) Assessment of residual risks:
(9) Detail procedure: the audit team needs to develop a written program for the detailed procedure.
(10) Closing meeting: the audit team needs to discuss all major observations with the auditee and rectify any error and omission if needed, results of this meeting must be documented.
(11) Reporting of audit observation (draft report): based on initial observation during the audit, a draft report is issued to the auditee for their reply within the due course of time.
(12) Issuance of final reports and audit rating: the final report is issued after considering the auditee's response over observation. The audit team sends unresolved observations to the Shariah board for corrective action.

8.4.1 Accounting and Auditing Organization for Islamic Financial Institutions (AAOIFI)

AAOIFI is a regulatory body established for governing Islamic financial institutions in 1991, and issuing a number of standards and guidelines on Shariah governance, accounting, auditing, and ethics for IFIs. AAOIFI has shed light on the Shariah audit and provided a comprehensive roadmap for the Shariah audit. AAOIFI's Auditing Standards highlight that the objective of a Shariah audit is 'to provide guidance on the performance of an independent assurance engagement (to be referred to in this standard as the external Shariah audit) to ensure compliance of an Islamic Financial Institution (IFI) with the Shariah principles and rules' (AAOIFI, 2010). This statement illustrates that the Shariah audit has comprehensive rules and guidelines for IFIs which pave the path for better governance.

Guidelines issued by AAOIFI on Shariah audit in IFIs are considered the most relevant guidelines in the available practices for Shariah audit frameworks. Besides the internal Shariah framework, the IFIs have an in-house Shariah supervisory board (SSB) which is responsible for certifying the adherence of Islamic financial institutions to Shariah. The internal Shariah audit has to be carried out by an independent Shariah department/division of the IFIs or part of the internal Shariah department (AAOIFI, 2010). This department/division operates within the IFI to evaluate and examine the extent of compliance with Shariah principles, fatwas (a ruling on particular points of Islamic law issued by recognized authorities), and guidelines issued by the SSB of the IFIs. The Shariah department works under the supervision of SSB directions and ensures adherence to Shariah compliance within the IFIs.

The internal Shariah audit framework in the IFIs is an integral part of the Shariah governance which operates under the umbrella of IFI's policies and guidelines that consists of a statement of purpose, a detailed outline of authorities, and responsibilities. This document is prepared by the management which conforms to the Shariah principles and is approved by the SSB, issued by the board of directors of the IFI, and needs to be reviewed regularly (AAOIFI, 2010). The Shariah audit practices in Malaysia, Pakistan, and the Middle East is explained in the next section.

8.5 Practices of Shariah Audit in Malaysia

In the Malaysian financial market, an accelerated development and expansion have been witnessed in Islamic financial institutions in the last few decades which amplified the need for comprehensive regulation and good governance (Isa et al., 2020). Bank Negara Malaysia (BNM) established Shariah Governance Framework (SGF) in 2010 which is used by Islamic financial institutions for the establishment of the governance structure and to improve their transparency. This document categorically provides the functions of Shariah audit which is one of the required businesses of the IFIs in addition to other activities, including Shariah Risk Management, Shariah Review, and Shariah Research.

In 2010, the Islamic Financial Services Board (IFSB) was created as an accounting and auditing agency to oversee Islamic financial institutions and make Islamic financial products (Khatib et al., 2022). The bank Negara necessitates commercial banks to conduct an internal audit by the department of internal Shariah audit and requires an external auditor in order to perform the daily transactions of these banks according to Islamic principles. The BNM Shariah Governance Framework reviews and audits distinct definitions. Shariah auditing is 'the periodic examination undertaken from time to time to give an impartial review and objective assurance meant to add value and increase the degree of compliance with regard to the IFI's business activities'. Shariah audits include organizational structure, financial accounts, and Shariah governance (SGF, 2010). The IFI's Shariah audit section has relevant expertise and training. The SGF (2010) defines 'Shariah review' as 'the periodical examination of the IFI's activities for Shariah compliance to guarantee that the IFI's activities and operations are Shariah-compliant'. A Shariah examination covers just the IFI's commercial activities and not the full statement. The difference between the two terms is evident from the above definitions of 'audit' and 'review'. 'Sharia audit' refers to an independent and periodic assessment of the financial statements, whereas in 'Shariah review' a regular assessment of the activities is compulsory rather than independent review' (meaning review is more frequent than an audit), and it is concerned about 'Shariah compliance' of the business activities and operations of the IFIs.

In reality, the main goal of the Shariah audit is to make sure that the Shariah is being followed, which is a key part of how an Islamic financial institution works. In 2013, an Act was passed to strengthen the oversight tasks of the Shariah committee and ensure compliance with the Shariah practices in IFIs. This act describes in detail the regulations and procedure of supervision of the IFIs, Islamic foreign exchange market, payment system, and relevant entities for enhancing financial stability, the providence of Shariah-compliant financial services, and related matters (Islamic Financial Services Act 2013).

It is noted that SGF 2010 does not explain in detail the areas of Shariah and types of Shariah knowledge required for the internal auditors to conduct Shariah audits (Isa et al., 2020). The Shariah Governance Policy Document (2019) states that IFIs must execute a Shariah audit by a competent person who knows the relevant Shariah principles. This paper demonstrates that the internal auditor may contact the Shariah officer to do his work effectively as long as the main audit aim is not compromised (BNM, 2010). The senior officer is responsible for the Shariah audit, which is part of IFIs' internal audits to ensure Shariah compliance and objective attainment. In reality, the board can choose anyone to do an external audit to give the board and Shariah Committee of IFIs independent assurance about how well operations, business, affairs, and activities comply with Shariah.

These developments in the Islamic financial services industry demonstrate great attention to the compatibility of financial services provided by these institutions with Shariah in Malaysia. These developments may bring more financial benefits, including attracting good investments in Malaysia, and obtaining benefits by sharing experience in Shariah audit and Shariah compliance practices with other countries.

8.6 Practices of Shariah Audit in the Middle East

Various Shariah audit procedures are now used in Islamic financial firms (IFIs). Some IFIs have a separate internal Shariah audit unit that conducts internal Shariah audits; other institutions contract with external auditors to carry out their internal Shariah audits; and yet other institutions do Shariah reviews rather than internal Shariah audits (Khalid et al., 2018). Reviewing the financial accounts of well-known IFIs based in Bahrain reveals that the majority of them performed a Shariah review rather than a Shariah audit (Shafii et al., 2015). The IFIs do, however, recognize the value of a Shariah audit.

Shariah audits and reviews are handled differently by AAOIFI, BNM, and IFSB. AAOIFI rules only use the word 'Shariah review' in reference to an IFI's conformity with Shariah in relation to the audit of its financial accounts. As a result, AAOIFI distinguishes between 'Shariah audit' and 'Shariah review'. In a Shariah audit, IFIs examine the financial information to determine whether or not the business operations they conduct comply with Shariah. While conducting a Shariah review, the SSB examines whether IFIs adhere to Shariah in all of their operations (Khalid et al., 2018).

In contrast, the IFSB's Guiding Principles for Shariah Governance Systems interchangeably use the terms 'Shariah audit' and 'Shariah review'. The terms 'audit' and 'review' were used interchangeably. For instance, the IFSB (2009) described review and audit as 'verifying that Shariah compliance has been fulfilled, during which any event of non-compliance shall be noted and reported, and as far as feasible, addressed and corrected'.

Since 1979, the Kingdom of Bahrain achieved various milestones in the Islamic financial sector and became the hub of global Islamic financial services. It was mandated for the Islamic banks to have the Shariah Supervisory Board at an earlier stage, anecdotal evidences show that from 2008–2010 and up until 2017, it was mandatory for the IFIs to have both Shariah Supervisory Board and internal audit function. In 2016, the centralized Shariah Supervisory Board (CSSB) was established by the Central Bank of Bahrain which issued new modules in 2017 entitled Shariah Governance Module. The regulators implemented new requirements for Shariah governance in IFIs which include two internal Shariah departments, implemented external Shariah auditing and mandated the SSB. It is also mandated by the Central Bank of Bahrain for IFIs to have three Shariah scholars in their SSB that is one of the requirements of AAOIFI. In term of Shariah audit functions in the IFIs, SG-4.1.4 mentioned the following categories that are needed to be examined when analysing the adherence business of the IFIs to the Shariah compliance requirements. They are as follows: (a) Sharia principles; (b) Shariah-related directives, regulations, and resolutions issued by the CBB; (c) the fatwas of the SSB, in addition to their pronouncements, instructions/recommendations, and guidelines; (d) AAOIFI Shariah standards; and (e) Shariah-related policies of the Islamic bank.

Saudi Arabian Monetary Authority (SAMA) regulates financial sector operations in Saudi Arabia. SAMA performs as the Central Bank of the Kingdom of Saudi Arabia that regulates the functions of Islamic financial institutions operating in the Kingdom of Saudi Arabia. SAMA has promogulated business rules for the Islamic banks to ensure adherence to the rules of Shariah, including Shariah audit functions. It is mandated for the

IFIs to conduct Shariah audit at least once a year that may be conducted as part of audit practices in the IFIs. The Shariah audit will be performed by internal Shariah auditors who have Shariah-related knowledge. In addition, the internal Shariah auditors may engage an expert Shariah officer to perform the Shariah audit, as long as the independence of the Shariah audit is not compromised at all. It is also mandatory for the audit committee to submit the internal Shariah audit findings and observations to Shariah committee and board audit committee.

8.7 Practices of Shariah Audit in Pakistan

In Pakistan, there is a broad Islamic banking movement across the nation. The switch-over plan was carried out in stages since it was such an enormous undertaking. Beginning on 1 July 1979, the activities of specialized financial organizations, including the Investment Corporation of Pakistan, the National Investment Trust, and the House Building Finance Corporation, were converted to an Islamic-based structure. On 1 January 1981, the commercial banks that had been taken over by the government and the one foreign bank each opened an interest-free counter to attract deposits based on how much money they made or lost. All commercial banking activities became 'interest-free' as of 1 July 1985. No Pakistani bank, even those from outside, was permitted to take any interest-bearing deposits after that day. All current bank deposits were handled as if they shared in the profits and losses. Foreign currency loans and deposits, however, were still managed according to interest rates. In the meantime, the government also passed the Mudarabah Companies Act of 1984, which let banks or businesses set up their own Mudaraba companies in a country.

The State Bank of Pakistan (hereafter, SPB) is the organization in charge of overseeing Islamic banking in Pakistan. To aid in the growth of IFIs, the SPB created the Islamic Banking Department (IBD), which works closely with the Inspection and Supervision Department and the Policy and Regulatory Department. The IBD collaborates with the rest of the SBP and the banking sector to provide helpful regulatory advice relating to general Shariah compliance and particular problems/challenges experienced by Pakistan's Islamic banks.

To provide clients and investors with trust in the Islamic banking sector, SBP has implemented a thorough and powerful multi-tiered Shariah compliance process. Shariah compliance has three main parts: (a) Shariah advisors in all banks who advise and reassure banks about Islamic financial services; (b) a Shariah Board at SBP that approves policies, guidelines, and qualifications for advisors; and (c) a Shariah audit system. The inspection handbook, which was created by Bahrain-based Ernst & Young in conjunction with their branch in Pakistan, forms the foundation for the Shariah audit system. It is highly detailed. The Shariah audit system is needed to make sure that the terms of

Islamic contracts, the fatwa on the transaction, and the order in which the agreement is carried out all follow Shariah law.

The financial statements are prepared in accordance with AAOIFI standards, and the inspection is focused on inspecting the transactions in accordance with these standards. In addition to the standard SBP examination, all Islamic banks will be subjected to the Shariah Compliance Inspection. Shariah compliance audits of Islamic banks look at their buildings, operations, services, goods, accounting records, and financial statements to make sure all transactions follow Shariah rules. To improve the Shariah compliance process in Islamic banking, the SBP makes sure that all applicable Shariah-compliant banking laws are followed both in letter and in spirit, as well as the Shariah Compliance Framework.

The Shariah Compliance Framework in Pakistan places a strong focus on Shariah considerations while also incorporating pertinent sections of the laws, rules, regulations, policies, and practices relating to Islamic Banking that are already in place. The rules and requirements must be included in the IFI's procedures in such a way that internal control structure includes monitoring and assessing concerns relating to Shariah compliance. All of the IFI's operations, goods, and locations should be under constant observation and scrutiny for Shariah compliance. Checking whether the IFI's transactions, procedures, and products adhere to Shariah and satisfy all relevant requirements as determined by the Shariah advisor is the main goal of this duty.

IFIs in Pakistan have set up an internal Shariah audit system to make sure that all the objectives of Shariah compliance are met. Depending on the extent of the IFI's activities, the internal Shariah audit may be conducted as a different unit from the standard internal audit. The main goal of the Internal Shariah Audit is to make sure that the IFI's management is carrying out its duties in accordance with the Shariah laws and guidelines as established by SBP and the IFI's Shariah advisor. By conducting an internal Shariah audit, an institution may ensure that its Shariah compliance internal control system is both theoretically and practically sound. This is done to make sure that all the goals related to following Shariah are met.

Shariah audits are conducted in accordance with Shariah norms and principles, as well as SBP recommendations and instructions. Internal Shariah auditors communicate directly and on a regular basis with all levels of management and the Shariah advisor. There are no restrictions on access to information, records, reports, and so on. The Internal Shariah Audit reports comprise observations and evaluations of Shariah-compliant systems and processes. The Shariah report will offer improvements and corrective actions. The IFI's Shariah advisor works to solve any disagreements between management and internal Shariah auditors. The Internal Shariah Audit report is presented to the Shariah advisors for advice on suitable corrective action, and then to the IFI's Audit Committee for consideration and appropriate remedial action as suggested by the Shariah advisors. In Pakistan's IFIs, the Shariah audit results are given a lot of attention through the Shariah Supervisory Report.

Depending on the size of the bank, SBP advises all IFIs to either allocate a small number of internal audit staff members to Shariah audits or establish a distinct Shariah internal audit department. This department is in charge of the Shariah audit in the primary. There are specific instances, such as PLS profit distribution, where SBP asks banks to have an external auditor and a Shariah Advisor (SA) jointly audit the whole process. Thus, it can be said that both internal and external auditors do Shariah audits in Pakistan. Additionally, Shariah audit results were not stated in the external auditor report on Islamic banking in Pakistan. This is justified by the fact that Islamic banking is still in its infancy and that any Shariah observations of this kind would harm both the bank and the industry as a whole. Therefore, the legislation does not require that Shariah findings be included in the report. Additionally, if Shariah observations are discovered by internal or external auditors, they notify SA, who may subsequently take the appropriate measures. Also, the SBP Banking Inspection team looks at how well the bank follows Shariah law. If any problems are found, SA is told and the right steps are taken.

8.8 The Challenges of Shariah Audit

In the governance framework of IFIs, Shariah auditors are crucial. All Shariah standards must be followed, and the auditors are in charge of making sure that goals are achieved, claims Karim (1990). Internal auditors who are adequately knowledgeable and skilled in Shariah-related matters may carry out the Shariah audit role. The internal auditors must play a role in ensuring that an internal control system is in place that is sound and effective and closely adheres to Shariah standards in order to accomplish the ultimate objectives. Shariah auditing provides stakeholders with a particular level of confidence. However, it has several flaws and problems, such as a lack of expertise in both finance and Shariah and independence from outside influences (Kasim et al., 2013; Khalid et al., 2019). Even though IFIs have to follow a number of laws, rules, accounting standards, and guidelines, more needs to be done to make sure that Shariah audit is governed by the right standards or a framework that can help IFIs be more uniform.

8.8.1 Adequacy of Standards for Shariah Auditing Procedures

The IFIs are required to adhere to Shariah standards, which forbid, among other things, the use of interest in economic transactions. This demonstrates the need for a comprehensive set of integrated Shariah auditing requirements. The accounting practices and standards used by IFIs to prepare their financial reports are not currently regulated. Due to this situation, the IFIs have created their own sets of rules and regulations for different commercial dealings based on consultations between the management, the SSB, and outside auditors. For instance, Abul Hassan et al. (2021) found that Al-Rahji had produced the Shariah Monitoring Guide and Shariah Control Guidelines to ensure proper monitoring and implementation of Shariah principles and decisions. But the fact that there aren't any auditing standards that take Shariah principles into account could lead to wrong interpretations of Shariah decisions and provide a strong argument against regulating IFIs.

8.8.2 Independence of Shariah Auditors

The apparent independence of the Shariah auditors themselves, both in appearance and behaviour, has led IFI stakeholders to see auditors as having integrity. If the Shariah auditors are independent enough to express views on the IFIs' standing with regard to Shariah compliance, their integrity may be further reinforced (Kasim et al., 2009). The (SSB) of IFIs monitors governance to ensure that transactions strictly comply with the Shariah's tenets (Toufik, 2015). The SSB performs audits to guarantee Shariah compliance, which is considered akin to what corporation auditors do, even though they have no direct control over the top management. In other words, the problem of independence and conflict of interest is raised when the SSB, who are paid by the organization where they work, audit their own work. Haniffah (2010) contends that the SSB's independence is compromised by its involvement in overseeing the operations and output of IFIs while also carrying out Shariah audits or reviews. AAOIFI's standards regarding the independence of the Shariah auditor clearly state that: 'It is the responsibility of the head of internal Shariah audit to ensure that his subordinates maintain independence and avoid conflict of interest, and are able to discharge their responsibilities without prejudice.'

8.8.3 Shariah Auditor's Qualification

Competency is the capacity or a group of specified behaviours that provide organized guidance to make it easier for people to identify, assess, and develop the behaviours necessary to do a job well. An auditor needs solid accounting and Shariah expertise in order to comprehend and complete a Shariah audit. For this reason, it is essential that Islamic institutions make financial investments in the education of their Shariah auditors in order to advance their knowledge and skills (Ahmad & Al-Aidaros, 2015; Rahman, 2011; Shafii et al., 2014). Despite the fact that the members of the SSB are well-trained in the role of issuing fatwas about whether or not any financial items are permissible, Najeeb and Hameed (2013) contend that they are incompetent auditors due to a lack of the necessary credentials and training. The development of Shariah auditing and the Islamic financial industry as a whole may suffer from a shortage of auditing professionals who are proficient in both conventional and Shariah audits. As a result, it may not be possible to determine how Islam's vision and goals were upheld by the IFIs. Because of this, IFIs need certified Shariah-compliant auditors with experience in accounting and auditing as soon as possible.

8.8.4 Shariah Auditor's Accountability

Internal or external auditors with Shariah knowledge may perform Shariah audits (Yaacob, 2012). The IFIs' Shariah committee receives the report. Shariah committee members may only provide their opinions to the Board of Directors, which makes the final decision. Shariah auditors are thought to just create financial reports and not affect IFI decision-making. Shariah auditors would have been more responsible since they are accountable to shareholders, the community, the ummah, and Allah for all acts and inactions. The SSB committee reviews the financial report for Shariah-related problems before presenting it to the Board of Directors, which makes the final decision.

8.8.5 Shariah Auditor's Competence

Hameed (2008) highlights the problem of the capability of SSB members to undertake Shariah audits. The author says that members of the SSB are qualified to give fatwas about whether a financial instrument is legal or not, but they don't have the training and certification to act as certified auditors. In addition, it has been noticed that regularly planned meetings may not be enough to settle certain pressing problems facing the bank. Therefore, the authors recommend that the Shariah Committee undertake a full audit over a one-year period and publish a statement of Shariah's opinion in the annual report. Since the majority of members of the Shariah Committee have technical expertise in Islamic law, rapid product development makes it challenging to accommodate new financial products into the Shariah framework. Some cases, such as those involving a conflict of laws or iktilaf, as well as the fact that Shariah conclusions are based solely on Shafie-based scholars, cannot be universally accepted. It is thus a challenge for Malaysian practitioners to consider fatwas that are more internationally acceptable. Abdelgader et al. have also expressed another worry about the SSB's ability to undertake such an audit. They point out a few important things that auditors need to pay attention to, such as their responsibility to investors, their evaluation of management practices, social audit, and religious audit (which is meant to make sure that Islamic banks' operations follow Shariah principles).

8.9 Structure of Audit Framework

From the standpoint of the Shariah committee, external auditors, and internal auditors, Abdul Rahman (2008a) gives a helpful assessment of the problems, concerns, and limits in the application of Shariah auditing. Specifically, he highlights the necessity for a standardized Shariah auditing framework that would serve as a guide for all parties conducting such an audit. Having a framework would assist IFIs to build appropriate Shariah auditing protocols, procedures, and processes, as well as prerequisite requirements (like qualifications and certifications) for Shariah auditors. Shariah

8.10 Conclusion

Shariah audit is the key part of Shariah governance in the Islamic financial system, as the rules governing operations and activities of the Islamic financial institutions stem from the overall Shariah governing framework in which IFIs operate. The Shariah governing framework differentiates Islamic financial system from the conventional financial system, therefore, the governing bodies of the Islamic financial institutions give great importance to the Shariah governance. For this reason, scholars and practitioners documented various aspects of Shariah governance that enrich the knowledge of Shariah governance in the IFIs. This chapter highlighted the process of Shariah audit documented by AAOIFI for IFIs which consists of 12 different stages starting from planning a detailed Shariah audit procedure and ending with submitting the final report to the Shariah board for corrective action. Shariah audit practices in different countries are also documented which includes Malaysia, Pakistan, and the Middle East. This chapter discussed the key challenges of Shariah audit including independence of the Shariah auditor, adequacy of the Shariah auditor, qualification and accountability of the Shariah auditor. Shariah

Bibliography

AAOIFI (2010). GSIFI06 : External Shariah Audit (Independent Assurance Engagement on an Islamic Financial Institution's Compliance with Shariah Principles and Rules. Accounting and Auditing Organization for Islamic Financial Institutions, Manama.

Abul Hassan, M., Sadiq, S., & Md Mahfuzur Rahaman, M. (2021). Sharīʿah Governance and Agency Dynamics of Islamic Banking Operations in the Kingdom of Saudi Arabia. *ISRA International Journal of Islamic Finance*.

Abdul Rahman, A. R. (2008a). Issues in corporate accountability and governance: An Islamic perspective. *The American Journal of Islamic Social Sciences*, 15(1), 55–71

Ahmad, M. R., & Al-Aidaros, A. H. (2015). The need of independent Shari'ah members in Islamic cooperative banks: An empirical study of professional accountants in Malaysia. *International Review of Management and Business Research*, 4(1), 110–120.

Alama, K., Rahman, S. A., Thakur, O. A., Bashir, A., & Hosen, S. (2020). *The reasons behind the absence of a comprehensive* Shari'ah *Governance Framework of Islamic banks in Bangladesh*.

BNM (2010). Shariah Governance Framework for Islamic Financial Institutions. Bank Negara Malaysia, Kuala Lumpur.

Chapra, M. U., & Ahmed, H. (2002). *Corporate Governance in Islamic Financial Institutions*.

Embi, S., & Shafii, Z. (2018). The impact of Shari'ah governance and corporate governance on the risk management practices: Evidence from local and foreign Islamic banks in Malaysia. *The Journal of Muamalat and Islamic Finance Research*, 1–20.

Gambling, T., & Karim, R. A. A. (1993). *Business and Accounting Ethics in Islam.* New York.

Grais, W., & Pellegrini, M. (2006). *Corporate governance and* Shari'ah *compliance in institutions offering Islamic financial services* (Vol. 4054). World Bank Publications.

Hameed, S. (2008). The case for Islamic auditing. International Accountant, Issue 41, May 2008.

Haniffa, R. (2010). Auditing Islamic Financial Institutions. *QFinance Newsletter,* p. 14.

Haron, H., Chambers, A., Ramsi, R., & Ismail, I. (2004). The reliance of external auditors on internal auditors. *Managerial Auditing Journal.*

Hassan, Y. M. (2016). Determinants of audit report lag: Evidence from Palestine. *Journal of Accounting in Emerging Economies.*

Isa, F. S., Ariffin, N. M., & Abidin, N. H. Z. (2020). Shari'ah audit practices in Malaysia: Moving forward. *Journal of Islamic Finance, 9*(2), 42–58.

Kamaruddin, M. I. H., & Hanefah, M. M. (2021). An empirical investigation on waqf governance practices in waqf institutions in Malaysia. *Journal of Financial Reporting and Accounting.*

Karim, R. A. A. (1990). The independence of religious and external auditors: The case of Islamic banks. *Accounting, Auditing & Accountability Journal, 3*(3), 0–0.

Kasim, N., Ibrahim, S. H. M., & Sulaiman, M. (2009). Sharī'ah Auditing in Islamic Financial Institutions: Exploring the Gap Between the 'Desired' and the 'Actual'. *Global Economy and Finance Journal, 2*(2), 127–137.

Kasim, N., NuHtay, M. S. N., & Salman, S. A. (2013). Shari'ah governance for Islamic capital market: A step forward. *International Journal of Educational Research, 1*(6), 1–14.

Khalid, A. A., Halim, H. A., & Sarea, A. M. (2019). Exploring Undergraduate Students' Awareness of Internal Sharī'ah Auditing in Malaysia. *Humanities and Social Sciences Reviews, 7*(1), 461–468.

Khalid, A. A., Haron, H., & Masron, T. A. (2018). Competency and effectiveness of internal Shari'ah audit in Islamic financial institutions. *Journal of Islamic Accounting and Business Research.*

Khalid, A. A., Haron, H., & Masron, T. A. (2018). Competency and effectiveness of internal Shari'ah audit in Islamic financial institutions. *Journal of Islamic Accounting and Business Research.*

Khalifa, R., Sharma, N., Humphrey, C., & Robson, K. (2007). Discourse and audit change: Transformations in methodology in the professional audit field. *Accounting, Auditing & Accountability Journal.*

Khan, M. A. (1985). Role of the auditor in an Islamic Economy. *Journal of Research in Islamic Economics.*

Khatib, S. F., Abdullah, D. F., Al Amosh, H., Bazhair, A. H., & Kabara, A. S. (2022). Shari'ah auditing: Analyzing the past to prepare for the future. *Journal of Islamic Accounting and Business Research.*

Lahsasna, A., Ibrahim, S. H. H. M., & Alhabshi, S. O. (2013). Sharī'ah Audit: Evidence and Methodology in Islamic Finance. Available at: http://citeseerx.ist.psu.edu/view doc/download?doi=10.1.1.683.9097&rep=rep1&type=pdf (accessed 14 March 2023).

Lenz, R. and Hahn, U. (2015). A synthesis of empirical internal audit effectiveness literature pointing to new research opportunities, *Managerial Auditing Journal, 30*(1), 5–33.

Lewis, F. (2012). Auditing capability and active living in the built environment. *Journal of Human Development and Capabilities, 13*(2), 295–315.

Masruki, R., Hanefah, M. M., & Dhar, B. K. (2020). Shari'ah governance practices of Malaysian Islamic banks in the light of Shari'ah compliance. *Asian Journal of Accounting and Governance*.

Mattei, G., Grossi, G., & AM, J. G. (2021). Exploring past, present and future trends in public sector auditing research: A literature review. *Meditari Accountancy Research*.

Mirakhor, A. (2000). General characteristics of an Islamic economic system. *Anthology of Islamic banking, institute of Islamic banking and insurance, London*, 11–31.

Muneeza, A., & Hassan, R. (2014). Shari'ah corporate governance: The need for a special governance code. *Corporate Governance*.

Najib, S. F., & Ibrahim, S.H.M. (2013). Professionalizing the role of Shariah auditors: How Malaysia can generate economic benefits. *Pacific Basin Journal of Finance*, 28(1), 1–24.

Napier, C. J. (1997). *Auditing*. External Publications, University of London.

Othman, R., & Ameer, R. (2015). Conceptualizing the duties and roles of auditors in Islamic financial institutions: What makes them different? *Humanomics*.

Othman, R., & Ameer, R. (2015). Conceptualizing the duties and roles of auditors in Islamic financial institutions: what makes them different? *Humanomics*.

PWC (2012). Shariah Audit: Industry Insights. www.isfin.net/sites/isfin.com/files/shariah-auditsecured.pdf

Rahman, A.R.A. (2011). *Shariah Audit: An Analytical Perspective. Proceedings of International Shariah Audit Conference 2011*. Crown Plaza Mutiara.

Rana, T., Steccolini, I., Bracci, E., & Mihret, D. G. (2022). Performance auditing in the public sector: A systematic literature review and future research avenues. *Financial Accountability & Management*, 38(3), 337–359.

Salman, A., & Nawaz, H. (2018). Islamic financial system and conventional banking: A comparison. *Arab Economic and Business Journal*, 13(2), 155–167.

Shafi, Z., Abidin, A. Z., & Salleh, S. (2015). Integrated Internal-External Shariah Audit Model: A Proposal towards the Enhancement of Shariah Assurance Practices in Islamic Financial Institutions. Working Papers No 1436-7. The Islamic Research and Teaching Institute (IRTI).

Shafii, Z., Salleh, S., & Shahwan, S. H. (2010). Management of Shari'ah non-compliance audit risk in the Islamic financial institutions via the development of Shari'ah compliance audit framework and Shari'ah audit programme. *Kyoto Bulletin of Islamic Area Studies*, 3(2), 3–16.

Shafii, Z., Salleh, S., Zakaria, N., Hanefah, M. M., Ali, N. A. M., & Yunanda, R. A. (2014). Shari'ah audit certification contents: Views of regulators, Shari'ah committee, Shari'ah reviewers and undergraduate students. *International Journal of Economics and Finance*.

Sultan, S. A. M. (2007). *A Mini Guide to Shari'ah Audit for Islamic Financial Institutions- A Primer*. CERT Publications Sdn Bhd.

Toufik, B. B. (2015). The role of Shari'ah supervisory board in ensuring good corporate governance practice in Islamic banks. *International Journal of Contemporary Applied Sciences*, 2(2), 109–118.

Watts, R. L., & Zimmerman, J. L. (1983). Agency problems, auditing, and the theory of the firm: Some evidence. *The Journal of Law and Economics*, 26(3), 613–633.

Yaacob, H., & Donglah, N. K. (2012). Shariah audit in Islamic financial institutions: The postgraduates' perspective. *International Journal of Economics and Finance*, 4(12), 224–239.

Yahya, Y. (2018). A review of Shari'ah auditing practices in ensuring governance in Islamic financial institution (Ifis)–A Preliminary Study. *Advances in Social Sciences Research Journal*, 5(7).

Yahya, Y., & Mahzan, N. M. (2012). *The Role of Internal Auditing in Ensuring Governance in Islamic Financial Institution (IFI)*.

Yasoa, M. R., Abdullah, W. A. W., & Endut, W. A. (2018). Shari'ah audit effectiveness in Islamic Banks: A conceptual framework. *Auditing*, 2(10), 12–19.

Yussof, S. A. (2013). Prospects of a Shari'ah audit framework for Islamic financial institutions in Malaysia. *Islam and Civilisational Renewal (ICR)*, 4(1).

9 Shariah Governance for Islamic Financial Institutions

Imran Hussain Minhas

9.1 Introduction

The origin of the term 'governance' comes from the ancient Greek verb 'kubernan' which means 'to pilot' or 'to steer', and Plato used it for designing a system of rule (Mazhar et al., 2015). The word governance closely resembles the word government which is derived from the French word 'gouvernement'. Root of the word gouvernement is found in the early French word 'gouvernance' that was used to express the art of governing (Torfing et al., 2012).

Governance has been defined by the Commission on Global Governance as 'governance is the sum of the many ways individuals and institutions, public and private, manage their common affairs. It is a continuing process through which conflicting or diverse interests may be accommodated and cooperative action may be taken. It includes formal institutions and regimes empowered to enforce compliance, as well as informal arrangements that people and institutions either have agreed to or perceive to be in their interest.' The governance is a process instead of an activity or set of rules; it is based on coordination of public and private sector rather than a control only; the governance is ongoing interaction and not a formal institution (Keping, 2018).

Governance serves as a protection tool for the governments, public sector enterprises, corporates, business and non-business entities and working groups. It protects an organization from various known and hidden risks, events and problems threatening the administration, management, revenues, and smooth operations. It is claimed that no governance at all, or bad governance, leads to all evils including corruption, losses, failure, and collapse of the societies and organizations. Good governance is always based on a well-defined set of laws, rules, regulations, guidelines, and policies approved, implemented, and enforced by the public sector regulatory bodies, law-enforcing agencies or the corporates in their respective domains. Governance has been defined by the International Bureau of Education, United Nations Educational, Scientific and Cultural Organization (UNESCO) as 'structures and processes that are designed to ensure accountability, transparency, responsiveness, rule of law, stability, equity and inclusiveness, empowerment, and broad-based participation'. Governance also refers to the set standards, rules of game and values

DOI: 10.4324/9781003324836-9

necessary to manage the public affairs in participatory, transparent, and responsive manner (UNESCO, 2022).

The governance infrastructure introduced by the corporate regulators for their regulatees is known as corporate governance. It means presence of necessary legislation to ensure protection of the stakeholders, existence of effective risk management framework, clear and well-defined responsibilities and authorities, transparency and fairness in operations and reporting supported by the judicial system of accountability. Corporate governance is defined as 'Corporate governance involves a set of relationships between a company's management, its board, its shareholders and other stakeholders. Corporate governance also provides the structure through which the objectives of the company are set, and the means of attaining those objectives and monitoring performance are determined' (OECD, 2015). Regulators use corporate governance as one of the regulatory tools to evaluate and strengthen the legal and regulatory framework of the corporate sector to ensure financial stability, investors' protection along with sustainable economic growth besides the accountability of wrongdoers.

Islam upholds the concept of governance and accountability. It gives a complete code and guidance, which are close to the concept of governance framework, to human beings as to how spend their lives. Accountability is one of the major themes of Islam in this world and hereafter. In this world punishment of many social crimes has been prescribed for example 'cutting the hands off thieves' and 'death penalty to murderer' and for some crimes where complete justice is not served, on the Day of Judgment the criminals will have to face God as well. For violation of commandments of the Quran and Sunnah of the Holy Prophet Mohammad (peace be upon him) or any misdeed, mankind is accountable to God as mentioned in the Quran in the following words:

يَا بُنَيَّ إِنَّهَا إِن تَكُ مِثْقَالَ حَبَّةٍ مِّنْ خَرْدَلٍ فَتَكُن فِي صَخْرَةٍ أَوْ فِي السَّمَاوَاتِ أَوْ فِي الْأَرْضِ يَأْتِ بِهَا اللَّهُ إِنَّ اللَّهَ لَطِيفٌ خَبِيرٌ (١٦)

Oh my child (said Luqman) Surely if it (your deed) is the very weight of the grain of a mustard-seed, even though it is in a rock, or in the heavens or in the earth, Allah will bring it (before you in your life film on the Day of Resurrection). Surely Allah is Subtle (owner of subtleties), all-aware.

(Al-Quran 31:16)

On doomsday everyone will be asked for his/her actions and deeds he/she performed in this world and will get reward or punishment for their good or bad deeds, even if they are the tiniest. The concept of accountability given in the above verse of Quran can be considered as the foundation of every law and governance framework in Islamic Shariah.

Literally, Shariah means the path to water (reference), in religious context it is the righteous path derived from the teachings of Quran and Sunnah. It is divine law that provides necessary guidelines to spend lives within the sphere of Islam. The implementation of Islamic Shariah in the corporate governance is called Shariah governance.

Shariah governance as per Islamic Financial Services Board (IFSB) is 'the set of institutional and organizational arrangements through which an international/national IFIs ensures that there is effective independent oversight of Shari'ah compliance over issuance of relevant Shari'ah pronouncements/resolutions, dissemination of information on such Shari'ah, and an internal Shari'ah compliance review for verifying that Shari'ah compliance' (COMCEC, 2020). Shariah governance is simply defined as 'the set of institutional and organizational, arrangements, policies, processes, procedures rules, regulations and laws which lead the organization towards Shari'ah compliance' (Minhas, 2012). Shariah Governance Framework (SGF) has been defined by the Malaysian banking regulator as 'the Shari'ah governance framework is a set of organizational arrangements through which Islamic financial institutions (IFIs) ensure effective oversight, responsibility and accountability of the board of directors, management and Shari'ah committee' (BNM & FSPSR, 2009).

Governance is a way to manage affairs in the best interest of the stakeholders whereas corporate governance is a set of regulations for the regulators and boards for stable operations, productivity, reduce risks, improve performance and reputation of the business. In addition to the corporate governance, compliance of Shariah requirements is a mandatory part of Islamic business and the only reason for existence of the Islamic financial institutions. The unique feature of IFIs is the Shariah governance which, being an integral part of the IFIs, ensures stability, public confidence, satisfaction of the users and business management in conformity with the principles of Islam. Although Shariah compliance is a permanent challenge for the management of the IFIs, a sound and well-functioning Shariah governance framework can minimize the risk of Shariah non-compliance.

9.2 Importance of the Shariah Governance in IFIs

Shariah governance framework should provide a complete solution to the Shariah-related issues by ensuring all possible compliance with the Islamic principles not only in the operations, products, processes and systems of the IFIs but also in the policies, strategies and documents. The concept of Shariah governance cannot be undermined and ignored in the Islamic finance industry. It is closer to the concept of Hisbah in Islam that means an act of counting or evaluating a thing or to perform an act for seeking reward after death or good deed for the common cause. The concept lies in the Quranic verses (3:104 and 3:110) where it is said:

'الامر بالمعروف والنهي عن المنكر'

It means enjoining the good and forbidding the evil. Two important duties have been assigned to the human by the God; one is to promote good and the other to prevent evil. SGF serves the same purposes for the players and stakeholders of Islamic financial system (IFS).

The globalization of Shariah-compliant industry has reinforced the mysticism of Islamic values and the Islamic financial industry has witnessed a tremendous growth in all of its segments including Islamic banking, Islamic fund management, takaful and sukuk industries during the last three decades. This growth is not restricted to Islamic countries only, as with its presence in more than 75 jurisdictions, it is a worldwide subject now. The global Islamic finance assets are consistently showing double-digit growth and have reached to US$2.7 trillion in 2020 (IFSR, 2021) from US$826 billion in 2010. S&P expects consistent growth pattern in the future as well and has projected 10% to 12% growth in global Islamic financial assets in 2021–2022. Rapid growth, increase in numbers of Islamic financial institutions, growing demand, accumulation of a sizeable amount of assets and competition with the conventional counterparts have increased the chances of errors and misdirection. Any compromise on Shariah issues may greatly expose the IFIs to Shariah non-compliance risk (SNCR) which arises due to failure of internal controls, system and people and broadly covered under the operational risk. IFSB has defined the SNCR as the risk of loss due to the 'failure of the IBs to comply with the Shariah rules and principles determined by the Shariah board or the relevant body in the jurisdiction in which the IB operates'.

Shariah non-compliance risk has become a crucial risk for the IFIs more than ever and it is most difficult to manage. There is no scientific method to manage and mitigate the Shariah non-compliance risk as compared to other banking risks like credit, market, operations, liquidity and rate of return except to put in place a comprehensive and effective SGF within the IFI. SGF can help to ensure maximum Shariah compliance and minimum SNCR in the IFI. In the absence of Shariah compliance there is no reason for the IFIs and Shariah-compliant products to exist. Shariah governance is very important for compliance of the Islamic values and principles while practising Islamic banking and finance (IBF). Some of the areas which are highly important for the SGF are summarized below:

(a) Shariah compliance is the only reason to introduce a new banking system parallel to the conventional which is possible with the existence of reliable SGF.
(b) Shariah compliance is the nucleus for confidence and trust building of the users of Islamic financial products.
(c) Shariah governance framework can serve to raise early warning signals where compliance is weak or compromised due to any reason including insufficient knowledge and incapacity of the operational management.
(d) SGF is essential to provide comprehensive guidelines on role, responsibility and accountability of the board of directors (BoD), Shariah board, executive management, Shariah advisors, Shariah compliance officers and Shariah auditors.

(e) Shariah governance is imperative for fair and transparent reporting, disclosure and confidence of the investors, promoters and collaborators.
(f) Growing size and numbers of the Islamic financial industry necessitate transparent, fair and trusted system to regulate Islamic financial business and products in accordance with the Islamic principles.
(g) Shariah governance is significant to offer truly Shariah-compliant products and services and execute the financing, selling, renting and agency transactions within strict parameters of Islamic business.
(h) Shariah governance is important to minimize unnecessary charities of legitimate income of the IFI.
(i) SGF is a key to mitigate Shariah non-compliance and reputational risks of the Islamic finance industry.

Shariah governance framework helps the faith-based customers to park their money in the financial system for economic growth of the economy, which otherwise is locked at home in order to avoid *Riba*. Shariah governance has its cost as well which is associated with the appointment of Shariah board, Shariah compliance reviewers, Shariah auditors and Shariah training experts. These costs are in addition to all other costs of management and infrastructure which a conventional financial institution incurs. This is actually the cost of doing Islamic financial business and we may call it the cost of Shariah. Some investors may view cost of Shariah as unnecessary, undesirable and expensive but it has its own advantages and the foremost benefit is compliance with the commandments of Allah (swt). Shariah governance is also beneficial and for the worldly business as it attracts a large number of masses who do not wish to deal in *Riba*. In short Shariah governance framework serves the business and humanity in both ways – one for worldly gains and second, but the most important, for the blessings of Allah (swt). All the time it provides guidance and charter to ensure Shariah compliance in financial transactions with complete transparency, efficient oversight and effective control. It provides the governance foundations to practice banking, capital market operations, insurance, fund management and any other businesses in Islamic way.

9.3 Evolution of Shariah Governance Framework

The purpose of SGF is absolute Shariah compliance which can be achieved with the chained and coordinated efforts. The compliance process starts from the BoD and comes to an end with the annual report of the Shariah supervisory board of the IFI. There are lots of stages, and processes between these two ends which need to be established and facilitated through a reliable SGF, capable to establish, assess, guide, operate, examine, rectify and report the affairs of Islamic financial institution. It is important to clearly prescribe, in SGF, the role, responsibilities and functions of each and every segment of the IFI. It is necessary that members of the BoD are qualified enough to understand and implement the requirements of Shariah in the financial institution. Second, an independent Shariah board, capable senior management and trained staff, can guarantee successful operations of a Shariah-compliant institute.

The concept of Shariah board was started in 1976 by the Faisal Islamic Bank, Egypt, followed by some other Islamic banks in Jordan, Sudan, Kuwait and then the rest of the world practising Islamic banking. Some independent entities such as Accounting and Auditing Organization for Islamic Financial Institutions (AAOIFI) in February 1990 in Bahrain and the Islamic Financial Services Board (IFSB) in November 2002 at Kuala Lumpur, Malaysia, were also established to standardize and harmonize the Islamic financial products, practices and strengthen the Shariah governance framework and regulations (Zulkifli, 2012).

Islamic banking and finance started its journey towards Shariah compliance from self-governing compliance of Islamic principles by appointing Shariah advisors or boards, voluntarily in the IFIs. The regulatory bodies introduced proper regulations and Shariah governance frameworks after the birth of Islamic banking in their jurisdictions in majority of the cases. Islamic banking increased in numbers and size gradually and consequently the regulatory bodies realized the importance of regulations and Shariah governance. Initially the regulatory bodies prescribed minimum requirements for the IBF, some of the regulators prescribed requirements of Shariah board of the IFIs; others set up their own Shariah boards as well. Early risers towards the legislation of Islamic finance who ultimately moved towards effective Shariah governance frameworks are discussed below.

In 1980, the Government of Pakistan, in order to promote true Islamic financial institutions, promulgated the 'Modarabas Companies (Floatation and Control) Ordinance 1980' (Modaraba Ordinance, 1980; SECP, 1980) to enable the incorporation of modaraba companies, the non-banking Islamic financial institutions which were authorized to undertake Islamic financing, trading of goods and commodities, or manufacturing business. The modaraba companies were also allowed to accept deposit from the general public in the form of certificates of investment. Section 9 of the Modaraba Ordinance 1980 (SECP, 1980) stipulates the requirement of Religious Board for Modaraba Companies (RBM). It was first example in the world of any legislation for the Islamic finance industry and RBM was the first Shariah board which was established at the national level under any law. Shariah compliance of the businesses of Modarabas was the responsibility of the RBM (SECP, 1980; Modarabas, 1980). On the other side central bank of Pakistan (SBP) issued proper policies and criteria for the promotion and establishment of Islamic banking institutions (IBIs) in 2003. The policies contain three categories to undertake Islamic banking business in the county, (a) stand-alone Islamic Banking Institutions; (b) IBI as subsidiary of the conventional bank; and (c) independent Islamic banking branches (IBBs) of the conventional banks. For Shariah governance purposes, compulsory Shariah board was the requirement of the first two categories whereas the Islamic banking under category three was allowed under the supervision of a Shariah advisor or Shariah supervisory committee. SBP also established its own Shariah board in 2003 (BPD Circular No. 1, 2003) which has been renamed as Shariah Advisory Committee in 2018 (IBD Circular Letter No. 1, 2018).

The corporate regulator of Pakistan, Securities and Exchange Commission (SECP), being regulator of the nonbanking Islamic financial industry and Islamic capital market, introduced SGF for the first time as Shariah Compliance and Shariah Audit Mechanism (SCSAM) for Modarabas (non-banking IFIs) in 2012 which had three parts for effective Shariah compliance: (a) Shariah Compliance, it describes the responsibilities of the management towards Shariah compliance, different avenues of investments and screening method and income purification process; (b) Shariah Advisors, this part includes the qualification, appointment, role, responsibilities, powers, reporting, and performance review process for the Shariah advisors along with the dispute resolution mechanism; and (c) Shariah Audits, it tells the role, duties and reporting of Shariah auditors and compliance framework of the Shariah audit reports. Violation of any provision of the said framework was a criminal offence (SCSAM, 2012). In 2018, SECP enhanced the scope of SCSAM for Shariah-compliant companies in addition to the non-banking IFIs, by issuing Shariah Governance Regulations 2018 (SECP, 2018).

Malaysia is another example where proper law, Islamic Banking Act 1983, for IBF was introduced. It was the first law to regulate the Islamic banks (IBs) in Malaysia and the oldest in the world for the Islamic banking industry. Requirement to establish Shariah advisory board for the Islamic banks was also introduced under this law (Laldin, 2018). In 2013, Malaysia repealed the Islamic Banking Act 1983 by issuing Islamic Financial Services Act. The Malaysian Securities Commission, the Islamic capital markets regulator and the Bank Negara, Islamic banking regulator, constituted their separate Shariah Advisory Councils (SAC) in 1996 and 1997 respectively.

UAE is the other jurisdiction which follows Shariah as the major source of law, and the Law No. 5 of the UAE Federal Law of 1985 ('the Law 1985') recognizes the Islamic financing contracts whereas Law No. 6 of the Law 1985 is concerning Islamic banking, its article 5 contemplates the concept of considering Higher Shariah Authority in the country to oversee Shariah compliance in the financial sector of the country (Amjad et al., 2019).

The Government of Sudan also decided in 1989 to replace the conventional banking system with Islamic banking and in 1991 the central bank of Sudan promulgated the Banking Business (Organization) Act, stating that all banks and banking transactions must be conducted according to Shariah. Prior to this Act, in 1984 the Sudanese Court of Appeal declared that charging interest is a criminal offence and the whole banking system was made Shariah based (Fady et al., 2011).

Many other jurisdictions issued regulations for the Islamic financial industry and prescribed requirement of Shariah boards in the regulations, like central bank of Kuwait issued law number 30 of 2003, to add special section for Islamic banking and prescribed requirement of the Shariah supervisory board at the central bank's level for Shariah governance purposes (CBK Law 30, 2003). Dubai Financial Services Authority (DFSA) issued a law 'Regulating Islamic Financial Business DIFC Law No. 13' in September 2004 and prescribed Islamic Finance Rules (IFR) under the law. Clause 3.5 of the IFR prescribes the requirement of Shariah supervisory board of at least three scholars for Shariah governance purposes (DFSA Rule Book, IFR). Qatar Finance Center and Central Bank of Bahrain also introduced Islamic Finance Rules in 2005. Central bank of Libya amended The Banking Law 2005 in 2012 to introduce regulated Islamic banking in Libya, along with other requirements such as the requirement to set up a Shariah Supervisory Authority in IBI is also introduced for the Shariah governance purposes (Zainab et al., 2018). Central bank of Nigeria introduced full-fledged Islamic banking in 2012 and issued regulations to govern Islamic banking which required that IBI shall appoint an Advisory Council of Experts (ACE) to oversee the Shariah compliance functions in the Islamic banks (Sadad et al., 2021).

United States introduced amendments vide Office of the Comptroller of the Currency Interpretive Letters No. 806 and No. 807 from 1999 and 2001 to allow banks use of Islamic contracts of rent (Ijarah) and sale (murabahah) to finance the housing sector. Similarly, the UK Financial Services Authority since 2004 regulates murabahah, Ijarah and diminishing musharakah as Regulated Mortgage Contracts for home financing and Home Purchase Plans (Lee, 2016; Dar, 2004).

9.4 Shariah Governance Frameworks of AAOIFI and IFSB

In this part, popular SGF prescribed by the two globally prominent bodies, AAOIFI and Islamic Financial Services Board (IFSB) which are engaged in the development and standardization of Islamic financial system are discussed. AAOIFI and IFSB are the independent bodies established in 1991 and 2002 respectively with the objectives of issuing and setting standards for the global Islamic banking, capital market, takaful industries and the regulators. AAOIFI is the first body at global level which is established as a non-profit organization to support Islamic finance industry by issuing standards for different operational areas of Islamic finance industry. AAOIFI is supported by over 200 organizations including regulatory bodies, IFIs, private audit and law firms from 45 countries. The second organization, IFSB, was founded by the Islamic Development Bank and a consortium of central banks to set standards, provide guidance and awareness to Islamic finance regulatory bodies on the issues that could hamper the growth of Islamic finance. It has 187 members including 81 supervisory and regulatory bodies, 10 government organizations and 96 corporate bodies and exchanges from 57 countries. Both the organizations are considered as high-level standards-setting bodies for the IBF sector with slightly different mandates. Major work of the AAOIFI is for the industry players whereas work of the IFSB is largely for the use and guidance of regulatory and supervisory bodies.

9.5 Governance Standards of AAOIFI

AAOIFI has a Shariah board (the Board), comprising 20 top Shariah scholars from all over the world. No standard is issued by the AAOIFI without approval of the board. The board is responsible to review, examine and approve all the standards according to the principles of Islam. AAOIFI, focusing on the individual IFIs, has issued 100 standards including 57 Shariah, 29 accounting, 5 auditing, 7 governance standards and 2 codes of ethics for IFIs and their professionals to harmonize and standardize the practices, modes and products of global Islamic finance industry. The standards are not compulsory for the members to adopt but the members may opt to follow the whole or partial standards voluntarily. A member may also choose to follow the standards set by the AAOIFI after making some changes in the provisions of the standards, if the Shariah scholars of the member countries do not approve the standard as a whole or some of its provisions. Presently all the leading IFIs in the world and many of the regulatory bodies are following the standards issued by the AAOIFI in one or the other forms.

In the late 1990s AAOIFI took the task to standardize SGF for IFIs by issuing guidelines on the basic framework of Shariah governance in the Governance Standards GS 1 to 5. Now there are 13 governance standards out of which GS-6 covers Statement on Governance Principles, GS-7 is on Corporate Social Responsibility, GS-8 discusses the role and responsibilities of Central Shariah Board for the Regulators, GS-10 is on Shariah Compliance and Fiduciary Ratings, GS-12 prescribes Sukuk Governance framework, GS-13 prescribes Governance framework for Waqf. The rest of the standards which are directly related to the SGF of the IFIs are discussed below.

GS-1 outlines the requirements for the independent Shariah Supervisory Board (SSB) for the IFIs, was declared effective for the financial statements in the financial period starting from 1 January 1999. It laid down the requirements regarding issuance of the Shariah report of the SSB, the appointment of the SSB, its composition, term, role and dismissal process of the SSB of the IFI. GS-1 stipulates that every IFI shall appoint SSB, consisting of three to five members, with the approval of the shareholders on the agreed terms and conditions. The members of the SSB should be specialized in Fiqh ul Muamulaat; however, the SSB may include one member, expert in the area of IBF and have some knowledge of Fiqh ul Muamulaat and shall be authorized to seek services of the external experts in law, banking, economics or accounting. The duties of SSB should include directing and supervising the functions of IFI to ensure Shariah compliance and decisions of the SSB shall be binding on the IFI. The SSB shall submit its report on the affairs, operations, earnings of the IFIs to the stakeholders as per components of the report given in the GS-1. GS-5, which is effective from 1 January 2008, prescribes that SSB should be free from conflict of interest, independent, intellectually honest, fair and perform their duties in public interest for the better public confidence. The SSB members should not be involved in managerial or executive decision making as well.

GS-2 provides guidance to SSB in conducting Shariah reviews of memorandum, and articles of associations, contracts, policies, products, financial statements and audit reports, it requires the SSB shall consider the circulars of the supervisory bodies, Islamic principles, previous fatwas, decision and rulings before forming opinion thereon. The standards guide on process and planning of Shariah review, executing procedures, preparing working papers and submitting review report. The standard holds management of the IFIs responsible for the Shariah compliance. The standard is effective from 1 January 1999.

GS-3 is about internal Shariah review (ISR) and requires that ISR should be carried out by an independent auditor or division to assess that management is performing their duties as desired by the SSB of the IFI. The ISR department must have purpose, approved charter and full support of BoD and management of the IFI. The staff of ISR should be qualified and must comply with the AAOIFI's code of ethics to exercise due care while performing their job. The head of internal Shariah review will submit written report to the BoD, SSB and the management of the IFI. The standard is effective from 1 January 2000.

GS-4 is about audit and establishment of governance committee at the board level, to enhance public confidence with transparency, proper disclosure in the financial reports, and internal audit reports, internal controls accounting practices, etc. The standard stipulates that the committee should consist of at least three knowledgeable members reporting to the BoD of the IFIs by ensuring integrity of reporting in the best interest of the stakeholders. Effective date of the standard is 1 January 2002.

GS-9 prescribes requirement for Shariah compliance functions under the Shariah Compliance Department (SCD) within the IFI. The standard stipulates that management must ensure proper Shariah compliance system exists and functions on preventive and detective control approaches in the IFI. The standard also discusses the structure, key functions, compliance review process, independence, compliance techniques and tools regarding reporting, escalation and follow-up of the issues. SCD should have qualified staff to serve as secretariat to the SSB. The standard is effective from 1 July 2021.

GS-11 is the improved version of GS-3 for Internal Shariah Audit (ISA). It was issued and adopted in June 1999 and stipulates framework for the Internal Shariah Audit (ISA) and internal controls of the IFIs. The ISA will perform its work according to approved manual and SOPs. The standard discusses the qualification of auditors, audit functions, its scope, plans, engagement, process flow, working, papers, materiality of reporting, sampling mechanism and IT audit techniques along with some other related areas. The standard allows establishing in-house ISA department or outsourcing the same function to professional firms with the reporting line to the audit committee and the SSB (GS–AAOIFI).

9.6 Shariah Governance Framework of IFBS

IFBS is responsible for promoting stability and soundness of the Islamic finance industry by introducing international standards, guiding principles, conducting trainings, research and maintaining database on the Islamic finance by adhering to Shariah principles, for adoption of mainly the regulatory bodies on voluntary basis but some work may be for the use of Institution offering Islamic financial services (IIFS). Its work covers the areas of corporate governance, risk management, capital adequacy and transparency. IFSB has issued 'Guiding Principles on Shariah Governance Systems for Institutions offering Islamic Financial Services' ('the Guiding Principles'). The Guiding Principles covers Shariah governance system, requirements of the Shariah board and other segments. It requires that Shariah governance should not only be the responsibility of the Shariah board but the management, regulatory bodies, clients and all other stakeholder shall also join hands to achieve the objective of Shariah compliance in the IFIs.

The Guiding Principles have five parts. Part One discusses the general approach for SGF and good governance practices including requirements for the Shariah boards. Part Two relates to the area of competency, expertise, skills, professional development and performance of the board. Independence of the Shariah is discussed in Part Three to avoid any conflicts of interest. Part Four focuses on the confidentiality and Part Five is about professionalism of the board members to enhance credibility of the SGF.

First part of the Guiding Principle requires every IIFS to have Shariah board, with clear scope and responsibility regarding Shariah compliance in all the offered products and services of the institution. Supervisory authorities may decide about the responsibilities of the Shariah board with regard to governance and client protection for effective management of the system. It also prescribes to appoint a minimum three members of the Shariah board from different schools of thoughts having some exposure to banking, commerce or finance by fulfilling the fit and proper criteria ('F&P') prescribed by the supervisory authorities.

Part One of the Guiding Principles also sets out that the Shariah boards of IIFS must have clear mandate, responsibility and terms of reference regarding operating procedures, reporting line, observance of professional code of ethics and accountability towards the stakeholders. The Principles strongly recommend IIFS to build in house capacity for Shariah compliance by having internal Shariah compliance unit, comprising of the appropriately experienced and qualified staff, to serve as first contact point for the Shariah board and serve as secretarial office of the Shariah board. The Code of ethics for the Shariah board members is another important area which can be addressed through adoption of internationally recognized codes or by developing the codes in house. The supervisory authorities may prescribe requirements of the code of ethics for the Shariah board members for their working and to avoid any possible conflicts of interest with the IIFS.

Part two of the Guiding Principles prescribes that, for public confidence the person authorized to oversee the Shariah governance should meet the F&P, commonly used by the regulators. The F&P may include the requirements of (a) good character based on reputation, honesty and integrity demonstrated over time, and (b) competence and capability; that the person responsible to implement Shariah Governance Standards technically understands the business and its risks. This may be assessed by setting requirements of qualification, experience and consistency in past and present judgments. The BoD may consider other important factors, if deemed fit, on a case-to-case basis while appointing the Shariah board members. If the products and size of Islamic business operations of the IIFS are limited and small, the IIFS may also outsource the function of Shariah compliance to some external Shariah advisory firms and the BoD will be responsible to ensure and periodically check the level of competency of the staff working in such firms.

The IIFS should also facilitate professional development of Shariah board members and officers of the compliance unit on continuous basis through arrangement of training programs or other similar capacity enhancement events. Training needs must also be assessed, and necessary training on latest developments in Islamic markets should be given to the Shariah board on ongoing basis enabling them to update and strengthen the internal controls according to changing demands. Performance of the Shariah board should also be evaluated, on the basis of comparison with the peer groups and criteria already agreed, and communicated to them to give an idea as to what is required to the IFI. Shariah board may also be allowed to carry out self-assessment to effectively contribute towards their core duties. BoD should review the performance evaluation of the Shariah board for consideration of retention, termination or adding new members in the board if their performance is not found satisfactory.

Part Three of the principles is about independence of the Shariah board for a strong unbiased oversight of Shariah matters. Decision making should be independent and without any duress from the internal or external management or authority. To achieve this objective an appropriate and transparent conflict resolution system between Shariah board and the BoD or the executive management of the IIFS should be in place. In such situation the supervisory authorities should also have a conflict resolution system in place. Independence should also be ensured by discouraging the appointment in the Shariah board, of any close relative of BoD and senior management and the persons having substantial shareholding in the IIFS. In case of Shariah advisory firms, there should also not be any related party relationship between the firm and the IIFS, its directors and senior management. The members of the Shariah board should also not be the full-time employees of the IIFS. Shariah board must be given access to all the necessary information at all levels of management along with adequate support to provide the information in timely manner to enable the Shariah board to fulfil its official responsibilities in an efficient and smooth manner. Shariah board, at the expense of IIFS, must be free to seek independent opinions on legal and financial matters where deemed necessary.

Part Four of the Guiding Principles is about confidentiality of internal information which must be ensured by the members of the Shariah board while performing their duties for the IIFS. Confidential information includes the information which is not public yet like, among others, information about any new product, internal decisions of management, contents of important conversation and/or information about the customers of the IIFS. Strict professional code of ethics should be followed by the Shariah board members regarding sensitive information of the IIFS and it must not be used against the interest of the IIFS and to gain any personal benefit out of it. The terms of reference (TOR) agreed and accepted by the Shariah board members or Shariah advisory firm must expressly contain the clause to maintain secrecy and confidentiality of the business of IIFS, and consequences upon breach of this requirement may also be made clear in the TOR.

Part Five of the Guiding Principles is about consistency in the Shariah interpretation of the rules, which also reflects professional competency of the Shariah board. Decisions should be made with the consensus of all the members and the rule of simple majority may only be allowed where the decision-making process has a prolonged or reasonable time period that has elapsed in achieving the consensus. Shariah board and firms should know process of announcing or disseminating the decision or information to the general public. Whereas consistency should be ensured by following the rulings of the central Shariah boards of the regulatory bodies, decisions of internationally recognized Shariah boards or bodies like AAOIFI, OIC Fiqh Academy or national level Shariah bodies, Islamic counsels, Shuras or religious boards. The Shariah board members must be able to answer the questions of shareholders, customers, general public, associations and others regarding Shariah matters, products, processes and their decisions. Shariah compliance-related information, rulings and fatwas should be disseminated to the stakeholders through the annual reports (IFSB-10, 2009).

Shariah governance and compliance is a brain of Islamic financial system and only a capable brain can allow the body to properly live and function. The IFIs cannot accurately function, survive or exist for long in the absence of a reliable SGF. Over time, many developments and improvements in the SGFs have been witnessed. The SGFs given by AAOIFI and IFSB provide comprehensive set of principles and guidelines to the IFIs.

9.7 Jurisdictions with Forward-Looking SGF

Shariah compliance is the most critical area for the regulators and the IFIs. Some of the regulators are still relying on the bare minimum Shariah compliance requirements or on the oversights of the Shariah boards, committees and Shariah advisors of the regulatees. However, if the regulatory body prescribes effective SFG for the regulatees it may serve as a legitimate tool for deep regulatory oversight and Shariah compliance environment in the country. Therefore, many of the jurisdictions have now introduced forward-looking models and approaches to manage Shariah non-compliance risk, safeguard interest of the investors, enhance public confidence and trust in the Islamic financial system. Malaysia, Pakistan, Oman, Dubai and Bahrain took the lead in SGF followed by many others. Basic points of SGFs of some of the jurisdictions are discussed below.

Bank Negara Malaysia (BNM) has introduced proper SGF for regulatory oversight, which is mandatory to be followed by the IFIs, including Islamic banks, takaful operators and the financial institutions licensed to participate in Islamic banking schemes like the development of financial institutions. BNM issued first SGF for the IFIs in 2010 which had two-tier infrastructure of Shariah governance in the form of Shariah boards, one at the central bank's level and the second at each IFI's level. BNM provided guidelines for the Shariah committees on different important aspects including appointment, functions, roles and accountability, etc. In 2019, BNM revised the SGF and introduced certain controls for Shariah compliance culture besides responsibilities of BoD and Senior Management. The main controls include the followings:

(i) Shariah Committee (SC) consisting of minimum five members for full-fledged IFI and three members for window operators, as per the fit and proper criteria, with clear objectives to provide sound, quality and consistent advice on the business affairs of the IFIs to ensure Shariah compliance;
(ii) Control functions to manage, monitor and report SNCR;
(iii) Shariah review process;
(iv) Shariah audit for independent opinion on effectiveness of internal controls; and
(v) Transparency and disclosure to disclose the IFI's state of Shariah compliance to the stakeholders.

BoD of the IFI is responsible to provide support, resources and required information to the SC besides implementation of the SGF and decisions of the SC in the operations of IFIs. Non-compliance of the SGF is a criminal offence which may put the responsible persons behind bars for up to eight years or declare him/her liable to pay a fine up to 25 million ringgit or both as per section 29(6) of the Islamic Financial Services Act 2013.

In Pakistan, the SBP has Shariah advisory committee at national level to approve rules, regulation, standards, modes and other requirements for Islamic banking industry in the country. To ensure Shariah compliance in IBIs, the SBP in 2008 introduced Shariah compliance guidelines followed by SGF in 2014 and 2015. SBP continued all possible efforts to introduce an effective mechanism of Shariah governance in the IBIs and revised the SGF in 2018 which is applicable on Islamic banking industry of Pakistan now. The framework, besides holding the BoD responsible to implement Shariah compliance and accountability culture with the help of the executive management of the IBI, prescribes the following four main controls for effective Shariah governance:

(i) Shariah Board;
(ii) Resident Shariah Board Member;
(iii) Shariah Compliance Department supported by the product development and training department; and
(iv) Shariah Audit.

BoD of the IBI is responsible to appoint an independent SB for three years, consisting of minimum three members, qualified as per the F&P of the SBP, to supervise all the Shariah-related matters. All support shall be provided by the management to the SB and after a careful review and examination of Shariah review and audit reports, the SB will issue a report on the status of Shariah compliance to publish in the annual accounts of the IBIs. It is also required to appoint a full-time RSBM to look after Shariah affairs of the IBI on regular basis to provide guidance and to ensure compliance of the rulings and decisions of the SB. SCD, being secretariat of the SB, shall continuously watch the Shariah compliance of the IBI and for this purpose it may conduct Shariah review on sample basis to submit reports to the SB. Shariah audit, internal or external, shall conduct periodical audits and all Shariah-related reports shall be submitted to the SB for comments and guidance. Unlike the SGF of Malaysia, this SGF does not provide clear legal provisions for any penal action against the persons responsible for Shariah non-compliance (SGF 2018).

Central Bank of Oman (CBO) regulates the activities of Islamic banks and Islamic windows of the conventional banks. CBO issued Islamic Banking Regulatory Framework (IBRF) in 2012. Part 2 of the IBRF covers proper SGF for Islamic banking entities (IBEs). It stipulates that the key elements of SGF are the Shariah Supervisory Board (SSB), of the licensee, Internal Shariah Reviewer, Shariah Compliance and Audit Units, the Board and the management. The SGF prescribes that the Head of Islamic banking should be adequately qualified and have basic knowledge of Islamic banking and its products. The licensee should have its own SSB consisting of a minimum three expert Islamic scholars to be a responsible authority for all the Shariah-related matters. The small sized entities may outsource this function. To perform its function effectively, the SSB is authorized to use the reports of the internal Shariah review, compliance and audit in order to assess the level of Shariah compliance in the IBEs. BoD of the Licensee will approve the scope, composition, charter, functions and the reporting mechanism of the SSB as per F&P prescribed by the CBO. The Licensee will also be responsible to appoint Internal Shariah Reviewer (ISR) and set up Internal Shariah Compliance (ISC) and Shariah Audit (SA) Units. The SGF stipulates the role and responsibilities of these functions and defines the F&P for the ISR and the staff working in

ISC and SA units. The CBO has also established a High Shariah Supervisory Authority to give opinion on Shariah matters, facilitate sukuk issues, and faster the process of product development (IBRF, 2012).

The Central Bank of UAE (CBUAE) introduced the 'Corporate Governance Regulations for Banks' and 'Corporate Governance Standards' in 2019 (together 'the Regulations') applicable to all the licensed banks. The Corporate Governance Regulations in Article 14 cover governance requirements for the IFIs. The CBUAE issued Shariah Governance Standards (SGS) for IFIs in May 2020 which outline minimum requirements for the banks, conducting all or part of their business, according to the Shariah. The Higher Shariah Authority (HSA) of the CBUAE and Internal Shariah Supervisory Committee (ISSC), constituted by the IFI as per prescribed criteria to take care of the Shariah-related matters of the IFI. However, BoD is mainly held responsible to ensure Shariah compliance according to the rulings of both the Shariah advisory bodies. BoD's Risk Committee is entrusted with the task to supervise the Shariah non-compliance risk whereas its Audit Committee is responsible to evaluate the adequacy and effectiveness of the audit and policies relating to Shariah compliance. The Regulations prescribe that ISSC shall be independent, having minimum five members, responsible for Shariah compliance and monitoring Shariah aspects of the IFI with the help of Internal Shariah Control Division (ISCD) and Internal Shariah Audit Division (ISAD). ISSC shall issue annual report which shall be reviewed and approved by the HAS before presenting it to the shareholders of the IFI. ISCD shall perform various functions like consultation and secretarial services to the ISSC, conduct research and training, perform Shariah compliance activities for the IFI. ISAD shall undertake Shariah audits and monitoring of compliance along with reporting to ISSC and BoD's audit committee. The Standards fulfil the deficiency of regulations and Shariah compliance framework for the IFIs in UAE (SGS, 2020).

Saudi Arabia had no parallel or separate regulatory framework for the IFIs, they were considered similar to the conventional banks previously but in May 2021, the Saudi Central Bank (SAMA) issued Shariah Governance Rules (the SGR) for the financial institutions engaged in financing of real estate, assets, SME, lease, credit cards, and consumer collectively called as 'Regulated Activities'. The purpose of SGR is introducing governance framework for the FIs engaged in one or more of the Regulated Activities. The SGR also aims to comply with the principles of Shariah, by setting out clear responsibilities of the BoD and the management in respect of Regulated Activities even if the finance provider is a conventional entity. Setting up of a Shariah Committee ('the SC') to supervise compliance is a mandatory requirement under the SGR even though the BoD of the IFIs is responsible to implement policies and develop information system to be followed by the senior management regarding the compliance of the SC's rulings in Islamic facilities. The SGR also prescribes provisions to appoint committee members, their requirement, numbers, functions, responsibilities as well as the election process. Alternatively, the IFIs are also allowed to outsource the functions of the SC to external Shariah consultants, as per the SGR (Ahmed et al., 2022).

In the above jurisdictions where even, the regulators have their own CSA, the Shariah boards of IFI are free to decide Shariah matters and implement Shariah rulings as per their own judgment within their respective institution. It sometimes brings difference judgments in two IFIs in the same case. For example, it is observed that in one jurisdiction, the Shariah board of one IFI allows tawarruq and *bai al inah* based products whereas the Shariah board of another IFI, working in the same jurisdiction, does not allow both the products. The different judgments on one product create negative impact on the public perception. In such cases the role of CSA becomes very important and it must use its authority by deciding and opting one judgment, to bring clarity, uniformity and standardization within its jurisdiction. For the purpose of true Shariah compliance, greater public confidence and trust and effective and sound SGF is necessary.

After studying various Shariah governance systems it is discovered that effective Shariah compliance, based on the footprints of the real Islamic principles and values, is only possible if it is supported with the existence of necessary legislation capable to provide an enabling environment, and support of the regulator. To achieve the objective of true Shariah compliance setting up a central Shariah board under the supervision of regulatory bodies and issuance of comprehensive SGF containing strict accountability process are vital for harmony, standardization, implementation of Islamic principles and values in the financial sector. Based on the different studies, practices for Shariah governance and outcomes in various jurisdictions, we may suggest drawing major structure and components of an effective SGF on the four basic pillars which are discussed below.

9.8 Basic Pillars of an Effective Shariah Governance Model

Globally the Islamic finance industry is operating in different forms that include IFI being an independent legal entity, IBBs and windows under the conventional banks and use of selected Islamic products by the conventional financial institutions. Therefore, one standard Shariah governance model fit for all forms of Islamic financial industry will not be feasible. Thus, the countries already practising Islamic finance or looking forward to develop a viable, sound and practicable Islamic financial market must consider and prescribe requirements for Shariah governance keeping in view the actual operating model of the institution.

Presence of comprehensive Islamic finance law and Central Shariah Authority (CSA) are the vital requirements for all models of Islamic banking and finance whether it is operating as full-fledged Islamic institutions, IBB, Islamic Windows or operating with selected Islamic banking products. The

CSA should be an independent body, consisting of at least five competent scholars of Islamic Shariah and finance for regulatory oversight of the Islamic finance industry in any country. The CSA should prescribe and approve legal, regulatory and Shariah compliance frameworks, modes of financing, major products and broad process flows, documents and agreements, basic operational structure and nonfinancial activities for the IBF industry. CSA should be the sole authority to issue final Shariah verdict on all matters of inconsistency and conflicts among the Shariah scholars, products, practices and procedures of the industry players (Minhas, 2012). CSA is also necessary to help courts and government agencies in resolution of the cases and issues relating to the Shariah. The author is of the view that a trustworthy Shariah governance framework is based on following four main pillars which should be made part of every SGF.

9.8.1 Board of Directors and Senior Management

BoD and key executives serve as the first pillar for the good Shariah governance framework and their main objective is to protect the interest of the stockholders by directing and managing organizational affairs in such a manner that ensure permissible (halal) and best returns on the investments of shareholders and the depositors. The BoD should approve and communicate a clear vision, objectives and policies for smooth and uninterrupted Shariah compliant operations of the IFI. One must keep in mind that true Shariah compliance cannot be ensured without the support of dedicated, determined and competent management. Hence, the regulators must define minimum qualification, role and responsibilities of BoD and key executives of the regulated Shariah compliant entities, which may include the following.

(a) Fit and proper criteria for BoD and key executives of the IFI, containing minimum relevant academic qualification, experience, proven track record of honesty, integrity and character free from any fraud, forgery and criminal history. The regulators must also ensure that the management is willing and committed to work for the true values of Islamic Shariah and the purpose of entering into Islamic financial business is not only to earn money but also to serve Islam. All such sponsors and key executives who are averse to Islamic values must not be allowed play with the money of investors and depositors in the name of Islamic Shariah.
(b) Approval of business policies, product manuals, code of conduct and ethics, fair and transparent process of appointment, replacement, termination and compensation of the key executives.
(c) Fair and transparent business operations by clearly defining major roles and responsibilities including the implementation of Shariah governance framework. The decision making, implementation of approved policies and decisions of the regulator, must be free from personal interests, of the BoD and the key executives.

(d) Performance evaluation and accountability: The BoD should approve put in place just and fair process of performance review of the key executives and the SBMs to oversee effectiveness of SGF. In case of any misrepresentation, deception to the shareholders, depositors and the BoD, non-compliance of Shariah standards, guidelines, rules and regulations issued by the regulators, violation of instructions and policies of the bank; and inconsistency and non-implementation of the ruling and fatwas of the Shariah board a fair process of accountability and punishment of key executives and SBMs should also be part of the performance evaluation policy. Performance evaluation of SBMs should be based on the evaluation of the products, frameworks, guidelines, internal controls, Shariah rating mechanisms, and policy documents approved by the Shariah board and assessing the quality and consistency in the Shariah rulings and decisions. The IFI must share performance evaluation report to the CSA for comments before implementing any decision regarding reward or punishment against the SBMs. It will serve as a natural process of accountability and further appointment of weak and incompetent members of the board can be avoided for better Shariah compliance environment in the country.

(e) Provide all the required resources and infrastructure within the IFI, to Shariah board in order to ensure adequate internal controls and undertake the business strictly according to the principles of Shariah.

9.8.2 Shariah Advisory Board

Shariah advisory board (SAB) is the second pillar of the SGF and it is the backbone of any Shariah governance model, framework, approach or system. There is no concept of SGF without existence of the Shariah board or Shariah advisors in the IFI. An independent IFI or a conventional bank operating IBBs must have its own SAB consisting of at least three Islamic scholars besides experts from other relevant disciplines at the choice and requirement of BoD of the IFI. However, where any financial institution is operating a small network of Islamic banking windows or deals in selected Shariah compliant products like Sukuk or Musharakah based certificates, such institutions may be allowed to outsource Shariah advisory or operate with one or two Islamic scholars.

The regulatory bodies must specify some major requirements for the independent SAB of the IFIs including but not limited to the following.

(a) Fit and Proper Criteria (F&P) for Members of the SAB: The F&P must specify minimum academic qualification for the members of SAB including in Shariah, *Fiqh ul Muamulaat* and *usul al fiqh* and *Takhassus Fi al Fiqh* besides the requirement of experience in issuance of fatwas, competency in assessing the financial matters, transactions, and documents according to the requirements of Shariah. The members must not carry bad reputation and should not be involved in fraud, forgery or in offenses of criminal nature. The members should be committed to work for the true values of Islamic finance and demonstrate high moral, ethical and religious values.

(b) Appointment and Composition of the SAB: Members of the SAB must be appointed according to the F&P and for at least three uninterrupted years, comprising at least three qualified Islamic scholars and further two industry experts at the choice of the BoD of the IFI. Three years period of the members should be protected from any unfair removal and termination from the SAB. However, in case of sheer negligence, violation of code of ethics, conduct and conflict of interest, the BoD should define a transparent process of removal or termination of the member from the SAB.

(c) Scope of SAB: The SAB should be assigned a clear mandate to ensure Shariah compliance in fair and transparent manner in the IFI in line with the verse 2 of Surah Al-Maidah in the Quran says, which states:

> Help ye one another in righteousness and piety, but help ye not one another in sin and rancour; Fear Allah, for Allah is strict in punishment.

The scope of the SAB should cover review and approval of all the matters relating to Shariah starting from the policies, products, investments, risk management, operational manuals, contracts, dealing with the complex situations by giving consistent advice in the form of Shariah rulings, guidelines, interpretations and comments.

(d) Meetings, Quorum and Decisions: The SGF should mention periodicity of the meetings, requirements of quorum and process to arrive at a final decision, should it be a simple majority or consensus of all the members of the SAB. Decisions, rulings and fatwas of the SAB should be binding on the respective IFI.

(e) Rating mechanism of the SBMs: Based on the true and fair evaluation system the central bank should introduce rating mechanism of Shariah advisors for their future appointment on different advisory board of the IFIs.

(f) Ethical Values: The SBMs must show high ethical values and avoid any conflict of interest and maintain required level of integrity and secrecy while performing their official obligations towards the IFI.

Development of human capital is another important area for effective Shariah governance framework. Survival of any business depends on the qualified and trained Shariah advisors and staff. IBF is very sensitive in this respect as the first contact person in the IFI leaves positive or negative image of the Islamic banking on the customer. If the person dealing with the customer is unable to satisfy the concerns of the customer about Islamic banking and its products, he will be the first reason for negative promotion of the IBF. On the other side an untrained staff will never be able to ensure Shariah compliance while executing asset-based financial transactions resulting in charity of legitimate income and loss to the IFI. Therefore, a proper learning and development department should function under the direction and supervision of a competent Shariah board for continuous capacity building of the staff working in the IFI.

Training of Shariah board members on latest developments and preparing Shariah scholars for the future of IBF is also an important area to address. For working experience in assets, liabilities and foreign trade and to prepare a good nursery of the competent Shariah advisors the central banks should encourage the financial institutions to launch Shariah advisors practical training and internship programs of not less than one year. Special courses on selected branches of Islamic Shariah, banking and finance can also be introduced at university level to produce a certain skill set in the area of Shariah advisory in the country.

Research and product development is an important area for innovation and growth of the existing products, practices, systems and controls. It should be an ongoing process under the supervision of the Shariah board and Islamic finance industry should invest in research and product development for sustainable future growth of Islamic banking and finance.

9.8.3 Shariah Review and Internal Reporting

The third important pillar of SGF is review of working, operations and Shariah compliance of the IFI supported by a team of compliance reviewers, internal and external Shariah auditors. Shariah reviews are conducted to ensure that appropriate internal controls are in place and they are functioning in line with the approved policies and risk appetite of the IFI. In general Shariah compliance function is performed by the Shariah reviewer or Shariah compliance department (SCD) which works under the direct control and authority of the executive management of the IFI. Shariah compliance serves as management's second defence line and the management must define proper systems and strategies to conduct Shariah reviews, its periodicity, reporting and rectification process at all departmental and operational levels.

SCD works under the supervision of the Shariah board and prepares reports on implementation status of the Shariah standards, fatwas, instructions, directions, guidelines, ruling and directions of regulatory bodies and SAB. It also examines the transaction execution process of the assets and liability products to confirm that all transactions are being conducted according to the approved standard operating procedures, manuals, process flows and other requirements of Shariah.

The reports of the SCD are submitted to the senior management for review, comments and compliance. The Shariah board through one of its full-time active member monitors the whole Shariah compliance culture of the IFI on regular basis and reviews all important issues in the periodical meetings.

Shariah Internal audit (ISA) performs the functions of audit under the supervision of the BoD and its committee on internal audit. ISA highlights the Shariah violations and makes it part of its report for BoD oversight on the Shariah-related matters. However, final authority to decide the fate of reported Shariah violations remains with the Shariah board. Finally external Shariah auditors conduct audit of the IFI and submit an independent report to the BoD, the shareholders and investors of the IFIs.

The regulator must define minimum qualification for the people working in the functions of Shariah compliance and Shariah Audit. The reporting and rectification mechanism of Shariah-related violation must also be clearly defined. All the violations pointed out by the external Shariah auditors should also be submitted to the CSA along with the SAB but SAB should not be the final authority to decide on the violations pointed out by the external Shariah auditors.

SAB should submit a report on the overall Shariah violations to the BoD, its Committee on Shariah compliance and senior management on periodical basis to communicate with the top management and to inform them on the status of Shariah compliance and seek help for compliance and to remove barriers, if any.

9.8.4 Transparency, Disclosure and Accountability

The last and fourth pillar is transparency, disclosure and accountability. Transparency ultimately leads towards accountability. It is very important to cover this aspect in SGF as it is vital to give a true and fair picture of the business affairs to the stakeholders. Fair, positive and timely disclosures about the state of Shariah compliance can help in better reputation of the IFI. Greatly Shariah-compliant institutions have the benefit of easy access to more and cheaper liquidity, increase in stock prices, growth in business whereas qualified reports with timely disclosures can help the investors to adjust their exposures accordingly.

Full disclosure and accountability can save the IFI and investors from the future losses and enables the BoD and the regulator to initiate appropriate steps against the negligent staff and the management. The regulators must prescribe timely, precise, relevant and appropriate disclosure requirements about the financial and non-financial affairs of the IFIs which are directly related to Shariah compliance. Generally, regulators require annexing Shariah compliance reports of the SAB with the annual accounts of the IFI whereas financial accounts of listed IFIs are published on quarterly basis. To give enhanced confidence, on the purity of profit SAB should also submit a Shariah compliance certificate (SCC) to be published in the quarterly accounts for the shareholders containing all outstanding and major Shariah violations of the IFIs. SCC is essential for satisfaction of the investors and faith-based depositors who invest their money for the sake of halal (permissible) earning only. Transparency may help in preventing disputes and frauds in financial transactions and are significant for improved Shariah governance.

Regulators must also prescribe clear accountability process for the responsible persons and office holders of the IFIs including the BoD and Shariah board. The BoD should reflect the similar accountability process for senior management and staff if they are found responsible for any gross Shariah violation.

To conclude, Islamic banking and finance is rapidly growing sector on the globe specifically in the Islamic world. It is a relatively new idea compared to the conventional finance. Shariah compliance is the soul of Islamic banking and finance which must be adhered to at all levels for its consistent growth, attention of the world and trust of the users. Shariah compliance is possible with the help of a suitable and legally enforceable SGF. A good SGF is about Islamic laws, competency and independence of the Shariah board and executive management, compliance, review, transparency, reporting and accountability.

References

Ahmed B., & Marwa A. (2022). New Shari'ah Governance Rules For Financial Institutions: Do You Need A Shari'ah Committee? *Mondaq.* 14 February 2022. www.mondaq.com/saudiarabia/islamic-finance/1150572/new-Shari'ah-governance-rules-for-financial-institutions-do-you-need-a-Shari'ah-committee-

Amjad, A., & Rahat, D. (2019). The legal and regulatory framework governing Islamic finance and markets in United Arab Emirates. *Lexology.* 14 October 2019. www.lexology.com/library/detail.aspx?g=88c2b316-ad1f-49eb-aa4c-d6f549ff601c

BNM, FSPSR (2009). Financial Stability and Payment System Report 2009. The New Shari'ah Governance Framework p. 99. www.bnm.gov.my/documents/20124/856392/cp03_003_whitebox.pdf

CBK Law 30 (2003). Central Bank of Kuwait. www.cbk.gov.kw/en/images/low-islamic-30-2003-1_v00_tcm10-147862.pdf

COMEC (2020). Improving Shari'ah Governance Framework (SGF) in Islamic Finance. Proceedings of the 14th Meeting of the COMCEC Financial Cooperation Working Group *COMEC Coordination Office, Ankara, Turkey* (October 2020). http://ebook.comcec.org/Kutuphane/Icerik/adc9ab88-78b5-4101-afb8-ffea3ad14a59.pdf

Dar, H. A. (2004): Demand for Islamic Financial Services in the UK: Chasing a Mirage? Loughborough University. Preprint. https://hdl.handle.net/2134/335

Fady, B., Hitham, A., Eldeen M., & Shahid, E. (2011). Islamic Banking in Sudan. *SSRN Electronic Journal*, September 2011.

IBRF (2012). Islamic Banking Regulatory Framework. *Central Bank of Oman.* Laws and Regulations. https://cbo.gov.om/Pages/IslamicBankingRegulatoryFramework.aspx

IFBS-10 (2009). Guiding Principles on Shari'ah Governance Systems for Institutions Offering Islamic Financial Services (December 2009). www.ifsb.org/published.php

IFSB (2021). Islamic Financial Stability Report 2021. Islamic Financial Services Board.

Keping, Y. (2018). Governance and Good Governance: A New Framework for Political Analysis. *Fudan Journal of the Humanities and Social Sciences, 11*, 1–8.

Laldin, A., & Hafas, F. (2018). Islamic Financial Services Act (IFSA) 2013 and the Shari'ah-compliance requirement of the Islamic finance industry in Malaysia. *ISRA International Journal of Islamic Finance*, 10 (1), 19 June 2018.

Mazhar, M. S. (2015). Issues of Good Governance in South Asia. *South Asian Studies A Research Journal of South Asian Studies*, 30(2), July–December 2015, 125–160.

Minhas, I. (2012). Shari'ah governance model (SGM) and its four basic Pillars. Islamic Finance News Malaysia Published by Red Money Publication. Available at https://ssrn.com/abstract=2153106

OECD (2015), G20/OECD Principles of Corporate Governance. OECD Publishing. http://dx.doi.org/10.1787/9789264236882-en

Sadad, I., & Muqaddam (2021). Shari'ah Governance in Islamic Financial Institutions in Nigeria: An Empirical Study. *Advances in Economics, Business and Management Research, volume 194* (December 2021). www.researchgate.net/publication/356665041_Shari'ah_Governance_in_Islamic_Financial_Institutions_in_Nigeria_An_Empirical_Study

SECP (1980). Modaraba Companies Modaraba Floatation Control Ordinance. Retrieved March 2023, from Security and Exchange Commission of Pakistan. www.secp.gov.pk/document/modaraba-companies-modaraba-floatation-control-ordinance-1980/

SECP (2018). Shari'ah Governance Regulations 2018. *Securities and Exchange Commission of Pakistan*/Laws. www.secp.gov.pk/laws/regulations/,

SECP (2012). SCSAM 2012. *Securities and Exchange Commission of Pakistan*/Laws. www.secp.gov.pk/laws/circulars/

SGF (2018). Shari'ah Governance Framework. *SBP Circulars/Notifications-Islamic Banking.* www.sbp.org.pk/ibd/2018/C1.htm

SGS (2020). Standard Re. Shari'ah Governance for Islamic Financial Institutions. Central Bank of the UAE. www.centralbank.ae/en/laws-and-regulations/regulations/banking

Torfing, Jacob, B., Peters, G., Pierre, J., & Eva, S. (2012). *Interactive Governance: Advancing the Paradigm.* Oxford University Press.

UNESCO (2022). Concept of Governance. *International Bureau of Education.* www.ibe.unesco.org/en/geqaf/technical-notes/concept-governance

Zainab., B., et al. (2018). Legal and Regulatory Framework of Islamic Banking in Libya. *Al Mashalih–Journal of Islamic Law*, 1(2), December 2018. www.researchgate.net/publication/330102366_legal_and_regulatory_framework_of_islamic_banking_in_libya

Zeno, M. R. (2015). The Path to Water: Shari'a revisioned. *Boom: A Journal of California*, 5(4), 100–103. https://doi.org/10.1525/boom.2015.5.4.100

Zulkifli, H. (2012). Shari'ah Governance in Islamic Banks. Edinburgh University Press Ltd. Chapter 3.3 Institutionalization of the Shari'ah Board.

Index

Note: Page numbers in **bold** refer to tables and those in *italic* refer to figures.

Abu Bakar 116, 119
accountability, Islamic concept of 153
Accounting and Auditing Organisation of Islamic Financial Institutions (AAOIFI): auditing guidelines 133–6, 139–40, 142, 144, 148, 161; definition of Shariah board 86; definition of Shariah governance 3; disclosure requirements 22, 24, 25; fatwa standard 41, 43, 45, 47; internal Shariah review, guidelines for 161; role of 159; Sharia board of 160; Shariah boards, guidelines for 6, 13, 87, 160–1; Shariah compliance departments, guidelines for 161; standardization of governance frameworks 160; standards, issuance of 160
Ahle–Sunnah Wal Jamah 119
Akhuwat 95, 107
al-amr bi al-maʿrūf wa al-nahy ʿan al-munkar 4–5
al-Baghawi 39
al-Juwaini, Imam al-Haramayh 38
Al-Rajhi Bank 145–6
Amdi 40–1
Amidi, Saifuddin 39

Bahrain 83, 103, 142
Bai Inah 102
Bangladesh 66, 68, 91
Barzali 42
bayʿal-Inah 44, 45, 58, 59
Bay ʾbithaman ajil 5
Bank Negara Malaysia (BNM) 6, 13, 14, 140–1, 165

bin Umar, Abdullah 115, 116
Brunei 125

centralized Shariah governance framework (CSGF, Turkey): Board of Directors 76, 77; certificate programs 72–3, 77; coherence of, criticized 73–4; Communiqué on Compliance to the Principles and Standards of Interest-Free Banking 65–6; defining boundaries of Shariah standards 70, 77; difficulty of coordinating with secular regulations 74; fair competition ensured by 69, 70; harmonization of Shariah standards 70–1; independence of Advisory Board 74–5, 77; members of Advisory Board 75–7; non-compliance risk decreased by 70, 77; Participation Bank Association of Turkey (PBAT) 65, 71–3, 75; Shariah audit 76–7; structure and procedures of Advisory Board 71–2, 77; uniqueness of 66; *see also* Turkey
corporate governance, definition of 153

distributional impacts of IBIs: commercialization, dominance over moral economy 95–7; external environment not conducive to social goals 97; improved access to credit where conventional banking development is low 96; involuntary excluded segments of population, failure to serve 94–6, 99; Islamic distinctness, benefits of strengthening 107; Islamic form, emphasized over

Islamic substance 97–8; microfinance, lack of enthusiasm for 95, 96, 100; similarity to conventional banking 98–100, 103; social principles of Islamic finance 97; stricter criteria for creditworthiness 103; urban bias 96, 100
Dubai 12, 15, 24, 55, 90, 159, 165

Faisal Islamic Bank 6, 157
fatwa: borrowing between schools 45–7; concept of, in classical tradition 37–8; end-results, consideration of 49–50; hiyal (stratagems), avoidance of 44–5; maqasid al-Shariah 47–9, 81; revision due to error or change of circumstances 50; Shariah concessions 43–4; sources and evidence, use of 43; *see also* fatwa in IBIs; mufti
fatwa in IBIs: Bay'Mu'ajjah of Sukuk, fatwa on 58–9; Mudarabah Sukuk, fatwa on 55–8; PMEX Murabahah Transaction 59–61; radical reform needed 63; Running Musharakah (RM), fatwa on 60–2; severe criticism of Shariah boards' use of 36–7, 63
fiqh mu'amalat 5, 6

Gangohi, Rashid Ahmad 46
Ghazali 38–9, 47, 113
globalization of Shariah-compliant industry 155
governance, definition of 152–3

Hisbah 5, 115–16, 131–2, 154

Ibn Abidin 42, 45
Ibn al-Humam 46
Ibn-al-Qayyim 40, 42, 45, 48
Ibn Arafa 42
Ibn Taymiyyah 45, 47
Ijarah contract 2, 42, 62, 99, 103–5, 159
Indonesia 24, 63, 68, 125
isitsna 2
Islamic Development Bank 86, 159
Islamic Financial Services Board (IFSB): auditing guidelines 142; Guiding Principles on Risk Management 5; role of 140, 159, 162; Shariah boards, guidelines for 6, 162–4; Shariah governance, definition of 2–3, 84, 154; Shariah non-compliance risk, definition of 155

Kuwait 159

Libya 159

Malaysia 12–13, 84, 140–1, 147, 154, 158; *see also* Bank Negara Malaysia
Maqasid al-Shariah 1–16, 21–31, 36–63, 65–77, 80–91, 94–108, 110–25, 131–48, 152–74
Mit Ghamer Savings Bank 110
mu'āmalah 4
Mudarabah 55–77, 98, 99, 114, 143, 157
mufti in IBIs: certification, lack of 53; conflict-of-interest issues 53–5, 63; qualifications for 51–3, 62–3; radical reform needed 63; remuneration 63
mufti: mujtahid *vs.* muqallid 38; obligations of 37–8; qualifications of 38–40, 62; qualities and characteristics of 41–2, 62; remuneration 42; specialization in particular fields 40–1, 62; *see also* fatwa; mufti in IBIs
muhtasib 132
Murabaha 59–60, 61, 98, 100, 103
Muraqabah 137
Musharakah 49, 57, 60–2, 98, 99, 159, 170

Nasser Social Bank 110
Nigeria 159

Oman 166–7
Organisation for Economic Co-operation and Development (OECD) 1, 153

Pakistan: interventionist approach to Shariah governance of IFIs 13; Mudarabah Companies Act 143, 157; Securities and Exchange Commission (SECP) 158; Shariah Compliance Framework 144; Shariah Compliance and Shariah Audit Mechanism (SCSAM) 158; Shariah Federal Court 13; Shariah Supervisory Report 144; switch-over to Islamic banking 143; *see also* State Bank of Pakistan
price competitiveness of IBIs: asset-light structures, development of 106; balancing redistribution of payoffs 107; benchmark risk with slack in repayments 101; costly inefficient intermediation 95, 96; documentary levies in contracts for multiple asset

transfers 101; faith premium, reliance on 105; fintech for efficiency 106–07; growth to avoid scale disadvantages 105–06; high average financing costs 99, 102; high spread 94, 95, 97, 100, 102; liquidity risk for funding liquidity shortfall 101–02; low average return on investment 99; maintaining higher asset quality 103, **104**; non-remunerative accounts, reliance on 95, 96; operating expense to net spreads 102–03; opportunity costs, restricted by strict Shariah compliance 107–08; Shariah compliance cost 94, 100–01, 156; tax neutrality, advocacy for 103–05; as widespread source of apprehension about Islamic banking 94

Qarafi 46
Qatar 12, 159

Rahmani, Khalid Saifullah 46
rapid growth of Islamic financial industry 155
Razi 41
research and development of Islamic financial products 125, 172
Riba, prohibition of 15, 44, 45, 47, 49, 58, 83, 95, 110, 156
Running Musharakah (RM) 49, 60–2, 98

Salam 2, 61, 96, 99, 100
Saudi Arabia 12, 142–3, 167–8
shareholder vs. stakeholder governance models 81
Shariah audit: AAOIFI guidelines 133–4, 139–40, 142, 144, 148; accountability of auditors 147; adequacy of standards 145–6; competence of auditors 147; IFSB guidelines 142; independence of auditors 146; internal audit 134–6, 173; as key oversight mechanism 8, 84, 85; Malaysian practices 140–1; Middle Eastern practices 141–3; objectives 135; Pakistani practices 143–5; process 138–9, *138*, 148; qualification of auditors 146; role of auditors 136–7; as role of Shariah board 88, 146; scope of 136; standardized auditing framework, need for 147; traditional financial audit, overlap with 133, 136;
traditional Islamic audit practices 131–2; zakat audit 137
Shariah boards: appointment procedures 13–14, 163, 171; as basic pillar of Shariah governance 80, 85, 86, 88, 110–11, 115, 117, 124, 170; capacities required by *124*; central boards 86–7; clear framework and structure essential to 3; competency of members 9–10, 89, 90, 164; confidentiality 164; consistency of decisions 164; decisions binding 84, 171; definition of 86; disclosure of basis for rulings 90–1, 164; disclosure of member profiles 125; fiduciary duty 88; foreign members 123; independence 10–11, 89, 125, 163; international boards 86; IBI boards 87; knowledge of financial accounting 121–2; mufti, presence of 122; multiple board membership, as confidentiality risk 89, 90, 122; professional development 9, 163, 172; qualifications of members 5–6, 86, 160, 163, 170–1; remuneration 89, 125; role of 14–15, 87–8, 120, *121*, 160; scope of 171; size 123–4; as Shura 119; *see also* fatwa in IBIs; mufti in IBIs
Shariah compliance certificates 173
Shariah compliance departments (SCDs) **27**, 80, 85, 161, 166, 172
Shariah-compliant investment, increasing global interest in 1
Shariah-compliant vs. Shariah-based products 2
Shariah, definition of 2
Shariah disclosure: essential for Muslim customers 21, 23, 173; indexes, various, developed for 23–4; regulators, role of 173; reputational importance of 173; research gap 22; survey design as method for study of 24; *see also* Shariah Disclosure Index
Shariah Disclosure Index (ShDI): binary or dichotomous value scoring of themes 26; coding of themes for 26; developed to compare expected with actual practices 26; formula for calculation of 25; key themes identified for 26, **27**–**30**; rankings of Pakistani Islamic banks 29, **31**; scoring individual banks 28
Shariah governance of IBIs: Board of Directors and management

7–9, 84, 85, 156–7, 163, 169–70, 174; centralized approach 67, 83; central Sharia authority (CSA) essential to 168–9; conflict resolution systems 163; decentralized approach 67; definition of 2–3; diverse models required for different countries 168; functions of 15–16; holistic culture of Shariah compliance 8–9; human capital development 171–2; hybrid approach 68, 83; internal *vs.* external 80, 85–6; interventionist approach 13, 67, 83–4; legislation necessary for success of 168; minimalist approach 12, 83–4; passive approach 12, 83–4; principles of governance *4, 117*; proactive approach 12–13, 83–4; reactive approach 12, 83–4; self-regulation approach 83, 91, 157; Shariah board crucial to 3; as tool to mitigate Shariah non-compliance risk 5, 155–6; stakeholder *vs.* shareholder model 81, 120; ultimate success of economy promoted by 16; unique issues generated by 22; *see also* Accounting and Auditing Organisation of Islamic Financial Institutions; Islamic Financial Services Board; Shariah audit; Shariah boards; Shariah review

Shariah non-compliance risk: crucial for IFIs 155; increased by rapid expansion of Islamic finance 155; investment jeopardized by 83, 155; Shariah governance as tool to mitigate 5, 67, 155–6

Shariah review 8, 84, 85, 88, 120, 141–2, 172

Shatibi 47, 49

Shura 80, 82, 118–20

State Bank of Pakistan (SBP): audit system 143–5; Bay'Mu'ajjah of Sukuk 58–9; criteria for Shariah advisors 6, 51–2; Islamic Banking Department 143; Shariah board of 158; Shariah disclosure standards 26; Shariah governance framework 165–6; Shariah leadership by, need for 63

Sudan 6, 14, 105, 106, 157, 158

Takaful 8, 49, 54, 114, 155, 159, 165

tas'ir (price fixation) 48

Tawarruq 5, 96, 102, 168

Tawhid 80–2

training of bank staff 125

Turkey: Banking Regulation and Supervision Agency (BRSA) 65, 71–3; constitutional secularism 67; historical decentralized approach to Shariah governance 65, 67, 69, 70; rapid growth of participation banks 65; *see also* centralized Shariah governance framework

uniformity, need for 1, 63, 145, 168

United Arab Emirates (UAE) 14, 90, 158, 167

United Kingdom 12, 90, 159

United States 159

Usmani, Muhammad Tadi 47

Uṣul al-fiqh 5, 6, 51, 113

Wa'ad-based sales 99

zakat 15, 48, 53, 58, 77, 114, 136, 137

Zuhaili, Wahhab 46, 47